State, Rural Women, and Domestication in Korea

This book explores the dynamic interactions between the state and society during the industrialization of South Korea in the 1960s and 1970s, focusing on rural women as a marginalized social group.

By illuminating rural women's interactions with the state and their aspirations for entering the middle class, it effectively reveals insights into the gender and class perspectives of industrialization in South Korea. Utilizing an analysis of personal letters from peasant movement activists, documents and periodicals issued by the Korean Catholic Peasant Women's Organization, as well as in-depth interviews with farmers, housewives, activists of the peasant movements, and governmental officers, this book represents a reconsideration of state–society relations, as well as a reinterpretation of housewife ideology theory.

Highlighting the often-invisible experiences of marginalized rural women, this book will be of great interest to students and scholars of Korean Studies, Women's Studies, and Rural Studies.

Jaok Kwon is a research fellow in the Centre for East Asian Studies at the University of Heidelberg, Germany. Her research interests include the sociology of development, labor and gender in East Asia, and transnational labor migration.

Routledge Advances in Korean Studies

53. South Korea's foreign aid
The domestic politics of middle power diplomacy
Hyo-sook Kim

54. Commons Perspectives in South Korea
Contexts, Fields, and Alternatives
Edited by Hyun Choe, Ja-Kyung Kim, Hun-Gyo Jang, Yea-Yl Yoon and Suh-Hyun Park

55. Confucian Reform in Chosun Korea
Yu Hyŏngwŏn's Pan'gye surok
Authored by Yu Hyŏngwŏn and edited by Woosung Bae

56. Social Policy Dynamics in South Korea
Soon-Yang Kim

57. Korean Film and Festivals
Global Transcultural Flows
Soon-Yang Kim

58. Power and the Elite in North Korea
Paektu and Kanbu
Jae-Cheon Lim

59. State, Rural Women, and Domestication in Korea
The Aspiring Middle Class
Jaok Kwon

For more information about this series, please visit:
www.routledge.com/asianstudies/series/SE0505

State, Rural Women, and Domestication in Korea

The Aspiring Middle Class

Jaok Kwon

Routledge
Taylor & Francis Group
LONDON AND NEW YORK

First published 2025
by Routledge
4 Park Square, Milton Park, Abingdon, Oxon OX14 4RN

and by Routledge
605 Third Avenue, New York, NY 10158

Routledge is an imprint of the Taylor & Francis Group, an informa business

British Library Cataloguing-in-Publication Data
A catalogue record for this book is available from the British Library

Library of Congress Cataloging-in-Publication Data
Names: Kwon, Jaok, author.
Title: State, rural women, and domestication in Korea : the aspiring middle class / Jaok Kwon.
Description: Abingdon, Oxon ; New York, NY : Routledge, 2024. | Series: Routledge advances in Korean studies | Includes bibliographical references and index.
Identifiers: LCCN 2024005528 (print) | LCCN 2024005529 (ebook) | ISBN 9780367627195 (hardback) | ISBN 9780367627225 (paperback) | ISBN 9781003110538 (ebook)
Subjects: LCSH: Industrialization--Korea (South)--History--20th century. | Women--Korea (South)--History--20th century. | Korea (South)--Economic conditions--1960-1988. | Korea (South)--Rural conditions--20th century. | Middle class--Korea (South)--History--20th century. | Korea (South)--Social policy--20th century.
Classification: LCC HC467.95 .K858 2024 (print) | LCC HC467.95 (ebook) | DDC 330.95195--dc23/eng/20240325
LC record available at https://lccn.loc.gov/2024005528
LC ebook record available at https://lccn.loc.gov/2024005529

ISBN: 978-0-367-62719-5 (hbk)
ISBN: 978-0-367-62722-5 (pbk)
ISBN: 978-1-003-11053-8 (ebk)

DOI: 10.4324/9781003110538

Typeset in Times New Roman
by Deanta Global Publishing Services, Chennai, India

Contents

Acknowledgments

This research dates to my doctoral dissertation project at the Graduate School of Social Sciences of Hitotsubashi University in Japan, entitled "Rural Development and Gender in the 1960s and 1970s in South Korea: Interactions between the State, Women's Movement, and Rural Women". The project aimed to shed light on rural women as a social group at the center of social changes during South Korea's industrialization in the 1960s and 1970s yet marginalized within the national economic success story. Professional bureaucrats, capitalists, and political leaders were widely considered the primary actors in this story, and it remains challenging to discern even the shadows of those who played essential roles beyond the public stage of industrialization. Despite scholarly attempts to illuminate the invisible, rural women, in particular, remain unseen. I hope this work provides insights into the gender and class perspectives of industrialization in South Korea by illuminating rural women's interactions with the state and their aspirations for entering the middle class.

During the long research journey toward finishing this book, I have benefited from the support of numerous people and institutions. First, I would like to express my deep appreciation to my interviewees, including rural women, former village leaders who participated in the state-led rural development projects, activists of the peasant movements, local governmental officers, politicians, and researchers. Even though their names have been made anonymous, I would like to thank them for their precious time and personal stories. The discussions helped me greatly in understanding everyday life in rural villages during the 1960s and 1970s and furnished insights to develop my research.

I am deeply indebted to my doctoral supervisors Shiro Kodamaya and Asami Yasuhito for their generous support, intellectual dialogues, encouragement, and patience. I would also like to thank all my colleagues at the Centre for Asian and Transcultural Studies at Heidelberg University for their kind support and for providing me with a great environment for research and teaching. Conversations with them in daily life and academic settings such as conferences and workshops provided me with the intellectual inspiration for developing the ideas in this book. I would like to express my deep appreciation to the researchers from diverse scholarly backgrounds who offered valuable feedback and suggestions to improve this manuscript. Soo-Hyun Mun of Hanyang University, a historian specializing in German history and women's history, provided detailed and insightful comments on the manuscript and offered continuous warm encouragement. Mihye Cho of Sungkonghoe University offered feedback and suggestions that enabled me to reconsider the theoretical framework from a sociological perspective. Finally, I am grateful to Nigel Swain of the University of Liverpool, who carefully read the entire manuscript and provided critical and constructive comments.

I was blessed with numerous grants in carrying out this research project. The completion of this research would not have been possible without the generous financial, institutional, and administrative support from various institutions. The Graduate School of Social Sciences of Hitotsubashi University supported fieldwork in Korea and Germany and an internship in Belgium spent conducting interviews. The Pohang Iron and Steel Company visiting fellow program at the East-West Center in Hawai'i gave me a precious opportunity to elaborate on the theoretical background of my research. Moreover, my appointment as a visiting scholar at the Seoul National University Asia Center (SNUAC) provided me with a great opportunity to access literature and fully concentrate on the completion of this manuscript. I am heavily indebted to the SNUAC for providing generous support and to the Korea Foundation for financially supporting my research stay at the SNUAC. I would like to thank my editor at Routledge for their kind, professional support. I am truly grateful to Agnes Conrad who kindly provided insightful and constructive suggestions to improve the language, arguments, and structure of my manuscript.

Parts of the theoretical portion of the introduction have been previously published elsewhere: "Modern Womanhood, the Ideology of Housewife, and Young Female Rural–Urban Migrants in the 1960s–1970s in South Korea", *European Journal of Korean Studies*, 19(1): 171–194 (2020). I am grateful to the editors and reviewers of the journal for the opportunities to share and refine my views. It should also be noted that this book could not have been realized without the financial support of the Academy of Korean Studies' publication grant program.

Finally, I would like to express my sincere gratitude to my family members for their emotional support. In particular, my parents always proved to be a lighthouse whenever I lose my way and cannot see forward. I owe immeasurable thanks to Henrik for his support, care, and great sense of humor, which I needed often during this project. Finally, I am indebted to my daughter, Marit Yuna, for being understanding that her mother had little time to spend with her and often had to sit in front of the computer while completing this book.

This publication was supported by the 2021 Korean Studies Grant Program of the Academy of Korean Studies (AKS-2021-P-005).

Notes on Romanization, Quotation, and Translation

Throughout this book, all Korean words have been romanized according to the McCune–Reischauer system, with a few exceptions. Exceptions include the names of famous figures such as presidents, generally known terms such as "Chosun" and "saemaul" and names of regions. The convention for writing Korean names in the main text, parenthetical citations, notes, and references follows the Korean practice of listing the surname first, followed by the given name without an intermediary comma. When citing literature written in Korean, the last and first names are listed. However, when citing literature written in non-Korean languages, only the surname is listed, even if the author has a Korean name. Single quotes are used to address idioms and discourses or to emphasize the meaning of words and phrases, while double quotes are used for direct citations from specific literature. Finally, all translations from Korean to English are my own.

Introduction

Modernization, the State, and Rural Women

Ideology of "Becoming a Housewife" Under the Park Chung Hee Regime

This book explores the under-researched nature of rural modernity and women in South Korea by focusing on the 1960s and 1970s. It answers the following questions: From a scholarly perspective, what did the modernization project of Park Chung Hee (1961–1979) signify for the marginalized social group of "rural women" in South Korea? Why were the rural population (especially, rural women) the main participants enthusiastically responding to Park's rural development project, despite not being the primary beneficiaries of his modernization project? How did Park Chung Hee's dictatorial regime create discourses on modernization to legitimize politically repressive rule and mobilize the rural working-class population in the modernization process without providing substantial financial support? How were rural women positioned relative to gendered relations, newly defined under Park Chung Hee's regime? Specifically, how were rural women positioned within the housewife ideology actively disseminated by the Park Chung Hee regime from the 1960s to the 1970s? In what ways did discourses on the housewife as the ideal of modern womanhood influence women who were not themselves stay-at-home housewives? Furthermore, how did rural women accept and interpret governmental intervention in everyday life, implemented in the name of development? Were rural women merely reactionary subordinates to governmental intervention, or were they active negotiators in accepting a "modern" ideology and in constructing gender relations? How did the Park Chung Hee regime interact with rural women in the 1960s and 1970s when South Korea faced urban-centered industrialization? What do the interactions between the state and rural women, who were marginalized social actors, tell us about the growth of the middle class and dis(continuities) of gender relations during the industrialization of the 1960s and 1970s in South Korea?

Per these research questions, this book maintains that the mechanisms of social mobilization during the Park Chung Hee regime in the 1960s and 1970s should be understood in the context of interactions between the developmental state and rural women: the state-led promotion of the "becoming a housewife" ideology and a strong bottom-up aspiration for the middle-class virtues of cities by rural women. By analyzing governmental documents and presidential speeches, this

DOI: 10.4324/9781003110538-1

research clarifies that the housewife ideology was forged by the Park Chung Hee regime as a clear and conceivable path toward the middle class for rural women. Meanwhile, drawing from magazines for women, daily newspapers, and in-depth interviews with rural women, this book delineates the governmental policies that regulated everyday lives, and the aspiration of rural women toward the middle class functioned as solid motivation for active participation in the modern nation-state building project of Park Chung Hee. This research empirically challenges the conventionally dichotomous interpretation of the relation between the Park Chung Hee regime and the population as *either* "oppressive mobilization from above" *or* "social consensus from the bottom" by analyzing mutual interactions between the state and rural women. It also elucidates that the gendered nature of state policy and intervention in the everyday lives of rural women during the Park Chung Hee era and rural women's negotiations with this interventionism have induced the (re) construction of gender relations during the industrialization in the 1960s–1970s period in South Korea.

Theoretically, this book contributes to the further development of Maria Mies' feminist theory of "housewifization" in the late industrializing countries. By expanding upon the relatively universal and monolithic concept of female domestication depicted within this theory, this book attempts to illustrate the diverse and dynamic processes at work in the creation of housewives through consensus, negotiation, and conflict among various actors, including the developmental state, rural women, the rural community, and family institutions. Specifically, this study demonstrates that the role of the state, the historical context, the diversity of women's experiences, women's agency, and the intersection of gender and class should be considered when examining the ideology of the housewife in the Asian context.

Industrialization, Women, and Domestication in Early Industrialized Economies

With the rise of industrialization and the shift toward wage labor in early industrialized countries, women were excluded from the formal labor market and confined to the domestic sphere.[1] Regarding women's domestication in the context of industrialization, Hall (1992) in her research on industrialization in Britain argues that the "housewife" idea emerged as a separate and domesticated figure, and its emergence as a social group influenced the nature of work and gender roles. Ochiai (2008, 4) in her research on industrialization in Japan and its impact on gender relations maintains that "modernization led to the gender division of labor between the "breadwinning" husband who labored in the public sphere and the housewife who specialized in housekeeping and childrearing in the domestic sphere". Modernization, in this sense, was marked by a change in gender roles, which meant that most married women were expected to assume the role of full-time housekeepers (Goldstein-Gidoni 2012). The discussion on the emergence of the housewife as a result of industrialization has developed into its relation to the construction of the middle class and women as housewives (Friedan 2013), women's domesticity and femininity as homemakers (Giles 2004), and the positioning of a housewife relative to non-housewives, such as the working-class and women of color (Hall 1992).

Additionally, the domestication of women means "becoming a housewife" whose main labor takes place in a private sphere and the devaluation of women's domestic labor, particularly by repositioning women's work as nonwork and deeming women as housewives. Hence, women's unpaid housework has been the center of the discussion in the study of women's labor in relation to capitalism. For instance, Secombe (1974) argues that housework is a form of unpaid work, even though it is indispensable to the reproduction of labor power and essential to the functioning of the capitalist system. She further argues that unwaged housework is the ground for the reproduction of unequal gender relations and the exploitation of women's labor under the capitalist system. Beechey (1987) also maintains that women's labor in the reproductive sphere is unpaid, devalued, and overlooked despite its important contributions, as the definition of work is confined to paid work.

In the context of late industrializing countries, the housewifization theory was proposed by the German sociologist, Maria Mies (1982, 1998), and has contributed to a better understanding of the fundamental roots of women's oppression under capitalism. Mies (1982), researching lace-makers in the city of Narsapur in India, defines the devaluation of women's labor as the "process by which women are socially defined as housewives, dependent for their substance on the income of a husband, irrespective of whether they are *de facto* housewives or not" (180). According to Mies' theory, the enhancement of the clear division of labor and segregation between the domestic and public spheres in industrialized countries because of modernization and industrialization was transferred to late industrializing countries through processes of colonialism and globalization, perpetuating global gender inequality and exploitation.

The process of capitalization in the industrialized world and the imposition of Western patriarchal values in the name of "development" policies in "developing countries" have been discussed by several researchers. In particular, Rogers (1980) and Mies (1998) argue that capitalism and Westernization have often resulted in a narrow definition of the "domestic" sphere, which redefines women's labor within the confined domestic place. Mackintosh (1981) maintains that the penetration of Western capitalism has induced an artificial division between the spheres of productive and domestic labor and their ideological reinforcement. Development practitioners easily assume rural women in developing countries to be housewives and, thus, ignore the productive role of women within households and the subsistence economy. Hence, they have been excluded from formal access to training, credit opportunities, land rights, education, and technology (Buvinić 1983; Kabeer 1994; Rogers 1980).

In this context, Mies (1998, 110) argues that "housewifization means the externalization, or ex-territorialization of costs that otherwise would have to be covered by the capitalists. This means women's labor is considered a natural resource, freely available like air and water". Thus, the domestication of women's labor is part of the functional logic of capitalism in which non-waged or underpaid labor in the domestic sector by women supports capital accumulation and patriarchy. Mies' theory is meaningful in that it tries to clarify how the housewife ideology in advanced Western societies is interconnected with the devaluation of the labor of working-class women in late industrializing countries (Mies 1998; Mies Bennholdt-Thomsen and Werlhof 1988). With women in the late industrializing countries thus defined as housewives who use their spare time to earn extra cash, the housewife ideology from advanced economies supports the integration of female workers in developing countries within an exploitative global production system.[2]

Domestication of Women in the Asian and Korean Context

Several empirical studies based on Mies' theory show that the domestication of women should be understood within varied sociopolitical and cultural contexts (see Barber and Bryan 2014; Ochiai 2014). For instance, Prügl (1996) demonstrates that the domestication of women is not necessarily an ideological construction that universally accompanies the development of capitalism but should also be "explored in socio-cultural and economic contexts, and cannot be stipulated as functional requirements of economic process" (ibid., 129). This notion is associated with the critics from Third World feminism, which argues that the diversity of women's experiences and the patriarchal orders should be considered (e.g., Mohanty 1984). The construction and proliferation process of the housewife ideology in the Asian (including Korean) context suggest five main important dimensions worth further elaboration to further develop the theory discussed as follows.

State-led Promotion for Becoming a Modern Housewife

The emergence of housewives has been considered to be, in part, a "natural" social consequence of industrialization and modernization in the general term. Ochiai (2008), therefore, identifies the domestication of women as a major indicator in the process of modernization in the West and Japan (ibid., 3), creating clear divisions of labor and a separation between the domestic and public spheres. This stance is apparent in analyses of cases in industrialized countries such as Japan (Bardsley 1999; Gordon 1997; Vogel 1965), Germany (Bridenthal 1984; Nolan 1990), and the Unitd States (Matthews 1987), where housewives have emerged as a social group *en masse.*[3]

Meanwhile, it is vital to pay special attention to the state's role in constructing the housewife ideology in the Asian context. One of the defining features of modernization in East Asia is that campaigns for social and economic development were often launched by the state (Kwon 2007). In this context, "movements" were not grassroot initiatives but governmental attempts to mobilize the population toward state-building goals. In China, the "New Life Movement" was initiated in 1934 by Chiang Kai-shek, the head of the government and the Chinese Nationalist Party. This government-led civic campaign of the 1930s in China aimed to promote sociocultural reforms and enhance Neo-Confucian social values, such as discipline, order, filial piety, frugality, and morality, and encouraged individuals to take personal responsibility for their own moral and spiritual development. The movement aimed to promote self-improvement and self-discipline to strengthen individuals and society. In Japan, the "Local Improvement Movement" was conducted from 1905 to 1925. Its campaigns continued under the "Moral Suasion Mobilization Campaign (1929–1903)", "National Spiritual Mobilization Movement (1937–1940)", and "New Life Movement" names in postwar Japan. State-led campaigns, including the "Life Improvement Movement (*saenghwal gaesŏn undong*)" during the colonial period and the "New Life Movement (*shinsaenghwal undong*)" in the 1950s, similarly spread in Korea. They continued through the "People's Movement for Nation Reconstruction" (*chaegŏn gungmin undong*), beginning soon after Park's military coup in 1961, and the "Saemaul Undong"[4] (hereafter New Community Movement), implemented in 1971, which is the main target for the analysis in this research. State-led campaigns influenced each other across East Asian countries. The New Life Movement of postwar Japan borrowed its name from its Chinese equivalent, and the same name was later used for government-led campaigns in 1960s Korea (Kwon 2007).

More importantly, East Asian countries share commonalities in that the housewife ideology was strongly promoted by the state within the state-led movements. For instance, via a series of state-led campaigns, Japanese minds were molded to devote their lives to the nation. Women were especially mobilized to become "proper" housewives under the Japanese government's strong interventions in people's daily lives (Garon 2006). In the Korean context, the creation of modern women was among the major goals of the modernizing, state-building project by the Park Chung Hee regime (Kim Hyŏnmi 2000; Kim Ŭnshil 1999; Yi Suja 2000). Housewives were at the center of the discussion on the idealized standard of modern womanhood under the Park Chung Hee era (Shin Kŏn 2001). Thus, the ideology of "becoming a good housewife" based on the idea of "housewife for the motherland" was strongly promoted. In this context, the South Korean case indicates that "housewife" was not merely an outcome of the industrialization of those who are naturally "born" but also an institutionalized ideology promoted by the state and, thus, was regulated, controlled, (re)defined, guided, and monitored by the state.

Moreover, *all* women (not only full-time housewives) were redefined as housewives (Kim Hyegyŏng 2009). In the 1960s and 1970s, Korean society began to witness the gradual emergence of full-time housewives alongside rapid industrialization, the proliferation of the nuclear family, and the birth of the middle class (Chang Migyŏng 2007; Paek Misuk 2015). Even though the ideology of becoming a housewife had already begun to spread in South Korea during the Japanese colonial period (1910–1945), it had been confined to a small number of middle- and upper-class women and intellectuals termed "New Woman" (*sinyŏsŏng*).[5] The ideology of the housewife did not truly begin to broaden in scope and extend to the general public until the modern nation-state building that followed the Korean War (1950–1953) (Kim Yŏnchu and Yi Chaekyŏng 2013). Furthermore, it was only at the end of the 1970s that a "typical" form of the middle class comprising housewives and salaried male workers with stable incomes emerged (Pae Ŭnkyŏng 2008). Of course, the term "middle class" and the figure of the modern housewife were suggested by the developmental state, "carrying images of affluence and modernity" as "a new model for development and national identity" (Yang 2018, 42).

Discourses on economic development and modern nation-state building were promoted in mass media, such as newspapers and magazines (Yang 2018). In particular, women's magazines were key to regulating modern womanhood by continuously defining women's identities (Beetham 1996), depicting the life of an urban middle-class housewife as a desirable achievement (Kim Yŏnchu and Yi Chaegyŏng 2013). Housewives were also portrayed as important social actors in building loving nuclear households. They were expected to have romantic relationships with their husbands, serve as modern educators for their children, and act as disciplined home managers and rational consumers who disseminated modern values to family members (Chang Migyŏng 2007; Ch'oe Kyŏnghŭi 2016; Kim Yŏnchu and Yi Chaegyŏng 2013; Paek Misuk 2015). The media attempted to define ideal housewives and "problematize" their behaviors regarding consumption, leisure, labor, and family planning. Given the everyday socialization of *all* women as housewives, even rural and urban poor women recognized themselves to be housewives, regardless of whether they were *de facto* housewives. Thus, housewives were romanticized as ideal figures in the discussion of modern womanhood and positioned as the center of the private sphere for all women (Coates 2016, 38).

Compressed Modernity and the Mixture of "Tradition" and "Modernity"

The domestication of women in Asia has occurred over a relatively short period and is, therefore, complex and disconnected. While the domestication of women is associated with the emergence of a huge middle class and a clear gendered division of labor under long-term industrialization in the early industrializing economies (as discussed earlier), the emergence of the middle class in East Asia and Southeast Asian economies (except Japan) has not been as extensively visible. This situation is partly because many Asian countries have experienced "compressed modernity" (Chang 1999). In compressed modernity, a series of social changes occur simultaneously over a short period. It means that the domestication of women's labor in Asia has occurred quickly in an intensive and complex way. For instance, the active participation of women in the labor market has occurred simultaneously along with the development of the domestication of women in Asia. Further, the idea of becoming a housewife has been complicated by industrialization, which occurred alongside globalization in Asia. Therefore, people's perceptions of "becoming or being a housewife" are enormously diverse and dynamic in Asia (Ochiai 2008).

Similarly, rapid industrialization has precipitated the coexistence of "tradition" and "modernity" in conceptualizing the housewife ideology in Asia. As Gordon (1997, 250) observes in the discourses on housewives within the New Life Movements in China and Japan, there existed a "complicated mix of traditionalism and modernity". This situation was also the case for South Korea, where the modern womanhood suggested by the Park Chung Hee regime was characterized by coexistence and conflict between the "traditional" and the "modern". On a discursive level, the Park Chung Hee regime adopted "traditional" gender norms such as "wise mother and good wife" for the creation of the idealized modern womanhood. For instance, Kim Suchin (2008) discusses how the historical female figure of Shin Saimdang (1503–1551) of the Chosun Dynasty (1392–1897), symbolized as an ideal role model for the "traditional" mother, was newly revived as a symbol for the "modern" motherhood and the "rehabilitation of the nation" during the Park Chung Hee era. Interestingly, women's social roles, especially for rural women, expanded to allow for greater participation in community development projects.

Pae Ŭnkyŏng (2008) argues that the generally accepted features of housewives in the Western context did not become pervasive among the general populace in South Korea during the industrialization in the 1960s and 1970s, despite the promotion of the ideal housewives by mass media. Generally accepted ideas accompanying what it meant to be a housewife included a romantic husband-wife relationship, changes in the socioeconomic status of children from being part of the labor force to individuals needing "protection" and "education" with the emergence of the caring concept of "intensive mothering" (Hays 1996), the strengthening of domesticity, and the idea of an amicable family based on love and intimacy. Meanwhile, despite obvious socioeconomic changes during industrialization, such as the rising number of nuclear families 1960s,[6] the continuation of the traditional familism, patrilineal familial networks, and the preservation of the traditional *hoju* household system, under which only male descendants could serve as household heads, all strongly influenced the housewife ideology in South Korea (Yi Chaegyŏng 2003). Therefore, the housewife ideology among lower working-class women played out between emerging modernity and strongly rooted traditional gender roles.

On this point, it is worth noting that late industrializing countries have a long history of adopting the ideology of becoming a housewife through colonialism. Korea was no exception. Though discussions on the emergence of full-time housewives in South Korea have concentrated on the 1960s to 1980s, when the number of nuclear families gradually increased, the introduction of modern familial concepts had already begun during the Japanese colonial period. Endeavors were made by the colonial government and intellectuals as part of the modernization initiatives to replace traditional values, structures, and emotions, while concepts of modern childcaring were introduced to upper and middle-class women during the colonial period (Kim Hyegyŏng 2006). For instance, the central ideology of 'wise mother and good wife' (*hyŏnmoyangch'ŏ*), which has strongly influenced the institutionalization of gender relations in Korea, originates from the equivalent Japanese term "good wife, wise mother (*ryōsai kenbo*)" during the colonial period (Hong Yanghŭi 2010; Kim Suchin 2008).

Rethinking Women's Labor: Varieties of Rural Women's Roles and Labor

It is important to contextualize women's labor in Asia within a broader sociocultural, economic, and policy context in the discussion of the formation of the housewife ideology. Especially, on the scope of rural women's labor, it is necessary to challenge gendered assumptions about work and recognize the diverse and often unrecognized roles and contributions of women to rural economies and communities. The scope of the labor by rural women during the industrialization covered farming, housework, and participation in the rural development and family planning program, community management, and organizational activities. In the 1960s and 1970s in South Korea, the everyday lives of women in rural villages underwent significant changes because of state-led rural development projects. It meant the significant broadening of the scope of labor by rural women. Beyond increasing the agricultural workload, rural women were encouraged to participate in community improvement projects, such as the repair of roofs and the improvement of roads. Roofs were renovated from thatching to colorful slate in the name of "rural housewives". Rugged soil roads in front of villages were paved with gray cement, and a saemaul public community center (*hoegwan*) was established in every village with a green saemaul flag on which three slogans – "diligence" (*kŭnmyŏn*), "self-help" (*chaju*), and "cooperation" (*hyŏptong*) – were written. Village residents – mainly rural women and children – were mobilized to clean the streets together early in the morning to the tune of the saemaul song. Rural women were encouraged to modernize by caring for children's nutrition and learning how to cook healthy foods with "modern" recipes. They were encouraged to practice family planning and use contraception to reduce the number of children. They were organized into "women's associations" (*punyŏhoe*) and were encouraged to become primary participants in the New Community Movement. Assignments for rural women's organizational activities varied from family planning; increasing productivity by planting high-yield varieties of a rice called unification rice (*t'ongilbyŏ*); purchasing modern agricultural machines; simplifying ceremonial occasions for weddings, funerals, and ancestral rites; and emphasizing work ethics. The activities were controlled and monitored from the village and administrative levels. Village leaders with green caps and armbands – one male and one female leader were appointed as saemaul leaders for each village – encouraged rural residents to participate in rural development projects assigned to the village. Local governmental officers visited each rural village to monitor and supervise the rural projects as part of the New Community Movement.[7]

Rural Women's Agency: Becoming a Housewife and Entering the Middle Class as an Aspirational Category

In the meantime, it is vital to pay special attention to the agency of rural women in understanding the proliferation of the housewife ideology. This research reevaluates the scope and emergence of the middle class in South Korea and Asia at large using the concept of "aspiration". In the 1960s and 1970s in South Korea, following the decline of the economy and society after the Korean War, the "narrative of the middle class as a mainstream social force was a discursive construct rather than an existing entity" (Yang 2018, 42) for most of the population. The aspiration to enter the middle class to support developmental goals was promoted by the state. Likewise, Goodman (2014) discusses the development of a comfortable middle-class lifestyle in China given the proliferation of the state-led discourse surrounding the emergence of the middle class. He argues that there is a clear state-sponsored discourse on the harmonious middle class and social changes more than a clear middle-class social structure in China. Schielke (2012, 47) describes the middle class in provincial Egypt as an "aspirational category" whose members are to "look forward to a better future and to work on the means of distinction and advancement to reach it". Meanwhile, he maintains that being in the middle class is an unfulfilled dream of many people in Egypt, as it is highly attractive and compelling. Heiman, Liechty, and Freeman (2012, 18) in their edited volume on the global middle class from late industrializing countries define the middle class as "not just an increasingly common category of self-identification, but – perhaps even more important – an *aspirational* category".

Callard (2018, 4) argues that aspiration is a "distinctive form of agency" and includes "the mental work of thinking, imagining, and reasoning". Davis (2004) employs this idea to analyze the rural middle class in late industrializing countries, as it focuses on the agency of the social actor. Davis demonstrates that "middle classes *shape* industrial and economic development, rather than being merely its product; and the particular ways in which middle classes shape themselves – and the ways historical conditions shape them – influence development trajectories in multiple ways" (ibid., 1, italics in original). In this sense, social class can be considered a process where "class boundaries and identities are constructed and reconstructed on a daily basis" (Yang 2018, 13).

Discussions on the agencies of social actors in the middle class are also connected with criticisms of the theory of the domestication of women's labor: women in late industrializing countries are often depicted as passive entities, contrary to the focus on female agencies in discussions on the domestication of women in early industrialized countries (see Goldstein-Gidoni 2012). Thus, this research attempts to illuminate the domestication of women not only as a creation of the state or a "natural" outcome of industrialization but also as the result of the aspiration of working-class women toward "becoming a housewife". Though the ideology of the middle class and the housewife remained "imagined" for most of the population in Korea (Kim Jaewŏn 2016), for rural women, the aspiration to enter the middle class and become a full-time housewife was strong and desperate. Moreover, according to Appadurai (2004, 67), even though aspirations "have something to do with wants, preferences, choices, and calculations, they are never simply individual". Instead, they are a collective outcome based on multilateral negotiation among various social actors in society. Thus, this research analyzes how the ideology of becoming a housewife was created, disseminated, and collectivized by the government and rural women.

Intersection of Gender and Class: "Rural Housewives" Versus "Urban Housewives"

The theory of housewifization should consider how gender and class intersect to produce different socialization in the process of becoming a housewife and unequal experiences of inequality. Gordon (1997), by analyzing the New Life Movement in postwar Japan, shows that the housewife ideology was applied to urban middle-class women and poor rural women. Within the housewife ideology, urban and rural women were regulated and defined differently. Rural women were actively mobilized for family planning, the modernization of life through sanitation and nutrition improvement, the democratization of family relations, ceremonial ritual simplification, and an emphasis on frugality (ibid.). Meanwhile, wives of salaried men in urban areas were educated to care for their working husbands to support their functioning as highly productive and efficient workers.

In the Korean context, the term "rural housewives" (*nongch'onjubu*) often appeared in the media and governmental documents as contradictory to "urban housewives" (*toshijubu*) in the 1960s. This situation might reflect the process of rapid urbanization and a clear division between the two social groups. In the construction and strengthening of the housewife ideology, discourses on rural and urban housewives were closely connected to definitions of labor, education, upward mobility, working ethics and leisure, ways of savings and consumption, and social organizing. As will be further investigated in this book, women were split into two dichotomous social groups of urban and rural housewives within which they were sometimes portrayed by the state as "partners" or "collaborators" and "competitors". "Social control" refers to "the capacity of a society to regulate itself according to desired principles and values" (Janowitz 1975, 82). This research highlights the fact that the Park Chung Hee regime attempted to maximize the effects of social control and promote social order by defining social groups in relation (opposition) to each other.

Despite state-level distinctions between urban and rural housewives, most Korean women in the 1960s and 1970s shared common experiences regarding economic challenges, working in informal sectors, and the (un)changing gender roles caught between tradition and modernity. In particular, unlike the domestication of women in the Western context, where "workers" and "mothers" were relatively clearly defined, during the early industrialization period, most married women in Korea occupied a gray area of "mothering" (Pae Ŭnkyŏng 2008). Furthermore, as most women were not actually "stay-at-home" housewives until well after the emergence of housewives as a dominant social group moved beyond the discursive level in the late 1970s (ibid.) and given the fact that most of the population was rural before this period, the urban–rural housewives divide was largely imagined during much of Park's rule.[8] Therefore, this research tries to examine the features of the ideology of becoming a housewife for rural women generated by Park's regime while carefully considering the common experiences of most Korean women during the 1960s and 1970s.

Looking Back on the 1960s and 1970s

Why Park Chung Hee? Why the 1960s and 1970s?: Connecting Past and Present

On March 10, 2017, the constitutional court upheld a parliamentary vote to impeach President Park Geun-hye (2013–2017) over corruption and cronyism scandals.[9]

The first daughter of former president, Park Chung Hee, who extensively profited from the Korean people's nostalgia toward her father in her election, thus, became the first democratically elected Korean president to be removed from office. The *Guardian* (McCurry March 10, 2017) judged Park's impeachment to be a victory for democracy and the end of Park Chung Hee's era in South Korea. However, Park Chung Hee has been at the center of conflicts between conservatives and progressives since the late 1990s, and his ghost is persistently present in South Korean society today. Any evaluation of the Park Chung Hee regime is connected, explicitly and implicitly, to current social issues; from different political stances between conservatives and progressives and deeply rooted intergenerational gaps and interpretations of Korean history to the building of national identity.

As Koreans suffered through the Asian Financial Crisis of 1997 and 1998, known as the "IMF crisis" by Koreans,[10] a strong nostalgia for Park Chung Hee emerged. Conservatives attempted to recast Park Chung Hee as a "national hero" (Podoler 2016) and glorify the "good old days" of the 1960s and 1970s, the period Korean society witnessed unprecedentedly rapid economic development. For these forces at play within right-wing populism in South Korea, Park Chung Hee consistently stands for "developmentalism", "economic achievement", and the "alleviation of poverty". During the presidencies of Lee Myung-bak (2008–2013) and Park Geun-hye (2013–2017), the Park Chung Hee commemoration was among the most important conservative agendas. The Park Chung Hee Presidential Museum was opened in Seoul in 2012, and the "Park Chung Hee Memorial Town" in Park's hometown of Kumi, Gyeongsang Province, which had been under construction since 2006, was completed in 2019. Honoring Park Chung Hee was not limited to Korea. The New Community Movement, initiated by the Park Chung Hee regime in 1971 to modernize the rural South Korean economy, was exported to developing countries as an international aid plan and promoted as a "successful" development model (see Doucette and Müller 2016; Jeong 2017; Schwak 2016).

For progressives, the Park Chung Hee regime is a historical legacy closely associated with the "memory of colonialism under imperial Japan", as he served as a high-ranking military officer under the Japanese Imperial Army during the Japanese colonial rule (1910–1945). Further, given the authoritarian characteristics of the regime, his ruling era has been depicted as "a dark age for democracy". Park Chung Hee declared a state of national emergency, known as "October *Yushin*", in October 1972, which continued through 1980. The *Yushin* Constitution's main features were martial law imposition, the suspension of the constitution, and the dissolution of the legislature. Moreover, the urban-centered industrialization and oppressive labor policies during his regime have been associated with "the emergence of economic disparities among social groups after the Korean War". After a series of democratization movements in the 1980s, including the Great Worker Struggle in 1987, in which over one million protestors yearning for democratization partook nationwide, President Noh Tae Woo proclaimed a "declaration of democratization" in the same year. In the late 1990s, when democracy blossomed after the democratization, the progressives attempted to rebuild a new national identity based on anti-colonialism and anti-authoritarianism. Accordingly, the "rebuilding of Korean History" project was initiated during the presidency of Kim Young-sam (1993–1998), which was the first administration directly elected by the people. Kim attempted to discard the historical legacy of Japanese colonialism by demolishing the Government-General Building (*chosŏnch'ongdokpu*), a symbol of Japanese imperialism, in 1995. The administration also restored Gyeongbokgung Palace, the royal palace of the Chosun Dynasty. The "rebuilding of Korean History" was further accelerated by the two liberal governments of Kim Dae Jung (1998–2003) and Roh Moo-hyun (2003–2008). During the Kim Dae Jung regime, the Institute for Korean Ethnic Nationalism (*minjok munje yŏn'guso*) worked for the official release of a list of "pro-Japanese collaborators" and protested against opening the Park Chung Hee Presidential Museum in 2000. Further, under the auspices of the progressive Roh Moo-hyun government, the "Presidential Committee for the Inspection of Collaborations for Japanese Imperialism" was officially established in 2005.

The varying interpretations and controversies associated with the Park Chung Hee regime indicate the importance of understanding how diverse social groups interacted with the state in the 1960s and 1970s to shape contemporary Korean society (Han 2004). In this sense, the 1960s and 1970s were an undeniably momentous period in defining contemporary Korean society (Cho Ŭnchu 2018).

Park Chung Hee and Modernization: Beyond the Dichotomy Between "Oppressive Mobilization from Above" and "Social Consensus from the Bottom"

Regarding the people's reaction to mobilization during Park's modernization, one finds two primary stances in scholarly discussions. First, involvement stemmed from an "oppressive mobilization from above", as exemplified during the *Yushin* (1972–1980), which provided dictatorial political power to Park Chung Hee without imposing any limits on re-election. Such views are strongly supported by progressive intellectuals and political dissidents in South Korea. Studies assuming this stance have shed light on the oppressiveness and coerciveness of governmental intervention in every sociopolitical dimension, from family planning (see Pae Ŭnkyŏng 2005) to the New Community Movement (Cho Hŭiyŏn 2004; Ko Wŏn 2006; O Yusŏk 2014; Pak Chindo and Han Tohyŏn 1999) to industrialization. Workers were considered to have been forced to provide labor in the name of the "economic development of the motherland" in exchange for low wages, long working hours, inhumane working conditions, and denial of workers' rights (see Yi Kwangil 1998).

Some have interpreted the regime's top-down social mobilization as a utilization of the Confucian order. This viewpoint posits the Park Chung Hee regime's modernization project as a marriage of Confucianism and authoritarian rule, within which Confucian elements such as "loyalty to the fatherland", "obedience to the power", and "filial piety" functioned as mechanisms of social mobilization for the people. Indeed, Asia's newly developing economies have even been characterized as exemplars of hypermasculine state developmentalism, where there exist "all the rights and privileges of classical Confucian patriarchy for the state while assigning to society the characteristics of classical Confucian womanhood" (Han and Ling 1998, 53). Hence, the Park Chung Hee regime is a prototype of the hypermasculine state (Kim 2001).

The second stance concerning the public's attitude toward the Park regime's governmental intervention focuses on the coerciveness of the regime and "social consensus from the bottom". Some scholars have approached this grassroots "social concord" through the lens of "fascism" as understood in the West (e.g., Chang Munsŏk and Yi Sangnok 2006; Im Jihyŏn 2004). They argue that 18 years of rule by Park Chung Hee cannot be explained merely by the oppressiveness of the regime, though they agree with the despotic characterization of Park's regime. They acknowledge that there certainly existed resistant forces and aspirations for democracy occasionally expressed through outcries from students, laborers, and progressive intellectuals. However, they raise the question of the silent public majority during a long period of dictatorial rule. This group of scholars suggests that the silence of the majority can be interpreted as a strong yearning for future prosperity, wherein a zealous longing for wealth induced *silent* "accordance", "agreement", and even "support" from the general public and made possible long-term rule by a dictatorship. This argument, the so-called "mass dictatorship theory (*taejungdokchaeron*)", continues to be discussed today.

There is also the explanation of "state populism" (Han 2004). Han (ibid., 80) argues that "'state populism' was fomented and practiced as a means of national mobilization. Economic equality and egalitarianism was to the 1970s as freedom and revolution was to the 1960s, and it pervaded every measure taken to arouse and sustain the New Community Movement". This stance views the implementation of egalitarian ethos as having stimulated the mobilization of the populace by providing an imagined projection of modernity, offering the betterment of individual lives. The "social consensus from the bottom" theory has been controversial, as it could accidentally induce the justification and glamorization of a dictatorial regime.

Despite the noted nuances, conventional debates on social mobilization mechanisms are largely dichotomous: they are either "oppressive mobilization from above" or the "social consensus from bottom". This book considers the oppressiveness of the regime and "consensus from the bottom" as factors for understanding social mobilization, as the consideration of both sides allows for a more systematic understanding of the mechanisms of the state-society "social contract" (Park 2010) and the dynamics of the state-society relations (Chang Munsŏk 2006).

Accordingly, an analysis must first be made of the multi-layered relationship between the state's pursuit of political legitimacy and social integration and the desire of the common people to ride the wave of rapid economic growth. Chang's (2012, 183, italics in original) work discusses the political contract between the citizenry and the state, under which "the state is expected to concentrate on economic development so that its citizens can *benefit as private economic players in the market system* – be workers, industrialists, or self-employed entrepreneurs". He further argues that so-called "developmental citizenship" is the basis for the state-society relationships in Third World countries. Moreover, Park (2010) provides great insights into manifold interactions between the state and society. He notes that few studies have investigated how developmental states in East Asia have set national goals, defined societal projects, and mobilized people to achieve these goals. He examines how the Park Chung Hee regime attempted to maintain "a high degree of mobilizational capacity as well as political legitimacy" (ibid., 596) and how the general public (in particular, the lower- and working-class who were the majority of the population at that time) responded to social policies. Park (ibid.), focusing on educational policymaking, elaborates that the Korean state implemented a series of egalitarian policies in the late 1960s and early 1980s, such as the introduction of a lottery-based allocation system in 1969 to replace entrance examinations for middle schools, the dissolution of elite high schools, and the implementation of the "High School Equalization Policy" in 1974.[11] Thus, Park (ibid.) posits that the state-society "social contract" in the educational sector is based on egalitarianism geared toward social integration of the general public and that this was achieved by oppressing the interests of the privileged middle class.

Second, it is necessary to consider the dynamics of the relationship between the state and society. Yi Sangnok (2006) argues that the multi-layered aspirations and agencies of the people have been overlooked in analyses of the stance of the masses to the Park Chung Hee regime given the noted dichotomous framework – "accord" or "resistance". He posits that more careful attention should be paid to complexities, conflicts, and divergences within the masses, as they simultaneously agreed with and resisted Park Chung Hee's rule. It is, thus, important to question how the Park Chung Hee regime's socioeconomic policies were interpreted among diverse social groups over time. For instance, in an analysis of "interactive developmentalism" between the state and society, focusing on South Korea's first generation of industrial workers, Kim (2013) provides important clues to understanding dynamic state–grassroots interactions. Kim (ibid., 591) depicts how "Industrial Warriors", who played a significant role as bulwarks of the developmental regime in the 1970s, had emerged as "the state shaped the national 'economy-first' psyche, by which grassroots Koreans willingly adopted new national values and discipline to establish a 'modern citizenship' or 'developmental citizenship' in return for a steady job and increased income". The same Industrial Warriors eventually became "Goliath Warriors", leading the democratization movements in the 1980s; the Goliath Warriors later gave rise to a "Labor Aristocracy" following the introduction of neo-liberalism to the labor market after the Asian Financial Crisis. Highlighting the nature of the populace's responses to and expectations of the Park Chung Hee regime can better illuminate discussions on the state–society relationship.

For a systematic understanding of the state–society relations, the concept of the "routinization of politics" helps explain the strategies socialist regimes use to encourage the general populace to internalize an ideology (Kim Chonguk 2009). Further, the "everyday life" concept (Haggard and Noland 2010) provides a better understanding of negotiations, challenges, and resistance from the bottom. As Steege et al. (2008, 362) maintain, "the history of everyday life draws explicit casual connections – in all their contradictory tensions – between the processes of the microhistorical context and the metanarratives of microhistory". This research attempts to examine how the state and society relationships had been built during the Park Chung Hee regime by paying careful attention to the "routinized politics" in everyday life.

Literature Review on Rural Women During the 1960s and 1970s in South Korea

A Marginalized Social Group in Research

In this research, members of the rural population are those whose socioeconomic livelihoods are based primarily on agricultural activities or whose daily lives are based in the countryside, regardless of whether they are agriculture producers, small-scale merchandisers, or landlords. Rural women are women who live and work in villages and small townships regardless of their socioeconomic background, economic activities, marital status, educational level, or age. However, married women will be the central focus of discussions in this book.

Despite continuous scholarly discussion on the Park Chung Hee regime in the political sciences, sociology, anthropology, and women's studies, few studies address the lives of rural women during this important period. While there is significant research on the participation of rural women in rural development projects, most of them were conducted by governmental bodies to mobilize rural women for the state-led modernization project. This lacuna can be explained by the fact that "rurality" and "women" are marginalized topical issues within scholarly discussion on South Korean modernization.

The marginalization of rural society and population in scholarly discussion is a common phenomenon observed in industrialized economies and is particularly apparent in the South Korean context. Sociologists have conducted fieldwork-based research to examine social changes and continuities in rural South Korean society during the rapid urbanization of the 1960s and 1970s (see Kim Chusuk 1994). However, with rapid city-centered industrialization and a shrinking rural population, rural sociology has declined as an academic field, even though at the dawn of industrialization in 1950, the share of the rural population was 81.6%. Despite decreasing to 72% by 1960 and 58.8% by 1970, the rural population comprised over half of the country's population until the mid-1970s (Pak Chindo 2003). The overrepresented proportion of the rural population during the 1960s and 1970s demonstrates how important it is to pay special attention to rural population involvement in the industrialization process in South Korea.

In the context of research on women, there have been significant scholarly attempts to highlight women's contributions to economic development during industrialization. Such attempts stem from the criticism of scholarly focus only on actors such as professional bureaucrats (see Cheng, Haggard, and Kang 1998; Evans 1995; Haggard 2004) or processes such as the interplay between the state and chaebol[12] (see Amsden 1989; Castells 1992; Evans 1995; Johnson 1987; Kohli 2004; Wade 1990; Weiss 1998; Woo-Cumings 1999). Since the transition to democracy in 1987, the "hidden heroes", workers who supported economic growth from the bottom up, have garnered much attention. Furthermore, criticisms that previous research on the Park Chung Hee regime lacked a gendered perspective, even within working-class discussions, have induced efforts to illuminate the "invisibles", including young female workers (*yŏgong*), who were the main labor force supporting labor-intensive export-oriented light industry in the 1960s and 1970s (see Chang Migyŏng 2004; Kim 2001, 2011; Kim Wŏn 2005; Koo 2001).[13] Young female factory workers are often considered the "hidden heroes" of the economic development of South Korea during early industrialization. The scope of the research on young female factory workers is broad, ranging from the sociocultural meaning of their labor as part of the modernization project of the Park Chung Hee regime (Chang Migyŏng 2004), to the cultural meanings of their residential spaces (Kim Ch'unsu 2005) to identity building and desires (Kim Wŏn 2004a), sisterhood among workers, organizational strategies for managing labor disputes (Kim Wŏn 2004c), and their positionality within the housewife ideology (Kwon 2020). Such research can broaden and deepen our understanding of the Park Chung Hee regime, as "the so-called 'industrial take-off' during this period would not have been possible without women's spartan industrial labor" (Chang 2010, 69).

One of the primary reasons previous studies on women's labor focus on young female factory workers is that labor at the factory is conventionally considered "work" in the formal or public sphere. Meanwhile, the experience and labor of women in the informal and private realms, as in the domestic sphere, rural areas, and the sex industry, are often socially considered "nonwork" (Chin 1998). There have also been endeavors to shed light on marginalized female workers such as bus fare collectors (Kim Chŏnghwa 2002; Kim Wŏn 2004b), housemaids (Kang Isu 2009; Kwŏn Kyŏngmi 2016), and sex workers (see Moon 1997; Yi Hayŏng and Yi Nayŏng 2015), working in the domestic and informal sector during the 1960s and 1970s. Previous research clarifies that labor spanning the domestic and informal sectors, such as the sex industry, was promoted by the developmental state as part of tourism for foreigners under the banner of "national security and economic growth" for the motherland (Soh 2003, 174). Meanwhile, such semi-formal laborers were the "Other" to urban middle-class housewives and, thus, were labeled a "social problem". Hence, some women stood at an ambiguous boundary – alternately and simultaneously considered the "shame of the motherland" and "patriots for the nation" (Yi Hayŏng and Yi Nayŏng 2015).

Studies on women's informal labor are typically marginalized in conventional discussions, but these recent scholarly attempts to shed light on the topic are meaningful in that the formal–informal sector border, as applied to women's labor in the earlier stage of industrialization, was not clearly defined (Chang Migyŏng 2004). Meanwhile, research on rural women's labor remains lacking. Rural women's diverse labor activities, such as productive and domestic laborers, family managers, and community managers during the industrialization process, have been overlooked even among feminist studies. In the process of (re)defining labor, work in the agricultural sector has also been considered "traditional" and, therefore, "informal" and "private". Thus, literature on Korean women during industrialization has focused on the work experiences of young rural–urban female factory workers or concentrated on "mothering" as a collective category in the context of Korean motherhood (Pae Ŭnkyŏng 2008).

The lacuna on rural women can also be attributed to the fact that women's movements have mainly focused on middle-class women's agendas since post-democratization. The progressive women's movement, which had directed much attention to the socioeconomic betterment of female workers from the lower class, has attempted to forge its own autonomous political space by keeping its distance from the conventional democratization movement forces since the 1990s, which were male-dominated. The movement even gave rise to further independent women's movements for middle-class women post-democratization, including housewives' movements, environmental movements, and labor-related matters of female office workers (Kwon 2018). During the professionalization, politicization, and institutionalization of middle-class-women-centered movements in the 1990s and 2000s, lower-class women issues, including rural women, have been somewhat trivialized within the women's movement (Cho-Yi Yŏul 2006). Thus, "this situation produced a polarization of women's movements, with lower-class movements and middle-/upper-class women's movements at opposite ends and led to the marginalization of lower-class women within mainstream women's movements" (Kwon 2018, 648). Alongside the marginalization of lower-class women issues in mainstream women's movements, research on rural women has also been undermined.

A Dichotomous Evaluation of the Labor and Involvement by Rural Women

Further, research on rural women's unrecognized labor during industrialization tends to take a dichotomous stance – "mobilization" under oppressive ruling or "participation" – when understanding the involvement of rural women in state-led rural development projects. This book discusses the interplay between the state and the variety of labor provided by rural women in the framework of becoming "good" housewives, including their productive and domestic labor, savings initiatives, and organizational activities. The dichotomous viewpoint on rural women's positioning during industrialization originates from the divided evaluation of the Park Chung Hee era, as discussed in the previous section. This section focuses on the literature on family planning and rural women's organizational activities to demonstrate how the conventional discussion was confined to a dichotomous perspective.

Since the 1990s, the discussion on family planning has considered women's rights – particularly the capacity to make decisions on reproductive issues to be crucial. Reproductive rights include the right to decide to give birth, decide when and how to give birth, and access information and services on birth control. In this context, issues of the violation of women's reproductive rights in various social and cultural contexts and how various actors have been involved in women's decision-making are now front and center (Hyodo 2002). A significant number of feminist scholars have raised questions on the impacts of state intervention on issues of women's bodies and sexuality (Gordon 1976; Savara 1983). In the

Korean context, many prior studies highlight the coercive and repressive nature of the family planning program of the Park Chung Hee regime (Cho 2016; Choi 2015; Pae Ŭn'kyŏng 2005). Previous research maintains that women's rights and reproductive autonomy were disregarded by the state for the economic development of the motherland (Hwang Chŏngmi 2001; Kim Ŭnshil 1999; Lee 2004; Moon 2005; Yi Migyŏng 1989; Yi Myŏngsŏn 1990). Meanwhile, in recent years, there have been attempts to examine women's agency and roles as active acceptors of family planning. For instance, Cho (2016) argues that South Korean women responded actively to family planning discourses and tried to make use of its program as an opportunity to express their desire for sexuality and associate it with the concept of love and relationships.

From the literature, the relationship between state intervention and women's sexuality has been well-explored. However, the following considerations are yet to be fully examined. First, family planning should be understood within a biological context and in social reproduction and the creation of "modern" motherhood during the "modern" nation-building process context (Ashford 2020). As family planning was considered part of national development for most postcolonial societies, it should be discussed in the broader context of how "modern" motherhood was (re)defined per the creation of nationalism (Yuval-Davis 1997). Next, even though family planning was commonly accepted as part of modern nation-building in postcolonial societies, perceptions toward family planning for women varied along with social class, educational level, urban-rural residency, and religion. For instance, for feminist middle-class women in India, family planning meant advancing free decision-making power in reproduction. Meanwhile, women targeted for family planning, who were mainly rural and working-class women, did not always comply with the nation-building logic and posited alternative interpretations of having multiple children, claiming that they were not a threat but a benefit to their family's welfare (Sreenivas 2021). For some urban women in Ghana, it was a means of self-expression (Ashford 2020). For others in Egypt, it was an expression of women's autonomy (Govindasamy and Malhotra 1996). Hence, we should raise the question of how rural women in South Korea interpreted family planning in the context of "modern" motherhood; in particular, in the context of strengthening their roles as "modern" educators and the importance of intensive mothering practices within the housewife ideology.

Moreover, regarding the organizational activities of rural women, the participation of rural women in state-led organizations during the Park Chung Hee regime has been evaluated from two perspectives. One scholarly view posits that the participation of rural women in the New Community Movement was an oppressive mobilization for national development and modern nation-building under the name of modernization of the motherland (see Shin Kŏn 2001). The other scholarly view considers the participation of rural women in rural development projects in a more positive light (see Chang Migyŏng 2008). This latter understanding has been informed by attempts to focus on rural women's viewpoints on their participation in the New Community Movement (Shin Hyŏnok 1999; Yokota 2002a, 2002b). In particular, Chang Migyŏng (2008) considers the participation of rural women in rural development projects as a process of experiencing, establishing, and negotiating with various identities, such as leaders, negotiators, and family members, by analyzing "successful stories" written by female saemaul leaders.

Previous research has furnished better insight into the gendered nature of state intervention and rural women's responses. However, it remains unclear in which context state-led organizational activities for rural women during the New Community Movement should be understood and in what ways rural women's involvement in rural development projects was connected with the (dis)continuation of gender relations in rural households. This book addresses such gaps.

Research Methods

This book addresses the stories of rural women in the 1960s and 1970s; stories that also regard the roots and origins of the middle class, state–society relations during the industrialization period, and the (dis)continuities of gender relations in current Korean society. It draws on three different sets of fieldwork data collected between 2005 and 2011. First, the study employs quantitative data such as official government statistics and surveys of previous research and media from the 1960s and 1970s to establish a broad picture of the society at the time. Such data indicate the overall situation of the labor market, urbanization, population structure, and saving habits and consumption behaviors on a macro level.

Second, it analyzes a wide range of archival data, including monthly magazines for rural women published by the government and civic actors, including major daily newspapers – *Chosun Ilbo*, *Donga Ilbo*, *Kyunghyang Shinmun*, *Maeil Kyungje* – popular magazines, governmental documents, and presidential speeches. Particularly, daily newspapers can help grasp everyday life in rural areas. The Park Chung Hee regime utilized every type of media as a means of proliferating the ideology of modernity to legitimize its dictatorship. In this context, women's magazines were among the most important components of Park's modernization project (Sŏ Yŏnju 2007). Given the gradual emergence of full-time housewives and the middle class in the 1960s and 1970s, there were numerous women's magazines available for urban middle-class housewives in the early stage of industrialization.[14] These women's magazines popularized the housewife as a "norm" and articulated middle-class housewives' lifestyles as "dreams" (Garon 2010, 331). There has been a significant amount of research on women's magazines for urban and middle-class women in Korea (see Chang Migyŏng 2007; Kim Hyŏnju 2007; Kim Poksun 2007). However, media discourses on rural women are under-researched. This book bridges the lacuna by analyzing monthly magazines for rural women, such as *Happy Home* (*kajŏng ŭi pŏt*),[15] published by the Planned Parenthood Federation of Korea. This magazine was published for rural women and sought to proliferate the ideology of the modern family, focusing on family planning in rural areas. In its first issue, the magazine clearly noted that its aim was "for the modernization of rural villages" (*Happy Home* 1968). It was particularly promoted in rural villages to increase family planning initiatives (Pae Ŭnkyŏng

2005). It was distributed to family planning mothers' clubs, which were established nationwide for housewives.

This book also analyzes personal letters from peasant movement activists and documents and periodicals such as *Rural Women*[16] (*Nongch'onbunyŏ*), issued by the Korean Catholic Peasant Women's Organization. Personal letters from peasant movement activists were collected by the author through personal communications. Documents were assembled from peasant organizations and the Korea Democracy Foundation, established in 2001 to collect materials related to democracy movements in Korea.

Finally, given the limited research on rural women in the 1960s and 1970s, this research draws on a qualitative research methodology through in-depth interviews with 32 informants in South Korea, Germany, and Belgium. These interviews were conducted by the author with farmers, housewives, activists of the peasant movements, governmental officers, managers, politicians, and researchers. Most participants were recruited using snowball sampling. Interviews took between one to three hours and were transcribed to facilitate analysis.

Structure of the Book

Chapter 1 describes the socioeconomic situation in the 1960s and 1970s in the rural areas in South Korea and the sociopolitical background of the New Community Movement. This chapter illustrates that the New Community Movement, a major national modernization project, was key to building relations between the state and rural society. It was accomplished under the banner of seeking "modernization of the motherland" through the "establishment of independent economy", "modern nation-state building", and "anti-communism ideology".

Chapter 2 elucidates how the work ethics established by the Park Chung Hee regime, as a "modern" concept, redefined the nature of labor for rural women under the housewife ideology. This chapter illustrates the process by which the labor performed by rural women in productive and domestic spheres was classified as domestic and consequently considered inferior under the housewife label. Additionally, the chapter explores the active adoption of work ethics, such as hard work, by rural women as a pathway to attain social mobility.

Chapter 3 illustrates the incongruencies between the state and rural women regarding ideal motherhood around the housewife ideology, promoted within the framework of the family planning program. It explores how family planning was strongly associated with rural women's aspiration toward achieving middle-class status through children's education, contrary to the state's intention to reduce the number of children.

Chapter 4 investigates rural women as financial managers (i.e., savers) as part of the housewife ideology. In particular, it analyzes how the Park Chung Hee regime intervened in everyday life to promote savings and collective drives. This chapter posits that rural women were promoted as managers for the household economy and rural communities. In a broader sense, they were positioned as the main agents responsible for accumulating the national capital for economic development. The chapter also clarifies that rural women attempted to capitalize on state-led saving initiatives to fulfill their aspirations toward becoming middle class.

Chapter 5 examines how rural women's participation in state-led organizational activities in the process of domestication of women in South Korea came to characterize the housewife ideology formation in a non-Western context. State intervention in rural women's everyday lives in rural society induced "unanticipated" consequences such as the strengthening of women's autonomy within the household economy. This chapter illustrates how state intervention was used to take the imaginary discourses on the middle class into daily life, transform living environments, and bargain with patriarchal order within the family and rural communities.

Chapter 6 highlights the fact that rural women's embrace of the "modern" housewife ideology should be interpreted as acceptance of the motherhood practices of urban housewives and as a gendered strategic negotiation of family structure to ensure their future social welfare and that of their family members. Further, this chapter shows that the increasing autonomy of rural women in the productive, domestic sphere; household economy; and rural communities did not necessarily lead to their "empowerment" or the deconstruction of local patriarchal orders given firmly rooted socioeconomic and cultural constraints. Thus, the scope of the bargaining power of rural women was restricted, and the consensus, compromises, and negotiations of rural women with the state intervention partially contributed to the (re)production of gender relations during the industrialization process in the 1960s and 1970s South Korea.

Finally, the conclusion summarizes the book's main arguments and theoretical contributions. Here, the study discusses the past and present (dis)continuities of gender roles and the socioeconomic significance of the analysis of rural women to the formation of the middle class in South Korea. It also presents the comparative implications of this research for general insight into the study of gender, class, and state–society relations in Asia at large.

Notes

1 On industrialization and the emergence of the housewife in early industrialized countries, see Davidoff and Hall (1987), Giles (2004), Tosh (1999), Friedan (2013), and Hays (1996).

2 In this sense, "anyone performing marginalized labor can be described as 'housewifized', even if that person performs wage labor or happens to be a male" (Ochiai 2008, 29). Mies' theory, thus, provides great insight into the current neo-liberalizing economy, under which "flexibility" and "deregulation" of the labor market have been extensively promoted on the global level.

3 There have been attempts to shed light on the multi-layered experiences of women from various social classes. For instance, Nolan (1990), Duchen (1991), and Gordon (1997) discuss the domestication process of women's labor regarding working-class women in Germany, France, and Japan, respectively. McCarthy (2020) explores the rise of the "working wife" in the United Kingdom and the motherhood of working-class mothers.

4 "Sae" literally means new and "maŭl" rural villages. In this book, saemaul undong will be translated as the New Community Movement. Elsewhere, saemaul is a proper noun when referring to leaders, organizations, or community building.

5 "New Woman" indicates women in Korea who attempted to define new gender roles for women during the Japanese colonial period. These young women from the upper and middle class, educated in higher education institutes, endeavored to raise sociocultural issues, such as gender relations, women's economic activities, relationship with male partners, and consumer practices of women, and political issues, such as independent movements from colonial powers. In fact, the emergence of New Woman was a common phenomenon in East Asia, along with the increase in education opportunities for women in the 1920s and 1930s, though the specific content of the activities of women's groups varied per sociopolitical situation.
6 The term "nuclear family" first began to appear in South Korea in the mid-1960s (Kim Hyegyŏng 2009).
7 Park Chung Hee attempted to strengthen administrative capacity by increasing the number of government officers. This move can be confirmed by the fact that the number of government officers doubled in 1971 relative to the 1950s. Particularly noteworthy is the increase in the number of public servants at the local level. The number of local public servants, including those at the rural village level, increased from 36,985 in 1953 to 90,625 in 1971, nearly tripling. This increase clearly demonstrated the intention of the Park Chung Hee regime to extend administrative power in rural villages (Kim Sŏnch'ŏl 1999, 40–41).
8 Until the mid-1970s, the rural population comprised over half of the whole population (Kim Hyegyŏng 2009). Even today, massive population migration during holidays, such as New Year's Day (*sŏllal*) and Korean Thanksgiving Day (*ch'usŏk*), indicate that the lives of most of the Korean urban population remain closely connected with rural areas. These migratory trends are also related to the fact that the history of industrialization in South Korea is much shorter than in other industrialized countries.
9 Park Geun-hye was released on December 31, 2021, through a special pardon by President Moon Jae-in after five years of imprisonment.
10 Regarding the socioeconomic impact of the Asian Financial crisis in South Korea, see Song (2009).
11 The High School Equalization Policy was introduced in 1974 to prevent highly heated competition among students and parents' overinvestment in children's education to secure entrance into selective prestigious high schools. Accordingly, all students were assigned by the Ministry of Education based on the district-wide lottery system.
12 Chaebol is a family controlled conglomerate that extensively dominates the economy in South Korea.
13 In recent years, there have also been attempts to highlight the relationship between female workers in the formal and informal sectors and their positions within broader discussions on women under Park Chung Hee's modernization project, such as domestic (see Kang Isu 2009; Sŏ Yŏnju 2007) and sex (Yi Hayŏng and Yi Nayŏng 2015) workers.
14 *Yŏwŏn* (1955–1970), *Yŏsang* (1962–1967), *Chubusaenghwal* (1965–present), and *Yŏsŏngdonga* (1967–present) are representative women's magazines published in the 1960s and 1970s in Korea.
15 The monthly magazine *Happy Home* was published from 1968 until 2005.
16 The *Rural Women* was published from 1976 until 1980.

Bibliography

Amsden, Alice. 1989. *Asia's Next Giant: South Korea and Late Industrialization.* New York: Oxford University Press. https://doi.org/10.1016/0305-750X(94)90111-2

Appadurai, Arjun. 2004. "The Capacity to Aspire: Culture and the Terms of Recognition." In *Culture and Public Action*, edited by Vijayendra Rao and Michael Walton Stanford, 59–84. California: Stanford University Press.

Ashford, Holly Rose. 2020. "Modern Motherhood, Masculinity, and Family Planning in Ghana, 1960–75." *Journal of West African History* 6, no. 2: 61–91. https://doi.org/10.14321/jwestafrihist.6.2.0061

Barber, Pauline Gardiner, and Catherine Bryan. 2014. "'Value Plus Plus': Housewifization and History in Philippine Care Migration." In *When Care Work Goes Global: Locating the Social Relations of Domestic Work*, edited by Mary Romero, Valerie Preston, and Wenona Giles, 29–44. London and New York: Routledge.

Bardsley, Jan. 1999. "Discourse on Women in Postwar Japan: The Housewife Debate of 1955." *U.S.-Japan Women's Journal* 16: 3–47.

Beechey, Veronica. 1987. *Unequal Work*. New York: Verso Books.

Beetham, Margaret. 1996. *A Magazine of Her Own?: Domesticity and Desire in the Woman's Magazine, 1800–1914*. London: Routledge.

Bridenthal, Renate. 1984. "Professional Housewives: Stepsisters of the Women's Movement." In *When Biology Became Destiny: Women in Weimar and Nazi Germany*, edited by Renate Bridenthal, Atina Grossman, and Marion Kaplan, 153–251. New York: Monthly Review Press.

Buvinić, Mayra. 1983. "Women's Issues in Third World Poverty: A Policy Analysis." In *Women and Poverty in the Third World*, edited by Mayra Buvinić, Margaret A. Lycette, and William Paul McGreevey, 14–31. Baltimore: The Johns Hopkins University Press.

Callard, Agnes. 2018. *Aspiration: The Agency of Becoming*. New York: Oxford University Press.

Castells, Manuell. 1992. "Four Asian Tigers with a Dragon Head: A Comparative Analysis of the State, Economy, and Society in the Asia Pacific Rim." In *State and Development in the Asian Pacific Rim*, edited by Jeffrey W. Henderson and Richard P. Appelbaum, 33–70. London: Sage Publications.

Chang, Kyung-sup. 1999. "Compressed Modernity and its Discontents: South Korean Society in Transition." *Economy and Society* 28, no. 1: 30–55. https://doi.org/10.1080/03085149900000023

Chang, Kyung-sup. 2010. *South Korea under Compressed Modernity: Familial Political Economy in Transition*. London and New York: Routledge.

Chang, Kyung-sup. 2012. "Developmental Citizenship in Perspective: The South Korean Case and Beyond." In *Contested Citizenship in East Asia: Developmental Politics, National Unity, and Globalization*, edited by Kyung-sup Chang and Bryan S. Turner, 182–202. London and New York: Routledge.

Chang Migyŏng. 2004. "Kŭndaehwa wa 1960–70nyŏndae yŏsŏng nodongja (Modernization and Women Workers in the 1960s and 1970s)." *Kyŏngje wa sahoe (Economy and Society)* 61: 100–126.

Chang Migyŏng. 2007. "1960–70nyŏndae kajŏngjubu (anae) ŭi hyŏngsŏng gwa chendŏ jŏngch'i: 'yŏwŏn', 'chubu saenghwal' japchi tamnon ŭl chungshim ŭro (The Formation of Housewives and Institutional Politics: Focusing on Magazine Discourse, 'yŏwŏn' and 'chubu saenghwal')." *Sahoe gwahak yŏn'gu (Social Science Research)* 15, no. 1: 142–180.

Chang Migyŏng. 2008. "Kaebal kukka shigi, saemaŭl undong punyŏ chidoja ŭi chŏngch'esŏng ŭi hyŏngsŏng kwa pyŏnhwa: punyŏ chidojaŭi sŏnggongsarye, sugirŭl chungshimŭro (Formulation and Transformation of Female Leadership Identity in the New Community Movement within the Developmental State: Examining Successful Cases and Essays of Female Leaders)." *Sahoe kwahak yŏn'gu (Social Science Research)* 16, no. 1: 426–660.

Chang Munsŏk. 2006. "Sŏron: sŏgu kŭndae ŭi t'eorema e taehan yŏksa (ch'ŏrhak)chŏk sŏngch'al (Introduction: A Historical and Philosophical Analysis of 'Teorema' in Modern Western Times)." In *Kŭndae ŭi kyŏnggye esŏ tokchae rŭl ikta: taejung dokchae wa pakchŏnghŭi ch'eje (Revisiting Park Chung Hee's Regime: Mass Dictatorship Theory and Park Chung Hee)*, edited by Chang Munsŏk and Yi Sangnok, 17–30. Seoul: Greenbee.

Chang Munsŏk, and Yi Sangnok (eds.). 2006. *Kŭndae ŭi kyŏnggye esŏ tokchae rŭl ikta: taejung dokchae wa pakchŏnghŭi ch'eje (Revisiting Park Chung Hee's Regime: Mass Dictatorship Theory and Park Chung Hee)*. Seoul: Greenbee.

Cheng, Tun-Jen, Stephan Haggard, and David Kang. 1998. "Institutions and Growth in Korea and Taiwan: The Bureaucracy." *The Journal of Development Studies* 34, no. 6: 87–111. https://doi.org/10.1080/00220389808422547

Chin, Christine. 1998. *In Service and Servitude: Foreign Female Domestic Workers and the Malaysian 'Modernity' Project'*. New York: Columbia University Press.

Cho, Eunjoo. 2016. "Making the 'Modern' Family: The Discourse of Sexuality in the Family Planning Program in South Korea." *Sexualities* 19, no. 7: 802–818. https://doi.org/10.1177/1363460715624455

Cho Hŭiyŏn. 2004. "Pakchŏnghŭi shidae ŭi kangap gwa tongŭi (Oppression and Consensus in the Park Chung Hee Era)." *Yŏksa wa bip'yŏng (History and Critique)* 5: 135–190.

Cho Ŭnchu. 2018. *Kajok kwa t'ongch'i (The Role of Family in the State's Ruling System)*. Seoul: Ch'angjak kwa pip'yŏng.

Ch'oe Kyŏnghŭi. 2016. "1960–70 nyŏndae yŏsŏngji rŭl t'onghae pon kŭndaehwa ŭi chendŏ yangsang yŏn'gu (Gendered Modernization through Women's Magazines in the 1960s–1970s)." *Han'guk munhwa iron kwa pip'yŏng (Korean Cultural Theory and Criticism)* 20, no. 4: 313–331.

Choi, Hyaeweol. 2015. "Constructions of Marriage and Sexuality in Modern Korea." In *Routledge Handbook of Sexuality Studies in East Asia*, edited by Mark McLelland and Vera Mackie, 87–100. New York: Routledge.

Cho-Yi Yŏul. 2006. "Chinbojŏk yŏsŏngdanch'e ŭi wigi (Crisis of the Progressive Women's Movement)." *Chinbo p'yŏngnon (Progressive Commentary)* 28: 240–255.

Coates, Jennifer. 2016. "How to be a Domestic Goddess: Female Film Stars and the Housewife Role in Postwar Japan." *U.S.-Japan Women's Journal* 50: 29–53. https://doi.org/10.1353/jwj.2016.0005

Davidoff, Leonore, and Catherine Hall. 1987. *Family Fortune: Men and Women of the English Middle Class*, 1780–1850. Chicago: University of Chicago Press.

Davis, Diane E. 2004. "An Introduction to Middle Classes, Discipline, and Development." In *Discipline and Development: Middle Classes and Prosperity in East Asia and Latin America*, edited by Diana E. Davis, 1–25. New York: Cambridge University Press.

Doucette, Jamie, and Anders Riel Müller. 2016. "Exporting the *Saemaul* Spirit: South Korea's Knowledge Sharing Program and the 'Rendering Technical' of Korean Development." *Geoforum* 75: 29–39. https://doi.org/10.1016/j.geoforum.2016.06.018

Duchen, Claire. 1991. "Occupation Housewife: The Domestic Ideal in 1950s France." *French Cultural Studies* 2: 1–11. https://doi.org/10.1177/095715589100200401

Evans, Peter. 1995. *Embedded Autonomy: States and Industrial Transformation*. Princeton: Princeton University Press.

Friedan, Betty. 2013. *The Feminine Mystique*. New York and London: W. W. Norton & Company.

Garon, Sheldon. 2006. "The Transnational Promotion of Saving in Asia: 'Asian Value' or the 'Japanese Model'?" In *Ambivalent Consumer: Questioning Consumption in East Asia and the West*, edited by Sheldon Garon and Patricia L. Maclachlan, 163–187. Ithaca: Cornell University Press.

Garon, Sheldon. 2010. "State and Family in Modern Japan: A Historical Perspective." *Economy and Society* 39, no. 3: 317–336. https://doi.org/10.1080/03085147.2010.486214

Giles, July. 2004. *The Parlour and the Suburb: Domestic Identities, Class, Femininity and Modernity*. Oxford: Berg Publishers.

Goldstein-Gidoni, Ofra. 2012. *Housewives of Japan: An Ethnography of Real Lives and Consumerized Domesticity*. New York: Palgrave Macmillan.

Goodman, David S. G. 2014. "Middle Class China: Dreams and Aspirations." *Journal of Chinese Political Science* 19: 49–67. https://doi.org/10.1007/s11366-013-9275-x

Gordon, Andrew. 1997. "Managing the Japanese Household: The New Life Movement in Postwar Japan." *Social Politics: International Studies in Gender, State & Society* 4, no. 2: 245–283. https://doi.org/10.1093/sp/4.2.245

Gordon, Linda. 1976. *Woman's Body, Woman's Right: A Social History of Birth Control in America*. New York: Grossman/Viking.

Govindasamy, Pavalavalli, and Anju Malhotra. 1996. "Women's Position and Family Planning in Egypt." *Studies in Family Planning* 27, no. 6: 328–340. https://doi.org/10.2307/2138028

Haggard, Stephan. 2004. "Institutions and Growth in East Asia." *Studies in Comparative International Development* 38, no. 4: 53–81. https://doi.org/10.1007/BF02686328

Haggard, Stephan, and Marcus Noland. 2010. "Political Attitudes under Repression: Evidence from North Korean Refugees." *East-West Center Working Papers, Politics, Governance, and Security Series* no. 21: 1–43. Honolulu: East-West Center.

Hall, Catherine. 1992. "The History of the Housewife." In *White, Male and Middle Class: Explorations in Feminism and History*, edited by Catherine, Hall, 43–74. Cambridge: Polity Press.

Han, Jongwoo, and Lily H. M. Ling. 1998. "Authoritarianism in the Hypermasculinized State: Hybridity, Patriarchy, and Capitalism in Korea." *International Studies Quarterly* 42, no. 1: 53–78.

Han, Seung-Mi. 2004. "The New Community Movement: Park Chung Hee and the Making of State Populism in Korea." *Pacific Affairs* 77, no. 1: 69–93.

Happy Home. 1968. "Nongch'on kŭndaehwarŭl wihan chapchi (A Journal for Rural Modernization)." August 5.

Hays, Sharon. 1996. *The Cultural Contradictions of Motherhood*. New Haven: Yale University Press.

Heiman, Rachel, Mark Liechty, and Carla Freeman. 2012. "Introduction: Charting an Anthropology of the Middle Classes." In *The Global Middle Class: Theorizing through Ethnography*, edited by Rachel Heiman, Carla Freeman, and Mark Liechty, 3–30. Santa Fe: School for Advanced Research Press.

Hong Yanghŭi. 2010. "Shingminji shigi hyŏnmoyangch'ŏron kwa modŏnit'i munje ('Modernity' and the Idea of 'Wise Mother and Good Wife' in Colonial Korea)." *Sahakyŏn'gu (Historical Research)* 99: 299–388.

Hwang Chŏngmi. 2001. "Kaebal kukka ŭi yŏsŏng chŏngch'aek e kwanhan yŏn'gu: 1960–70 nyŏndae han'guk punyŏ haengjŏng ŭl chungshimŭro (Women and the Developmental State: State Policy on Women in Korea in the 1960s and 1970s)." PhD diss., Seoul National University.

Hyodo, Chika. 2002. "Jinkōseisaku ni okeru raitsu gainen ni tsuite (A Study on Rights in Population Policy)." *Kosai Kyōryoku kenkyū (Contemporary Gender Studies)* 18, no. 1: 8–16.

Im Jihyŏn (ed.). 2004. *Taejung dokchae (Mass Dictatorship)*. Seoul: Ch'aeksesang.

Janowitz, Morris. 1975. "Sociological Theory and Social Control." *American Journal of Sociology* 81, no. 1: 82–108.

Jeong, Hyeseon. 2017. "Globalizing a Rural Past: The Conjunction of International Development Aid and South Korea's Dictatorial Legacy." *Geoforum* 86: 160–168.

Johnson, Chalmers. 1987. "Political Institutions and Economic Performance: The Government-Business Relations in Japan, South Korea, Taiwan." In *The Political Economy of the New Asian Industrialism*, edited by Frederic C. Deyo, 136–164. Ithaca: Cornell University Press.

Kabeer, Naila. 1994. *Reversed Realities: Gender Hierarchies in Development Thought*. London and New York: Verso Books.

Kang Isu. 2009. "Kasa sŏbisŭ nodong ŭi pyŏnhwa ŭi maengnak kwa shilt'ae (A Study on the Changing Work Structure of Domestic Service in Korea)." *Sahoe wa yŏksa (Society and History)* 82: 213–247.

Kim Chŏnghwa. 2002. "1960 nyŏndae yŏsŏng nodong: shingmo wa pŏsŭannaeyang ŭl chungshim ŭro (Women's Labor in the 1960s: Domestic Workers and Bus Fare Collectors)." *Yŏksa yŏn'gu (Historical Research)* 11: 81–107.
Kim Chonguk. 2009. "Puk'an kwallyo ŭi ilsang gwa ch'eje byŏnhwa (Systemic Transformation and the Everyday Life of Bureaucrats in North Korea)." *Hyŏndae puk'an yŏn'gu (Modern North Korean Studies)* 12, no. 3: 7–47.
Kim Ch'unsu. 2005. "1960–1970 nyŏndae yŏsŏng nodongja ŭi chugŏ konggan kwa tamnon (Discourses on the Residences of Female Factory Workers)." *Yŏksa yŏn'gu (Historical Research)* 15: 101–160.
Kim Chusuk. 1994. *Han'guk nongch'on ŭi yŏsŏng kwa kajok (Women and Family in Rural Villages in Korea)*. Seoul: Hanul Academy.
Kim Hyegyŏng. 2006. *Shingminji ha kŭndae kajok ŭi hyŏngsŏng kwa chendŏ (The Formation of Modern Family and Gender under Japanese Colonial Rule)*. Seoul: Ch'angjak kwa pip'yŏng.
Kim Hyegyŏng. 2009. "Pak chŏnghŭi ch'eje ha 'haekkajok tamnon ŭi pyŏnhwa gwajŏng gwa iwŏn gujo yŏn'gu (Discourses on the Nuclear Family and the Double Structure during the Park Chung Hee Era)." *Sahoe wa yŏksa (Society and History)* 82: 169–212.
Kim Hyŏnju. 2007. "1950 nyŏndae yŏsŏng chapchi 'yŏwŏn' kwa 'chedo rosŏŭi chubu' ŭi t'ansaeng (The Women's Magazine 'yŏwŏn' and the Birth of the 'Housewife' as an Institution in the 1950s)." *Taejung sŏsa yŏn'gu (Studies on Contemporary Society)* 13, no. 2: 387–416.
Kim Hyŏnmi. 2000. "Han'guk ŭi kŭndaesŏng gwa yŏsŏng ŭi nodonggwŏn (Modernity and Women's Working Rights in South Korea)." *Han'guk yŏsŏnghak (Korean Women's Studies)* 16, no. 1: 37–64.
Kim Hyung-A. 2013. "Industrial Warriors: South Korea's First Generation of Industrial Workers in Post-Developmental Korea." *Asian Studies Review* 37, no. 4: 577–595. https://doi.org/10.1080/10357823.2013.790341
Kim Jaewŏn. 2016. "1960nyŏndae Huban sŏulshi chut'aek chŏngch'aek kwa chungsanch'ŭng munje inshik (Housing Policy in Seoul and Perceptions of the Middle Class in the Late 1960s)." *Han'guksa yŏn'gu (Korean History Research)* 175: 319–363.
Kim Poksun. 2007. "1950, 60 nyŏndae ŭi yŏsŏng chapchi: 'yŏwŏn' ŭi munhwa tamnon (Women's Magazines in 1950s and 1960s Korea: Cultural Discourse in 'yŏwŏn')." *Yŏsŏng munhak yŏn'gu (Women's Literature Studies)* 18: 7–60.
Kim Sŏnch'ŏl. 1999. "70 nyŏndae saemaŭl undong kwa kukka-sahoe ŭi yŏn'gyesŏng (The New Community Movement and State-Society Relations)." Master Thesis, Yonsei University.
Kim Suchin. 2008. "Chŏnt'ongŭi ch'angan gwa yŏsŏng ŭi kungminhwa (The Invention of Tradition and the Nationalization of Women in Postcolonial Korea)." *Sahoe wa yŏksa (Society and History)* 80: 215–255.
Kim Ŭnshil. 1999. "Han'guk kŭndaehwa p'ŭrojekt'ŭ ŭi munhwa nolli wa kabujangsŏng (The Culture and Patriarchy Embedded in the Korean Modernization Project)." *Tangdae bip'yŏng (Contemporary Criticism)* 88: 79–100.
Kim Wŏn. 2004a. "Yŏgong ŭi Chŏngch'esŏng gwa Yongmang (The Identities and Desires of Female Factory Workers)." *Sahoe gwahak yŏn'gu (Social Science Research)* 12, no. 1: 44–80.
Kim Wŏn. 2004b. "Kŭndaehwa shigi chubyŏnbu yŏsŏng nodong e taehan tamnon (Discourses on Marginalized Female Labor in the Modernization Period)." *Ashia yŏsŏng yŏn'gu (Asian Women's Studies)* 43, no. 1: 181–236.
Kim Wŏn. 2004c. "1970nyŏndae yŏgong ŭi munhwa (Culture of Female Factory Workers in the 1970s)." *P'eminijŭm yŏn'gu (Feminist Studies)* 4, no. 1: 101–148.
Kim Wŏn. 2005. *Yŏgong 1970, kŭnyŏdŭl ŭi panyŏksa (Female Factory Workers: The 'Herstory' of Resistance)*. Seoul: Imagine.

Kim Yŏnchu, and Yi Chaekyŏng. 2013. "Kŭndae 'kajŏng jubu' doegi kkwajŏng gwa toshi chungsanch'ŭng kajog ŭi hyŏngsŏng (The Process of Becoming a Modern Housewife and the Construction of the Urban Middle-class Family)." *Kajok gwa munhwa (Family and Culture)* 25, no. 2: 29–61.
Kim, Hyun Mee. 2001. "Work, Nation and Hypermasculinity: The 'Woman' Question in the Economic Miracle and Crisis in South Korea." *Inter-Asia Cultural Studies* 2, no. 1: 53–68. https://doi.org/10.1080/14649370120039452
Kim, Mikyoung. 2011. "Gender, Work and Resistance: South Korean Textile Industry in the 1970s." *Journal of Contemporary Asia* 41, no. 3: 411–430. https://doi.org/10.1080/00472336.2011.582711
Ko Wŏn. 2006. "Pakchŏnghŭi chŏnggwŏn shigi nongch'on saemaul undong kwa kŭndaejŏk kungmin mandŭlgi (Nation-State Building and the New Community Movement in the Era of Park Chung Hee)." *Kyŏngje wa sahoe (Economy and Society)* 3: 178–201.
Kohli, Atul. 2004. *State-Directed Development: Political Power and Industrialization in the Global Periphery*. New York: Cambridge University Press.
Koo, Hagen. 2001. *Korean Workers: The Culture and Politics of Class Formation*. Ithaca and London: Cornell University Press.
Kwon, Jaok. 2018. "Forging Feminism within Labor Unions and the Legacy of Democracy Movements in South Korea." *Labor History* 59: 639–655.
Kwon, Jaok. 2020. "Modern Womanhood, the Ideology of Housewife, and Young Female Rural-Urban Migrants in the 1960s–1970s in South Korea." *European Journal of Korean Studies* 19, no. 1: 171–194. https://doi.org/10.1080/0023656X.2018.1470142
Kwon, Keedon. 2007. "Economic Development in East Asia and a Critique of the Post-Confucian Thesis." *Theory and Society* 36, no. 1: 55–83.
Kwŏn Kyŏngmi. 2016. "1970 nyŏndae yŏsŏng nodongja tamnon gwa pinodongja rosŏŭi kajŏngbu (Discourses on Female Workers in the 1970s and Domestic Workers as Non-workers)." *Hyŏndae sosŏl yŏn'gu (Studies in Modern Fiction)* 61: 5–35.
Lee, Jinock. 2004. "Rethinking Family Planning in the Development State from a Women's Perspective: The Case of South Korea 1961–1979." *Asian Women* 18: 167–183.
Mackintosh, Maureen. 1981. "Gender and Economics: The Sexual Division of Labour and the Subordination of Women." In *Of Marriage and the Market*, edited by Kate Young, Carol Walkowitz, and Roslyn McCullagh, 1–15. London: CSE.
Matthews, Glenna. 1987. *"Just a Housewife": The Rise and Fall of Domesticity in America*. New York: Oxford University Press.
McCarthy, Helen. 2020. *Double Lives: A History of Working Motherhood*. London: Bloomsbury Publishing.
McCurry, Justin. 2017. "Park Geun-hye: South Korean Court Removes President over Scandal." *The Guardian*, March 10.
Mies, Maria. 1982. *The Lace Makers of Narsapur: Indian Housewives Produce for the World Market*. London: Zed Press.
Mies, Maria. 1998. *Patriarchy and Accumulation on a World Scale: Women in the International Division of Labour*. London: Zed Books.
Mies, Maria, Veronika Bennholdt-Thomson, and Claudia von Werlhof. 1988. *Women: The Last Colony*. London and New York: Zed Books.
Mohanty, Chandra Talpade. 1984. "Under Western Eyes: Feminist Scholarship and Colonial Discourses." *Boundary 2* 12, no. 3: 333–358. https://doi.org/10.2307/302821
Moon, Katharine H. S. 1997. *Sex Among Allies: Military Prostitution in US-Korea Relations*. New York: Columbia University Press.
Moon, Seungsook. 2005. *Militarized Modernity and Gendered Citizenship in South Korea*. Durham and London: Duke University Press.
Nolan, Mary. 1990. "'Housework Made Easy': The Taylorized Housewife in Weimar Germany's Rationalized Economy." *Feminist Studies* 16, no. 3: 549–577. https://doi.org/10.2307/3178019

Oh Yusŏk (ed.). 2014. *Pakchŏnghŭi shidae ŭi saemaŭl undong: kŭndaehwa, chŏnt'ong kŭrigo chuch'e (Rural Saemaul Undong in the Park Chung Hee Regime: Modernization, Tradition, and Rural Population's Agency)*. Seoul: Hanwul Academy.

Ochiai, Emiko. 2008. "Researching Gender and Childcare in Contemporary Asia." In *Asia's New Mothers: Crafting Gender Roles and Childcare Networks in East and Southeast Asian Societies*, edited by Emiko Ochiai and Barbara Molony, 1–30. Kent: Global Oriental.

Ochiai, Emiko. 2014. "Leaving the West, Rejoining the East? Gender and Family in Japan's Semi-compressed Modernity." *International Sociology* 29, no. 3: 209–228. https://doi.org/10.1177/0268580914530415

Pae Ŭnkyŏng. 2005. "Kajok kyehoek saŏp gwa yŏsŏng ŭi mom: 1960–70nyŏndae ch'ulsan chojŏl pogŭp kwajŏng ŭl t'onghae pon yŏsŏng kwa kŭndae (Women's Bodies and the State Family Planning Programs in Korea: Examining 'the Modern' in Women's Lives through the Social History of Birth Control)." *Sahoe wa yŏksa (Society and History)* 67: 260–299.

Pae Ŭnkyŏng. 2008. "Kusul saengaesa rŭl t'onghae pon sanŏp'wa shigi han'guk ŏmŏni ŭi mosŏng kyŏnghŏm kyŏngjejŏk kiyŏ wa tolbom nodong, ch'injok kwan'gye kwalli ŭi kyŏrhap (Mothering Experiences of Korean Women in the Industrialization Period: Combining Economic Support, Care Work, and Relation Management for Family)." *P'eminijŭm yŏn'gu (Feminist Studies)* 8, no. 1: 69–123.

Paek Misuk. 2015. "1960–70 Nyŏndae chubu kyoyang p'ŭrogŭraem gwa t'ellebijŏn ŭi chendŏ chŏngch'i (The Housewife Culture and Gender Politics of Television in the 1960s–1970s)." *Ŏllon gwa sahoe (Media and Society)* 23, no. 4: 120–185.

Pak Chindo. 2003. "Inong ŭi chŏn'gae kwajŏng kwa kŭ ŭimi (The Process of Rural-Urban Migration and its Meaning)." In *Han'guk nongch'on sahoe ŭi pyŏnhwa wa palchŏn (Changes and Development of Rural Society in Korea)*, edited by Korea Rural Economic Institute, 79–101. Seoul: Korea Rural Economic Institute.

Pak Chindo, and Han Tohyŏn. 1999. "Saemaŭl undong gwa yushin ch'eje: pakchŏnghŭi chŏnggwŏn ŭi nongch'on saemaŭl undong ŭl chungshim ŭro (Saemaul Movement and Yushin System: Park Chung Hee Regime and the Rural Saemaul Movement)." *Yŏksa pip'yŏng (Historical Critique)* 5: 37–80.

Park, Sang-Young. 2010. "Crafting and Dismantling the Egalitarian Social Contract: The Changing State-Society Relations in Globalizing Korea." *The Pacific Review* 23, no. 5: 579–601. https://doi.org/10.1080/09512748.2010.522247

Podoler, Guy. 2016. "Who Was Park Chung-Hee? The Memorial Landscape and National Identity Politics in South Korea." *East Asia* 33: 271–288.

Prügl, Elisabeth. 1996. "Home-based Workers: A Comparative Exploration of Mies's Theory of Housewifization." *Frontiers: A Journal of Women Studies* 17, no. 1: 114–135.

Rogers, Barbara. 1980. *The Domestication of Women: Discrimination in Developing Societies*. London: Tavistock.

Savara, Mira. 1983. "Report of a Workshop on Women, Health and Reproduction." In *Third World Second Sex: Women's Struggles and National Liberation*, edited by Miranda Davies, 220–227. London: Zed Book.

Schielke, Samuli. 2012. "Living in the Future Tense: Aspiring for World and Class in Provincial Egypt." In *The Global Middle Class: Theorizing through Ethnography*, edited by Rachel Heiman, Carla Freeman, and Mark Liechty, 31–56. Santa Fe: School for Advanced Research Press.

Schwak, Juliette. 2016. "Branding South Korea in a Competitive World Order: Discourses and Dispositives in Neoliberal Governmentality." *Asian Studies Review* 40, no. 3: 427–444. https://doi.org/10.1080/10357823.2016.1193474

Secombe, Wally. 1974. "The Housewife and Her Labour under Capitalism." *New Left Review* 83: 3–24.

Shin Hyŏnok. 1999. "Kukka kaebal chŏngch'aek kwa nongch'on chiyŏk ŭi yŏsŏng chojik e kwanhan yŏn'gu (National Development Policy and Women's Organizations in Rural Areas)." PhD diss., Yonsei University.

Shin Kŏn. 2001. *1960–70nyŏndae Kŭndaehwa p'ŭrojekt'ŭ wa yŏsŏng damnon e kwanhan yŏn'gu (A Study on the Discourse on Women and the Modernization Project in the 1960s and 1970s)*. Master thesis, Yonsei University.

Sŏ Yŏnju. 2007. "Yŏsŏng sooe kyech'ŭng e taehan tamnon hyŏngsŏng yangsang yŏn'gu: yŏwŏn e nat'anan sahoe hyŏnshil inshik ŭl chungshim ŭro (How the Discourse on Marginalized Females Formed: Examining Social Reality Awareness in Yŏwŏn)." *Yŏsŏng munhak yŏn'gu (Women's Literature Studies)* 18, no. 18: 93–130.

Soh, Chung-Hee. 2003. "Women's Sexual Labor and State in Korean History." *Journal of Women's History* 15, no. 4: 170–177. https://doi.org/10.1353/jowh.2004.0022

Song, Jaesook. 2009. *South Koreans in the Debt Crisis: The Creation of a Neoliberal Welfare Society*. Durham: Duke University Press.

Sreenivas, Mytheli. 2021. "Feminism, Family Planning and National Planning." *South Asia: Journal of South Asian Studies* 44, no. 2: 313–328.

Steege, Paul, Andrew Stuart Bergerson, Maureen Healy, and Pamela E. Swett. 2008. "The History of Everyday Life: A Second Chapter." *The Journal of Modern History* 80, no. 2: 358–378. https://doi.org/10.1086/588855

Tosh, John. 1999. *A Man's Place: Masculinity and the Middle-Class Home in Victorian England*. New Haven: Yale University Press.

Vogel, Ezra. 1965. *Japan's New Middle Class: The Salary Man and His Family in a Tokyo Suburb*. Berkeley: University of California Press.

Wade, Robert. 1990. *Governing the Market: Economic Theory and the Role of Government in East Asian Industrialization*. Princeton: Princeton University Press.

Weiss, Linda. 1998. *The Myth of the Powerless State*. Ithaca: Cornell University Press.

Woo-Cumings, Meredith (ed.). 1999. *The Developmental State*. Ithaca: Cornell University Press.

Yang, Myungji. 2018. *From Miracle to Mirage: The Making and Unmaking of the Korean Middle Class, 1960–2015*. Ithaca and London: Cornell University Press.

Yi Chaegyŏng. 2003. *Kajok ŭi irŭmŭro: han'guk kŭndae kajok kwa p'eminijŭm (In the Name of Family: Feminism and Modern Family in Korea)*. Seoul: Tto Hana ŭi Munhwa.

Yi Hayŏng, and Yi Nayŏng. 2015. "'Kisaeng gwan'gwang': palchŏn gukka wa chendŏ, p'osŭt'ŭ shingmin chou ('Kisaeng Tourism': The Developmental State, Gender, and Postcolonialism)." In *Choguk kŭndaehwa ŭi chendŏ jŏngch'i: kajok, nodong, seksyuŏllit'I (National Development and Gender Politics: Family, Labor, and Sexuality)*, edited by Yi Chaegyŏng, 239–273. Seoul: Arche.

Yi Kwangil. 1998. "'Shingminji kŭndaehwa' esŏ minjuhwa kkaji: pakchŏnghŭi ch'ejeron pip'an (From 'Colonial Modernization' to 'Democratization': A Critical Analysis of 'Park Chung Hee Rule')." *Chŏngch'i pip'yŏng (Political Critique)* 3: 121–140.

Yi Migyŏng. 1989. "Kukka ŭi ch'ulsan chŏngch'aek: kajok kyehoek chŏngch'aek ŭl chungshimŭro (Birth Control Policy: The Family Planning Program)." *Yŏsŏnghak nonjip (Journal of Women's Studies)* 6: 49–78.

Yi Myŏngsŏn. 1990. "Kuk'oe Sokkirok e nat'anan Yŏsŏng Chŏngch'aek Shigak: kajok Kyehoek e taehayŏ (Policy on Women in the Documents of Parliament: Family Planning)." *Yŏsŏnghak nonjip (Journal of Women's Studies)* 7: 113–136.

Yi Sangnok. 2006. "Sŏron: Taejung Dokchaeron (Introduction: Mass Dictatorship Theory)." In *Kŭndae ŭi kyŏnggye esŏ tokchae rŭl ikta: taejung dokchae wa pakchŏnghŭi ch'eje (Re-reading Park Chung Hee's Regime: Mass Dictatorship Theory and Park Chung Hee)*, edited by Chang Munsŏk and Yi Sangnok, 221–229. Seoul: Greenbee.

Yi Suja. 2000. "Han'guk sahoe ŭi kŭndaesŏng e taehan yŏsŏng chuŭi munhwaronjŏk sŏngch'al (Feminist Cultural Reflections on the Modernity of Korean Society)." *Yŏsŏng yŏn'gu nonch'ong (Journal of Women's Studies)* 1: 169–188.

Yokota, Nobuko. 2002a. "'Kankoku ni okeru nōmin dōin to semauru undo (Mobilization of the Rural Population and the New Community Movement in South Korea)." In *Hendō no higashi ajia shakai (Changing East Asian Society)*, edited by Kitahara Atsushi, 131–160. Tokyo: Aokishoten.

Yokota, Nobuko. 2002b. "Kankoku ni okeru semauru undō to nōson josei no soshikika to dōin (Organizing and Mobilizing Rural Women in the New Community Movement in South Korea)." In *Kōhatsu Kōgyōkoku ni okeru josei rōdō to shakai seisaku (Women's Labor and Social Policy in Late-Industrializing Countries)*, edited by Murakami Kaoru, 129–157. Tokyo: Ajia Keizai kenkyūjo.

Yuval-Davis, Nira. 1997. *Gender and Nation.* London and Thousand Oaks: Sage Publications.

1 Rural Development in the 1960s and 1970s in South Korea

Park Chung Hee, who assumed power with a military coup on May 16, 1961, undertook "development" with the slogan of "modernization of the motherland (*choguk kŭndaehwa*)". Development had also been a major national agenda for Syngman Rhee's administration (1948–1960). However, for Syngman Rhee, economic development and the eradication of poverty on the heels of the Korean War meant a "return" to Korea's pre-war state with aid from the US (Yi Wanbŏm 1999). At the time of Park Chung Hee's inauguration, economic recovery was already somewhat progressing. Therefore, the Park Chung Hee regime needed to double down on development in earnest to set itself apart from its predecessor and establish political legitimacy following the military coup that brought the regime to power.

This chapter analyzes the New Community Movement as a government initiative to modernize the motherland and establish a new relationship between the state and rural society during the Park Chung Hee regime's industrial policy. It begins by describing how the commencement of the New Community Movement stemmed from the unstable socioeconomic and political situation in rural areas, which was closely associated with the urban-centered industrialization policy promoted by the Park Chung Hee regime. This description provides significant clues for understanding that the aspirations of rural populations toward the middle class were embedded in the context of the interconnectedness and the tension between rural and urban areas, which were rapidly identified via the industrialization policy initiated by the Park Chung Hee regime. Furthermore, this chapter demonstrates that the New Community Movement was not merely a rural development project but a governmental initiative with clear political and socioeconomic objectives. In this context, this chapter highlights that the Community Movement was designed to fulfill a broader national project – the "modernization of the motherland" proclaimed by the Park Chung Hee regime – and establish a new relationship between the state and rural society.

The Socioeconomic and Political Situation Before the New Community Movement

After 35 years of Japanese colonial rule (1910–1945), the traditional ruling class (*yangban*) during the Chosun Dynasty was gradually eliminated. Furthermore, the

DOI: 10.4324/9781003110538-2

introduction of the "Land Reform Law", a major land redistribution policy implemented in 1949, aimed to break up large landholdings owned by landlords and distribute the land to small farmers who had previously worked on the land as tenant farmers or sharecroppers. The land reform conducted between 1949 and 1950 established a limit on the amount of land that could be owned by an individual, with excess land being confiscated and distributed to those in need. The government hoped to increase agricultural productivity, reduce rural poverty, and create a more equal wealth and power distribution in rural society by breaking up large landholdings and redistributing the land to small farmers. Even though land ownership was reconcentrated, increasing from 26.4% in 1960 to 46.4% in 1981 given widespread farmland leasing practices (Ahn and Boyer 1988), there were no exploitative and absentee landowners (Brandt 1980). Therefore, land reform contributed to social and political stability in rural society through the relatively equitable distribution of land ownership. Beyond the unified land reform policy, rural–urban migration patterns were homogenizing the structure of rural society. Brandt (1980) maintains that "the stable, cohesive, homogeneous village structure comprising predominantly middle-level farm households" was established (ibid., 184) after the richest and the poorest farming households left rural villages in the earliest stage of industrialization. While land reform was an important step toward addressing issues of inequality in rural areas, alone, it did not provide a complete solution to the problems of poverty, unemployment, and limited economic opportunities faced by rural communities. The poor economic situation in rural areas was one of the factors that triggered the April 19 democratic revolution in 1960.[1]

After the resignation of Syngman Rhee given the April 19 democratic revolution, Park Chung Hee, a general in the army at the time, led a military coup on May 16, 1961, overthrowing the Yun Posun government (1960–1962) and seizing power. Park Chung Hee, who lacked political legitimacy, recognized the critical importance of attaining strong political support from the rural population, which accounted for over half of the total population at the time of his inauguration (Korean Research Association for Politics 1990). A series of efforts to gain recognition from the rural population were initiated during the early stages of the regime. For instance, the "Agriculture and Fishing Village High Interests Debt Dissolution Policy", the "Agriculture Product Price Maintenance Law", and the "Agriculture Cooperatives Law", introduced in 1961, were all agriculture policies targeting farmers. Political efforts to support the rural population were also well-reflected in agriculture policies, such as the establishment of the Rural Promotion Agency, the development of rural organizations, and the "Agriculture Restructuring Policies" of 1962 (Chŏng Myŏngch'ae et al. 1995). Moreover, to promote rural recovery, Park started the "Self-help Development Six-Year Plan (1966)" to foster leadership in rural villages, thus increasing the income of farming households and expanding government support (Yi Mankap 1981). Another policy implemented in the latter half of the 1960s was the "Promotion of Agriculture and Industry". This policy primarily aimed to develop a mutually beneficial and organic linkage between the industrial and agricultural sectors. This joining of agriculture and industry was embodied in the implementation of the "Special Project for Increasing Farmers'

Income" (1968–1971), the purpose of which was to improve farmers' income by supporting the cultivation of cash crops, promoting food processing industries, and developing agricultural products for the market. However, neither policy produced significant results, the former being limited in scope and the latter lacking demand for cash crops.

Moreover, the first and second Five-Year Economic and Social Development Plans (1962–1971) promoted alongside the various agricultural promotion policies throughout the 1960s and 1970s had negative impacts on rural economies and societies. Over seven Five-Year Economic and Social Development Plans were initiated by the Park Chung Hee regime from 1962 to 1996. They sought to achieve planned economic development and export-oriented industrialization; however, the latter of these goals resulted in an unequal growth rate between primary industries, such as agriculture and fishery, and secondary industries, such as light and heavy industries. The imbalance in growth between the agricultural and industrial sectors increased more during the second Five-Year Economic and Social Plan (1967–1971) than during the first Five-Year Plan (1962–1966). During the first Five-Year Plan between 1962 and 1966, manufacturing production expanded at approximately 14% per annum, while agriculture output grew at approximately 5%. Meanwhile, the growth rate in the industrial sector recorded 20.3% during the second Five-Year Plan between 1967 and 1971, while that in the farming sector was only 2.3% (Economic Planning Board 1986).

Another background for the collapse of the rural economy was the "Low Grain Pricing Policy". After the Korean War, a large quantity of surplus agricultural products from the US flooded into Korea. While these surplus products helped alleviate food shortages, they caused a sharp decline in domestic grain prices, dealing a huge blow to rural farming communities. In response, the "Agricultural Product Price Stabilization Act" was enacted on June 27, 1961, one month after the 5.16 military coup. The law was created to maintain agricultural product prices at an appropriate level and stabilize agricultural production and the rural economy. However, it remained a mere slogan. Even if some of the main slogans of the Park Chung Hee regime emphasized the "eradication of poverty of rural populations" and "enhancement of rural economy", import policies for agricultural products from foreign countries induced a decline in farming and put pressure on rural economies, as the government used the low-price grain policy to support the industrialization policy. This policy was implemented to entice rural populations to low-skilled factory jobs in urban areas by minimizing the profits they could make working in agriculture. Moreover, given the policy, the degree of food self-sufficiency in South Korea decreased from 91.8% in 1960 to 82.1% in 1968. Afraid of civil unrest among low-wage factory workers in urban areas, the Park regime increased food imports to manage inflation and ensure affordable food for low-wage workers.

The low-price grain policy and the rapid increase in food imports induced a price decline of local agricultural products and a rapid decrease in the household incomes of farmers (Kim Ilch'ŏl 1991). Consequently, the average farming household income, which had exceeded the household income of urban workers in the early 1960s, fell to 60.8% that of the urban household in 1968. The rural household income of small farmers was much lower than the mean rural household income, standing at 43.7% that of the urban household in the same year (Kim Chusuk 1981). Low-price grain policy, thus, became one of the strongest push factors for rural–urban migration, as residents of rural villages experienced feelings of relative deprivation alongside growing rural–urban disparities (Ho 1979). The sentiment of rural Korean society in the 1960s could be described as follows: "Rather than absolute poverty, however, it was a sense of relative deprivation, fed by radio broadcasts from Seoul and frequent trips to the city, that contributed to the growing discontent of the rural population" (Brandt 1979, 152).[2] Thus, in the 1960s, rural Korean society was full of anxiety given the deterioration of the rural economy and the rapid exodus of its young labor force (Kim Ilch'ŏl 1991). In a survey by a rural sociologist of six rural villages in Gyeonggi Province in 1969, 63.5% of participants replied that "[they] are not satisfied with the current agriculture policy". 40% of the respondents answered that "[they were] willing to migrate to cities" (Yi Mankap 1973, 85–88).

Given the limited economic opportunities in rural areas, migration from the countryside to urban areas began in the 1960s and gained momentum in the 1970s. Urbanization is clearly indicated in the population growth rate in urban areas, which was 6.8% between 1966 and 1970; it was 1.4% nationwide during the same period (Pak Taesik and Pak Kyŏngch'ŏl 2003). The increase in Seoul's population alone was 9.8% during this period (Chu Gwansu 1998). The deterioration of the economic situation in rural areas at the end of the 1960s also affected cities. Dispossessed farmers formed squatter settlements around cities, which led to frequent conflicts between the government and migrants over illegal settlements. In 1971, the urban poor who had migrated from rural areas resisted forced eviction, yielding violent demonstrations. The Park Chung Hee regime began to recognize urban–rural migration as a problem that could deplete the stability of society. Given the low working wages offered to workers who had migrated to cities and problems with poor working environments, the Park Chung Hee regime began to face resistance from the opposition and workers comprising farmers and the urban poor from circa 1970. Intellectual groups also organized the farmers who had been marginalized in the process of industrialization. Intellectuals had begun to develop a labor movement to improve working conditions and raise awareness of workers' rights. Thus, rural development and modernization were inevitable endeavors for the Park Chung Hee regime, as it sought to manage social unrest in rural areas. Although it could not be said that rural reconstruction was directly linked to economic development, it was a factor that could not be ignored from the broad perspective of the benefits the national economy reaped from the construction of a stable rural society.

From a political perspective, Park Chung Hee, who had gained political power via a military coup, faced the necessity of reviving rural society. Brandt (1979) notes the political threat Park Chung Hee faced given the economic imbalance between rural and urban areas in South Korea: "the extent to which farmers were being left behind in the development sweepstakes had become a kind of national scandal by the end of the first decade of Park Chung Hee's rule" (ibid., 152–153).

Park Chung Hee was re-elected as president in 1971 by a margin of only 7% of votes over the presidential candidate from the opposite party, Kim Dae Jung. The message was clear for Park Chung Hee that he did not have the absolute support of the population. Moreover, the ratio of seats of the Republican party in the parliament, the ruling party at the time, dropped to 14%. Further, the voting rate fell in urban and rural areas, which had hitherto been an important political base for the ruling party. Park Chung Hee was, thus, under pressure to increase his approval rating in rural areas (Pak Chindo and Han Tohyŏn 1999; Yi Mankap 1984).

The Commencement of the New Community Movement

The Park regime's lack of political legitimacy and the ensuing social unrest from city-centered industrialization triggered the initiation of a nationwide rural development project: The New Community Movement. This Movement was a political initiative and rural development project officially implemented by Park Chung Hee in 1971, but the idea had already been proposed as early as April of 1970.[3] During a presidential speech in October 1970, Park declared the implementation of village development projects based on the spirit of self-help and self-reliance. This speech marked the beginning of the New Community Movement; from October 1970 to June 1971, road expansion, embankment repair, well repair, and new infrastructure construction occurred in 33,267 villages nationwide. The government provided 335 bags of cement for each village as necessary materials for the projects. Under the slogans of diligence, self-help, and cooperation, the New Community Movement aimed to enhance the development of the rural sector and improve the standard of living in rural areas.

After adopting the *Yushin* Constitution in 1972, which codified *de facto* dictatorial powers held by Park Chung Hee by suspending the constitution and dissolving the legislature, Park Chung Hee began to secure a political support base in rural areas via the New Community Movement (Kim Ilch'ŏl 1991). His perception of the necessity of rural development was expressed in a 1973 presidential press conference: "October Restoration (October *Yushin*) is exactly the saemaul movement. Saemaul movement is the October Restoration". This statement by Park Chung Hee clarifies that he attempted to situate the New Community Movement as the symbol of his political identity. That is, rural areas had been a political support base for the Park Chung Hee regime since its inception, and rural modernization was indispensable in securing and maintaining a political base. Another important political background was the "North-South Joint Statement", adopted between South Korea and North Korea in 1972. At that time, both countries actively engaged in economic development supported by the competition between the Eastern and Western Blocs during the Cold War. South Korea achieved relatively successful results in the industrial sector through the first Five-Year Economic and Social Development Plan started in 1962. However, considering that the North-South Joint Statement was supposed to stimulate exchanges between North and South Korea, Park Chung Hee needed to rebuild rural villages in South Korea to a similar level as those in North Korea, as the rural economy in South Korea lagged behind North Korea at the time.

The early stage of the movement focused on improving basic services via "living environment improvement projects". Such projects included repairs of housing, roofs, and domestic sewage to dispose of water; the establishment of communal kitchens and laundromats; and the improvement of nutrition. The living environment improvement project included concrete improvements to living infrastructure and a simplification of ceremonial rituals in the name of the "rationalization of life" and the "scientific development of life". Under the New Community Movement, rocks and trees that were the object of folk religion were forcibly removed, and communal rituals held in village units, such as the *tongshinje*,[4] were abolished. Moreover, the rituals of shrines for familial ceremonies and the scale of ceremonial occasions among families were greatly reduced (Kim Kwangŏk 1984). The projects in the later stages focused on building infrastructure, such as installing electricity in rural areas. Further, fostering a "modern" mindset through a "spirit revolution project" was promoted throughout the whole project period.

The New Community Movement was split into three stages: The "Basic Infrastructure Establishment Stage (1971–1973)", the "Self-help Development Stage (1974–1976)", and the "Self-reliance Completion Stage (1977–1979)". Even though the project progressed under broad governmental guidelines, regarding the specific contents and timeline for each stage, every village was classified under one of the three categories – "basic", "self-help", or "self-reliance" – depending on the village's level of commitment to and performance on these projects. The distinctions were meant to streamline project efficiency and encourage local participation. Villages that achieved their goals could proceed to a "higher" stage and were often rewarded with more active governmental administrative and monetary assistance. Villages that could not fulfill the given goals had to remain in a "lower" stage. Fulfilling the goals aimed to attain self-sufficiency in managing rural development projects without governmental assistance. The classification of villages based on competition and the differential financial support provided by the government based on performance played a significant role in promoting the New Community Movement despite limited government funding (Davis 2004).

Intensive development of public facilities and infrastructure in rural villages was conducted in the "Basic Infrastructure Establishment Stage". During this period, institutions for the New Community Movement were established within central and local government organizations. The Ministry of Home Affairs oversaw integrating and coordinating the various government policies of the New Community Movement. The newly established Saemaul Movement Central Council promoted and managed general planning. Saemaul departments were set up for rural organizations and local administrative units such as provinces, cities, and village units, and a Saemaul Council was established for each administrative unit. Further, based on the assumption that the success or failure of the New Community Movement project depended on the capability of its leaders, the Saemaul Leader Training Institute was established in 1972.

The goal of the "Self-help Development Stage", the second stage of the New Community Movement project, was to improve the standard of living in rural areas and spread the spirit of the New Community Movement in rural society. It emphasized income-generating projects and paid particular attention to increased rice production, regional crop specialization projects, and methods for the joint production of agricultural crops. Meanwhile, special support was provided for living environment improvement projects, including housing and road maintenance. Resident organizations such as "women's associations", "youth agricultural experience club"[5], "forest associations", and "fishing village associations" were established for each village and were instructed to take charge of income-generating projects and living environment improvement projects.

The third stage of "Self-reliance Completion" sought to promote self-help and voluntary development efforts in rural areas. During this period, special guidance was given to design and manage unique projects for each village and accumulate capital to implement rural development projects without governmental assistance. The scope of the income-generating projects was also expanded to include agriculture-related and non-farming projects, such as the construction of small factories in rural areas.

In the 1960s, the government, private organizations, and foreign organizations conducted various rural development projects, but the result fell short of the goals set, indicating that systematic engagement did not necessarily guarantee active participation. However, since the mid-1970s, the active participation of farmers in the New Community Movement has become more visible regarding the number of participants, and the volume and scope of the projects.

Interconnectedness Between the "Rural" and "Urban"

The socioeconomic and political backgrounds of the New Community Movement demonstrate a clear rural–urban area interconnectedness in South Korea during the Park Chung Hee era and the whole industrialization process. Indeed, there is a scholarly perception that rural society is a "traditional", "static", and "unchanged" space, while urban spaces are the result of drastic changes. Under the growth-centered, modernizing ideology of the Park Chung Hee regime, and, particularly, in the early stages of industrialization, rural meant "backward", "unenlightened", "feudalistic", and "under-developed" and was, therefore, perceived as "bad"; something to be abolished and denied. However, urbanity was characterized as "industrialization", "progress", and "prosperity" and, thus, was glossed as "good" (Nemeth 1988, 15).[6] For Koreans trying to catch up with the Western modernization trend, urbanity epitomized "a bright future" and "an advanced space". Kim Sŏngjo (2017) argues that the image of rural villages as "under-developed", "passive", and "unproductive" spaces, as framed by the Park Chung Hee regime, contributed to a dissociation in scholarly discussions on rural villages and urban capitalists.

Davis (2004, 3) maintains that the marginalization of the rural and focus on the urban in the examination of development among late industrializers is based on the general assumption of contemporary development scholars that "cities are where one encounters what are generally thought to be the principal protagonists of industrial development and thus modern economic growth – ranging from owners of large manufacturing firms and their industrial workers to more affluent folk who consume these processed industrial goods", while rural villages stand in contrast. Scholars, urban-based administrators, and educators have failed to pay much attention to the knowledge, values, and attitudes of the rural population during South Korea's city-based industrialization. Rather, these actors promoted policies and ideas that induced rural community children to disconnect themselves emotionally and physically from rural life and agriculture, thereby deepening the rural–urban societal divide (Chang 2010).

Important to understanding the rurality–urbanity relation in South Korea is the fact that their division in time and space did not necessarily presume an entire disconnection. For instance, rural and urban areas were closely connected in time; that is, rapid industrialization, termed "compressed modernity" by leading Korean sociologist, Chang Kyung-sup (1999), was only made possible via the takeover of the "social transition costs of industrialization" by the rural population (Chang 2010, 84). Such costs included monetary support for rural–urban migrants from their families who had remained in rural villages during the early stage of industrialization, the provision of a well-educated and disciplined labor force through rural investment in children's education, and social safety networks during economic uncertainties (ibid.).

There were also complex interactions between rural and urban areas regarding space. Kim Sŏngjo (2017) discusses the entanglements of rural society, the state, and urban capitalists by illuminating how rural space was occupied with capital from urban manufacturers and fueled by the strong aspirations of small farmers toward modern urban life. Rural space was filled with "modern imaginaries" of urban lives suggested by the rural development projects in the name of "modernization of rural society". During South Korea's city-based industrialization, urban space became an aspiration of the rural population, who were offered a specific image of being or becoming middle class via the development of mass media.[7] Practically, rural space provided social security for urban industrial laborers by offering redress for issues such as sudden unemployment, housing problems, lack of food and childcare, and health problems (Chang 2010). Family members in rural villages could also support themselves with remittances sent by their rural–urban migrant family members, which compensated for the insufficient income they gained from agriculture (Kim Suyŏng 2001).

Modernization of the Motherland

To contextualize the New Community Movement within the national modernization project of the Park regime, it is essential to understand the goals and the contents of Park's "modernization of the motherland". This modernization, as advocated by Park Chung Hee, may be summarized using three slogans the government used to promote the project: "Establishment of independent economy", "modern nation-state building", and "anti-communist ideology".

First, the drive for the establishment of an independent economy was embodied in the Five-Year Economic and Social Development Plans, which commenced in 1962. Park Chung Hee's goal with the Five-Year Plans was to "liberate our people from poverty and become financially independent by establishing a self-reliant economy" (Park Chung Hee 1962, 101). Park criticized the previous regime of Syngman Rhee, describing it with political rhetoric, such as a "government that lost the sense of independence of our people, since it is dependent [on] Japan and the US" (Park Chung Hee 1963, 73), and claimed the construction of a national economy independent from international aid, even though Park's regime was extensively dependent on international aid from Western blocs in various forms, such as food aid, loan, and direct investments.[8] Suehiro (1998) characterizes development policies in Southeast Asian countries as a process of the "construction of economic nationalism", which refers to a set of strategies to promote and protect domestic industries and economies by prioritizing domestic production, trade, and investment, often through state intervention and regulation. In particular, such governments attempted to realize developmental policy by achieving food self-sufficiency, promoting industrialization plans, and strengthening infrastructure for economic development. Thus, the Park Chung Hee regime's approach was similar to that of many other Southeast Asian countries. That is, state management and the promotion of domestic capitalists stood at the center of the economic development shaping economic nationalism in South Korea (Amsden 1989; Dent 2000; Jones and Sakong 1980; Wade 1990; Woo 1991).

The Park Chung Hee regime's economic development plans were influenced by the domestic sociopolitical situation and global conditions. Circa 1957, the US foreign policy underwent major changes, emphasizing economic development agendas in Third World countries in the form of economic rather than military aid. That is, the US' rivalry with socialism, which was of paramount importance at the time, was an ideological conflict and a "competition between systems" over rapid technological development, systematic economic development plans, and visible economic growth in developing countries (Suehiro 1998). John F. Kennedy, the president of the US during this period, declared the 1960s the "Decade of Development". This idea was further systematized through official engagements by the UN in 1961. In the 1960s, UN member countries attempted to address issues of "development" in developing countries via measures such as UN resolutions and reports. Within a newly emerging global "inter-system competition" paradigm, the US was under pressure to take responsibility for stabilizing the sociopolitical situation and economy of South Korea in ideological and military opposition to North Korea. Hence, the US voiced support for the Five-Year Economic and Social Development Plans of the Park Chung Hee regime.

The next pillar of the modernization of the motherland was modern nation-state building grounded in "nationalism from above".[9] Park Chung Hee denounced Syngman Rhee's regime, describing it as a "deserted house" and referring to it as an assemblage of "corruption, old evil, and a vicious cycle of poverty". Thus, he attempted to legitimize the military coup of 1961 in the name of political efficiency and the building of a new society. Park Chung Hee also urged people to change their thinking through efforts such as the "People's Movement for Nation Reconstruction", which began in 1961. Advocated as a movement where all the people would cooperate and unite under the idea of democracy to build a welfare state and establish a new lifestyle characterized by a spirit of independence and self-help, plans for the People's Movement for Nation Reconstruction included the establishment of anti-communist ideas, the promotion of work ethos, and the improvement of national consciousness. Covering every socioeconomic dimension from the construction of infrastructure to the improvement of living standards for the whole population, its scope was so broad that it was ambiguous. The Syngman Rhee regime also worked on the construction of a modern nation-state through the top-down promotion of nationalism in the 1950s. However, Rhee's government initiated "modernization without industrialization", and the central focus of state-defined nationalism at the time was an anti-communist ideology. Meanwhile, Park Chung Hee declared that the nationalism advocated by his regime was based on an anti-communist ideology and aimed at mobilizing the people to support the so-called "modernization project" by emphasizing economic development and reforms in every social dimension (Pak Myŏngnim 1996).

Finally, anti-communist ideology was the primary national agenda in South Korea and many developing countries at that time. Especially in South Korea, divided into North and South given ideological differences, anti-communist ideology was even more deeply embedded into the nation-state building process than in other Third World countries. That is, the ideological confrontation between the East and the West explicitly penetrated domestic politics in South Korea. Indeed, the anti-communist ideology of the Park Chung Hee regime was extremely important to the modernization of the motherland.

Strengthening Relationship between the State and Rural Society: The Community Movement as Part of the Modernization of the Motherland

The New Community Movement is marked as a symbol of a new era of relations between the state and rural society. It is well indicated that rural development was promoted by the Park Chung Hee regime as key to the modernization of the motherland, and Park Chung Hee frequently made appeals for rural modernization in public. In a regular meeting of the National Agricultural Cooperative in 1967, he claimed that "we cannot expect modernization of our country without modernization of rural areas" (*Donga Ilbo* April 18, 1967). In the 1960s and 1970s, rural development served three important purposes within the national modernization project in South Korea: A demonstration effect for rural populations, an aid to industrialization through increased agricultural productivity, and a means of promoting nationalism among rural populations.

Suehiro (1998) states that one of the reasons the developmental dictatorships of East and Southeast Asian countries survived for such long periods was the "demonstration effect", with which the states attempted to visibly present the results of "development" in rural areas. Rural areas were separate from urban spaces, where changes from industrialization-centered policies were much more palpable. The gross national product (GNP) growth rate, the main goal of the economic development plans, was not directly related to people's daily lives in rural areas, thus risking dissatisfaction among farmers, which could easily induce social unrest (Suehiro 1994). Hence, an important goal of rural development projects was to instill the idea among the rural populations that they were not being overlooked by industrialization-centered policies. They were encouraged to adopt a growth-centered ideology within which they could see themselves as beneficiaries of national growth through highly visible projects.

Park Chung Hee used the New Community Movement to visibly manifest rural modernization. This goal was well-reflected in the infrastructure improvement projects undertaken in the early stages of the New Community Movement. For instance, in 1973, noticeable infrastructure improvement projects, such as cultivated land readjustment, road expansion, cooperative usage of agricultural facilities, repair of small rivers, and dissemination of agricultural machinery, accounted for 64.3% of all the movement's projects. Road expansion was the most important project among the infrastructure improvement projects conducted in the early stages of the New Community Movement, inducing a major change in rural society with the emergence of agricultural machinery. At the end of 1970, the total number of agricultural machines was about 150,000; in 1979, however, this number rapidly increased to 940,000. Thus, the infrastructure improvement project greatly contributed to a change in agricultural production methods.[10] The improvement in agricultural infrastructure closely affected the daily life of farmers, and the results were "visible". Such demonstration effects aimed to encourage voluntary participation among the rural population in national development (Pak Chindo and Han Tohyŏn 1999). Thus, the Park Chung Hee regime tried to help farmers feel that they shared in the fruits of development and the modernization of the motherland.

Second, rural development was considered a means to increase agricultural productivity and support a truly independent economy. While the Park Chung Hee regime promoted rural modernization to strengthen its political support base, city-based industrialization policies were left in place, as discussed in the previous section. Industrialization policies in the 1960s highly depended on the outside world in capital, factories, and technology. Under such conditions, low wages were fundamental to supporting export-oriented industries. In turn, low wages inevitably required a supply of cheap agricultural products to ensure workers were fed. Cheap agricultural products enabled price stability but also put pressure on the farm economy and promoted the abandonment of farming, consequently providing a stable supply of low-wage workers. Given the low-price supply policy for agricultural products, it is no exaggeration to say that the industrialization policy in South Korea was pursued at the expense of rural areas.

The city-based industrialization had not changed in the 1970s. Beyond the shift from free to paid food aid from the US in 1967, global food shortages in the early 1970s placed a considerable burden on grain imports. Thus, the government actively promoted a new variety of "unification rice" through the New Community Movement to motivate food production and food self-sufficiency. The cultivation began in 1969, and the cultivation area, which was 2,759 ha in 1971, had expanded to 600,000 ha in 1976. Unification rice was heavily promoted by the Park Chung Hee regime, occupying 76% of the country's total rice production in the late 1970s. The nationwide proliferation rate of unification rice demonstrates the fact that rebuilding the farm economy aimed to support industrialization, and the capacity of rural areas to promote further industrialization had changed little in the 1970s.

Agricultural policies such as agricultural mechanization, strongly promoted by the government in the 1970s, pesticide and fertilizer usage, forced cultivation of new varieties, development of agricultural irrigation systems, and development of agricultural production bases reflected the government's intention to supplement the lack of labor force in rural areas to avoid hampering industrialization while increasing food production. The "Promotion of Agriculture and Industry Policy", advocated by the government since the start of the 1970s, was enacted to eliminate the social instability from urban–rural income disparities through agricultural modernization. It is true that given the introduction of new varieties and price policies implemented since the beginning of the 1970s, self-sufficiency of stable grains was achieved around 1977, and farm income increased temporarily relative to the 1960s. However, it also sought to secure a political support base, as the rural modernization policy mobilized the rural labor force and capital toward export-oriented industrialization while stably securing food, resulting in an economic development system centered on industrialization.

Finally, rural development aimed to proliferate "nationalism from above"'. Park Chung Hee proclaimed at the national convention of the People's Movement for Nation Reconstruction in 1961 that "we will first develop our own revolution by promoting the movement with the goal of political independence, economic independence, and social stability". He also noted that "our people should have 'self-reliance' as individuals, and should establish a spirit of 'self-help' to develop their own destiny" (Park Chung Hee 1962, 242). Moreover, in a speech at the National Mayors' Conference in 1970, Park Chung Hee responded to the "Special Project for Increasing Farmers' Income" by claiming that "farmers with a strong spirit of self-help, participation, cooperation, unity, and working ethos will be prioritized" (*Kyunghyang Shinmun* March 12, 1970). Such values of "self-help", "cooperation", and "independence" were advocated as symbols of the modern nation and were directly reflected in the New Community Movement. Rural communities before the New Community Movement were depicted as "irrational" and "unproductive" "old villages". Farmers were characterized by "fateful inertia" and as "lazy and dependent" and "poor and ignorant". It was proposed that rural villages could be modernized through modern farming techniques, production infrastructure modernization, and living conditions improvement, but also through the cultivation of a "scientific", "productive", and "rational" way of thinking. The modern image of a peasant advocated by Park Chung Hee was a peasant who had acquired a modern way of thinking. Modern thinking included "hard work", "self-help", and "cooperation", core principles of the New Community Movement.

Indeed, a "consciousness revolution" or a "spiritual revolution" was key to rural development (Ministry of Home Affairs 1980). The significance of the "consciousness revolution" was clearly demonstrated in the saemaul leader education conducted between 1972 and 1978 nationwide at its regular base at the Saemaul Leader Education Training. The "saemaul spirit enlightenment" subject comprised 66.9% of the entire educational training (Saemaul Leader Education Training Center 1982). By propagating "saemaul spirits" to the everyday lives of the general rural population and providing regular and systematic education programs to village leaders, the Park regime attempted to encourage a spirit of nationalism from above based on the New Community Movement platform.

Conclusions

The "modernization of the motherland", as advocated by the Park Chung Hee regime, included the "establishment of an independent economy", "modern nation-state building", and an "anti-communist ideology". Rural development was an urgent agenda and played a major role in the modernization of the motherland. Accordingly, the New Community Movement was initiated in 1970 under the slogans of "diligence", "self-help", and "cooperation". It demonstrates the significance of understanding the rural–urban interconnectedness during the industrialization period. Further, the official commencement of the New Community Movement in 1971 marked a new era of relations between the state and rural society.

Notes

1 The April Revolution, also known as the April 19 Revolution or 4.19 Revolution, was a mass student-led protest against the corrupt and authoritarian government of South Korea's then-president, Syngman Rhee, in April 1960. The protests were sparked by widespread public outrage over allegations of electoral fraud in the presidential election, which was wildly believed to have been rigged in favor of Rhee. The protests quickly escalated into a nationwide movement, with millions of people taking to the streets to demand Rhee's resignation and the establishment of a new democratic government. The protests eventually forced Rhee to resign in the same month, in April 1960, and induced the establishment of a new government under a transitional regime until elections were held later that year. The April Revolution is considered a key moment in South Korean democratic history, marking the first successful popular uprising against an authoritarian regime and paving the way for the democratization of the country.

2 Meanwhile, even though economic inequality was relatively small during the early stage of industrialization in the 1960s, it had grown by the mid-1970s and had led to a sense of deprivation not only among the working class but the lower middle-class population (Campos and Root 1996).

3 The National Regional Ministers' Meeting, held for establishing countermeasures against drought on April 22, 1970.

4 *Tongshije* is a ritual for the village protector deity held on New Year's Day to pray for villagers' good health and a good harvest.

5 It is called the "4-H club" in Korea. It is a youth development program that focuses on providing hands-on learning experiences and skill-building activities to help young people develop knowledge and skills in areas such as agriculture, science, leadership, and community service. The program, initially established in the US, expanded to other countries, including South Korea.

6 Since the mid-1970s, rurality has represented "a shameful past" and "a backward space" while being, at times, romanticized as an antidote to the "materialism", "selfishness", and "individualism" believed to be characteristic of modernization (Hwang Pyŏngchu

2016). Such contradictory descriptions of rurality were often apparent within dialogues on the negative consequences of urbanization in the late 1970s. Conflicting ideas of rurality and urbanity might also have originated from the contradictory and complicated process of modernization during the Park Chung Hee regime, where the "tradition-modernity" lines were unclear (Kim Ŭnshil 1999).

7 Two surveys on changes in rural societies in six villages in 1958 and 1969 by rural sociologist, Yi Mankap (1981), clarify the proliferation of media in rural societies. A survey from 1958 found that villagers obtained information about the outside world primarily from village leaders (20%) and markets (14.9%), while 72% of respondents in a survey conducted in 1969 replied that they got information via radio.

8 Though the US strongly supported the economic development plans of the Park Chung Hee regime, Park Chung Hee attempted to distance his regime from Rhee's by mentioning that "the international aid from the US means the legitimacy of the political intervention by the US" (Park Chung Hee 1963, 35–36).

9 "Nationalism from below" is distinguished from "nationalism from above", the latter being advocated by the state. The former indicates a voluntary movement aimed mainly at democracy, liberation from colonial rule, challenges to authoritarianism, and labor movements as a means of building a nation-state (Pak Myŏngnim 1996).

10 In 1971, the Ministry of Agriculture and Forestry established the "Agricultural Machinery Five-Year Plan" to promote the localization and supply of agricultural machinery. In 1973, the ministry established the Agricultural Machinery Department under the Agricultural Development Bureau, which recommended and advised on agricultural machinery projects. A deliberation committee on agricultural mechanization was also established as an advisory body to the minister. In 1978, the Agricultural Mechanization Promotion Act was enacted by the government, laying the foundation for the continuous promotion of agricultural machinery projects (No et al. 2003). Even though the cost of the machinery was heavily subsidized by the government and the government provided low-interest loans to farmers to purchase the machinery, the financial burden remained significant for many farmers, especially for small-scale farmers who had to take out loans and sell assets to finance the purchase and cost of maintaining and repairing the machinery (Pak Chindo and Han Tohyŏn 1999).

Bibliography

Ahn, Byong Man, and William W. Boyer. 1988. "The Dilemma of Tenant Farming in South Korea." *Korean Studies* 12: 1–13. https://doi.org/10.1353/ks.1988.0016

Amsden, Alice. 1989. *Asia's Next Giant: South Korea and Late Industrialization.* New York: Oxford University Press. https://doi.org/10.1016/0305-750X(94)90111-2

Brandt, Vincent S. R. 1979. "Rural Development in South Korea." *Asian Affairs: An American Review* 6, no. 3: 148–163.

Brandt, Vincent S. R. 1980. "The Agricultural Sector in Contemporary South Korea." *Asian Affairs: An American Review* 7, no. 3: 182–194.

Campos, Jose Edgardo, and Hilton L. Root. 1996. *The Key to the Asian Miracle: Making Shared Growth Credible*. Washington, DC: The Brookings Institution.

Chang, Kyung-sup. 1999. "Compressed Modernity and its Discontents: South Korean Society in Transition." *Economy and Society* 28, no. 1: 30–55. https://doi.org/10.1080/03085149900000023

Chang, Kyung-sup. 2010. *South Korea under Compressed Modernity: Familial Political Economy in Transition.* London and New York: Routledge.

Chŏng Myŏngch'ae, Min Sanggi, and Ch'oe Kyŏnghwan. 1995. *Chuyo nongmin undong tanch'e ŭi hyŏngsŏng kwa chŏn'gae kwajŏng (The Organizations and Development of Major Peasant Movements in Korea).* Seoul: Korea Rural Economic Institute.

Chu Gwansu. 1998. "Chut'aek chaegaebal chŏngch'aeg ŭi pyŏnhwa gwajŏng e kwanhan yŏn'gu (Study on the Redevelopment of Housing in Korea)." Master thesis, Seoul: Korea University.

Davis, Diane E. 2004. "An Introduction to Middle Classes, Discipline, and Development." In *Discipline and Development: Middle Classes and Prosperity in East Asia and Latin America*, edited by Diana E. Davis, 1–25. New York: Cambridge University Press.

Dent, Christopher M. 2000. "What Difference a Crisis? Continuity and Change in South Korea's Foreign Economic Policy." *Journal of the Asia Pacific Economy* 5, no. 3: 275–302. https://doi.org/10.1080/13547860050175053

Donga Ilbo. 1967. "Nongsusanŏp ŭi kiŏp'wa (Commercialization of Agriculture and Fishery)." April 18.

Economic Planning Board. 1986. *Han'guk ŭi sahoe chip'yo (Social Index in South Korea)*. Seoul: Economic Planning Board.

Ho, Samuel P. S. 1979. "Rural-Urban Imbalance in South Korea in the 1970s." *Asian Survey* 19, no. 7: 645–659. https://doi.org/10.2307/2643987

Hwang Pyŏngchu. 2016. "Pakchŏnghŭi ch'eje ŭi kŭndaejŏk shigonggan inshik gwa shigoltoshi tamnon (Perceptions on Modern Time and Space and Discourse on Rurality and Urbanity in the Park Chung Hee Era)." *Yŏksa wa bip'yŏng (History and Critique)* 31: 303–342.

Jones, Leory P., and Il Sakong. 1980. *Government, Business, and Entrepreneurship in Economic Development: The Korean Case*. Cambridge: Council on East Asian Studies of Harvard University Press.

Kim Chusuk. 1981. "Nongch'on yŏsŏng munje sogo (A Study on Rural Women)." *Han'guk sahoehak (Korean Sociology)* 15: 49–60.

Kim Ilch'ŏl. 1991. *Han'guk ŭi sahoe wa pyŏnhwa (Society and Change in South Korea)*. Seongnam: The Academy of Korean Studies.

Kim Kwangŏk. 1984. *Saemaŭl Undong Iron Ch'eje Chŏngnip (The Theory of the Saemaul Movement)*. Seoul: Center for Saemaul Movement.

Kim Sŏngjo. 2017. "1970nyŏndae nongch'on chut'aek kaeryang saŏp ŭi chŏn'gae: chŏngbu, nongmin, chabon ŭi kwan'gye rŭl chungshimŭro (The State, Farmers, and Manufacturing Capital Dynamics in the Rural Housing Improvement Project in 1970s in South Korea)." *Yŏksa wa shirhak (History and Practical Science)* 64: 261–295.

Kim Suyŏng. 2001. "Han'guk ŭi sanŏp'wa gwajŏng gwa kajok, yŏsŏng (Family and Women in Industrialization)." *Chinbo p'yŏngnon (Progressive Critique)* 7: 57–75.

Kim Ŭnshil. 1999. "Han'guk kŭndaehwa p'ŭrojekt'ŭ ŭi munhwa nolli wa kabujangsŏng (The Culture and Patriarchy Embedded in the Korean Modernization Project)." *Tangdae bip'yŏng (Contemporary Criticism)* 88: 79–100.

Korean Research Association for Politics. 1990. *Han'guk Chŏngch'isa (The History of Korean Politics)*. Seoul: Paeksan Sŏdang.

Kyunghyang Shinmun. 1970. "Nongŏch'on kaebal orhae 2ch'ŏnŏk isang t'uja (Investment of Over 200 Billion Won for Rural Development This Year)." March 12.

Ministry of Home Affairs. 1980. *Saemaŭl undong 10nyŏnsa (Ten Years of the Saemaul Undong's History)*. Seoul: Ministry of Home Affairs.

Nemeth, David J. 1988. "The Walking Tractor: Trojan Horse in the Cheju Island Landscape." *Korean Studies* 12: 14–38.

No Sangha, Pak Wŏn'gyu, Kŭm Donghyŏk, and Han Wŏnshik. 2003. "Kungnaeoe Nongŏp Kigyehwa Chŏngch'aek (Domestic and International Agricultural Mechanization Policies)." *han'guk nongŏp kigye hak'oe haksul palp'yo nonmunjip (Proceedings of the Korean Society for Agricultural Machinery Conference)*, 3–41.

Pak Chindo, and Han Tohyŏn. 1999. "Saemaŭl undong gwa yushin ch'eje: pakchŏnghŭi chŏnggwŏn ŭi nongch'on saemaŭl undong ŭl chungshim ŭro (Saemaul Movement and Yushin System: The Park Chung Hee Regime and Rural Development)." *Yŏksa pip'yŏng (Historical Critique)* 5: 37–80.

Pak Myŏngnim. 1996. "Kŭndaehwa p'ŭrojekt'ŭ wa han'guk ŭi minjokchuŭi (Nationalism and the Modernization Project in Korea)." In *Han'guk ŭi kŭndae wa kŭndaesŏng pip'an (Modernity in Korea and Critiques of Modernity)*, edited by The Institute for Korean Historical Studies, 311–348. Seoul: The Institute for Korean Historical Studies.

Pak Taesik, and Pak Kyŏngch'ŏl. 2003. *Nongch'on chiyŏk sahoe ŭi pyŏnhwa tonghyang gwa chŏnmang (The Prospects of Social Change in Rural Society in Korea)*. Seoul: Korea Rural Economic Institute.

Park Chung Hee. 1962. *Minjok ŭi chŏryŏk (The Power of the Nation)*. Seoul: Donga.

Park Chung Hee. 1963. *Uri minjok i naagal kil (The Path Our People Will Take)*. Seoul: Dongmun.

Saemaul Leader Education Training Center. 1982. *Saemaŭl chidoja yŏnsuwŏn 10nyŏnsa (The 10-Year History of Saemaul Leader Education Training)*. Seoul: Saemaul Leader Education Training Center.

Suehiro, Akira. 1994. "Ajia kaihatsu dokusairon (Developmental Dictatorships in Asia)." In *Kindaika to kōzō hendō (Modernization and Structural Change)*, edited by Katusji Nakagane. Tokyo: Tokyo University Press.

Suehiro, Akira. 1998. "Kaihatsushugi, kokuminshugi, seityō ideorogī (Developmentalism, Nationalism, and Growth Ideology)." In *Kaihatsu to seiji (Development and Politics)*, edited by Junzō Kawada, Katsuhito Iwai, Takehiko Kamo, Keiichi Tsunekawa, Yōnosuke Hara, and Masayuki Yamauchi, 31–52. Tokyo: Iwanami shoten.

Wade, Robert. 1990. *Governing the Market: Economic Theory and the Role of Government in East Asian Industrialization*. Princeton: Princeton University Press.

Woo, Jung-En. 1991. *Race to the Swift: State and Finance in Korean Industrialization*. New York: Columbia University Press.

Yi Mankap. 1973. *Han'guk nongch'on sahoe ŭi kujo wa pyŏnhwa (The Structure of Rural Society and the Changes in Korea)*. Seoul: Seoul National University Press.

Yi Mankap. 1981. *Han'guk nongch'on sahoe yŏn'gu (A Study of Korean Rural Society)*. Seoul: Taragwŏn.

Yi Mankap. 1984. *Kongŏp palchŏn kwa han'guk nongch'on (Industrialization and Rural Society in Korea)*. Seoul: Seoul National University.

Yi Wanbŏm. 1999. "Kyŏngje kaebal 5kaenyŏn kyehoek ŭi iban kwa miguk ŭi yŏk'al (Planning the Five-Year Economic Development Plan and the Role of the United States)." In *1960nyŏndae ŭi chŏngch'i sahoe pyŏndong (Political and Social Changes in the 1960s)*, edited by the Academy of Korean Studies, 11–157. Seoul: Paeksan.

2 (Re)defining Work

Rural Women in Productive and Domestic Labor

During the early stages of industrialization in South Korea in the 1960s and 1970s, the aggregate working hours of rural women swiftly increased. This increase was based on the change in the structure of the working population in rural areas given the exodus of the male labor force and the younger generation from rapid industrialization and urbanization. Moreover, the working burden of rural women drastically increased with the implementation of the Park regime's rural development project: The New Community Movement. Meanwhile, in urban industrial factory complexes, the young female labor force – comprised mainly of young women from rural areas – was becoming the main support pillar for the labor-intensive, export-oriented manufacturing industry in South Korea. In short, the rural mothers in rural areas and their daughters who had migrated to urban areas had become a major component of the workforce given industrialization and "major members of the new proletarian class in South Korea" in the 1960s and 1970s (Kim 2011, 414).

Thus, during this time in modern Korean history, women's labor participation increased most rapidly (Chang Migyŏng 2001), with rural women engaging in agricultural production activities and young female rural–urban migrant workers engaging in the secondary manufacturing sector. However, contrary to the increasing importance of the female labor force, the 1960s to 1980s represented the time when the ideology of the housewife was intensively proliferated by the government:

> The modernization of gender hierarchy in industrializing South Korea during the period from the 1960s and 1980s hinges on the construction and maintenance of femininity and masculinity, tied to the ideology of housewife and husband-provider and the gender division of labor.
>
> (Moon 2005, 66)

Interestingly, according to a survey in 1987 (Kim Chusuk 1994), 57.8% of female farmers identified themselves as housewives, even though they were engaged in agricultural activities, while merely 10.1% of women interviewed responded that they were farm workers. The results of this survey show that the housewife ideology in South Korea during the industrialization period warrants a detailed investigation of the interplay between the state, class, and gender.

This chapter clarifies the process by which rural women's labor was redefined as a "modern" and gendered concept for the public and women in general

DOI: 10.4324/9781003110538-3

during Korea's industrialization. Given the country's rapid industrialization and the large migration of the rural population to urban areas, rural women became the primary labor force in rural productive and reproductive labor. However, rural women's labor was considered subordinate, docile, and inferior under the housewife ideology. The relabeling of women's work provides important insight into how non-housewives were mobilized as non-paid or underpaid workers during the industrialization process by being positioned as housewives. Even so, the work ethics of the housewife ideology for rural women should not be interpreted solely in terms of governmental intervention. Indeed, the idea of "becoming a hardworking productive laborer" was actively embraced by rural women as a class mobility strategy to fulfill their imagined aspirations of becoming urban middle-class "professional housewives" (stay-at-home housewives).

The (Re)Creation of Work Ethics

The creation of a shared national work ethic was fundamental to industrialization in the Western context (Weber 1968) and the proliferation of such ethics proceeded similarly in South Korea. During industrialization under Park Chung Hee, a positive attitude toward industrial work and industrialization was propagated through governmental slogans such as *jalsarabose* ("Let us work for a better life") (Kim and Park 2003), and this idea was extended beyond industrial workers to the whole population.

There had been a deep-seated negativity toward labor in general – particularly, manual work – under the half-century of sociopolitical Confucianism during the Chosun Dynasty and under Japanese colonial rule (Kim and Park 2003). However, as Thompson (1967, 57) maintains, the creation of a labor force during industrialization "entails a severe restructuring of working habits – new incentives, and a new human nature upon which these incentives could bite effectively". Needless to say, the Park Chung Hee regime was faced with no small task in transforming the negative perceptions the Korean population had toward labor.

Seeking to create a national "work ethic", the Park Chung Hee regime designated 1965 and 1966 as "years of work". The lyrics of the song, "The Year of Work", propagated by the Park Chung Hee regime at the time, demonstrate the feelings toward labor that the government hoped to imbibe in the population. The song emphasizes the importance of hard work and its transformative power in bringing happiness and prosperity. It underscores the idea that the current year is dedicated to diligent efforts to escape poverty and achieve a better life. The lyrics express the joy and excitement associated with labor, advocating for a collective commitment to working hard for individual and communal success. The sense of community and mutual support within the neighborhood is highlighted, emphasizing the collaborative pursuit of "shared" dreams through industriousness. Overall, the repeated refrain emphasizes that the focus and dedication to hard work are central to realizing happiness and fulfilling aspirations in the given year.

Although hard work had been a social value in rural villages before industrialization,[1] during the Park regime, it was newly defined as an ethos emblematic of the "modern" citizen and became part of a "nationalist historical mission" (Kim 2001, 55). Kim (ibid.) maintains that the Park regime stressed the importance of the work ethic of laborers and tried to position it as an essential part of the national collective mission. The new national work ethic was based on the idea that the commitment to industrial norms and values, such as hard work, diligence, and industriousness, could induce the realization of the wealth of the nation. The positioning of work ethic as part of the national mission for Koreans is depicted in the lyrics in the noted song, such as "let us get out of poverty", "let us enjoy our happy life", and "let us work for a better life". The "we"' spirit demonstrated in the song for the year of work promoted the economic prosperity of the community and the nation. "This 'in the same boat' mentality and the presumption of fair-sharing of the benefits of the economic growth" (Kim and Park 2003, 38) played a significant role in fostering a work ethic for the general public and, ultimately, in promoting industrialization in South Korea at large.

The Housewife Ideology, Women, and Labor

This section discusses the mechanisms by which women's labor is subsumed as subordinate to men's under the housewife ideology systematically promoted by the Park Chung Hee regime. Based on the discussion, it demonstrates that the productive and domestic labor by women in general – regardless of whether they are urban or rural women – was positioned within the context of newly defined work ethic and national economic development. Specifically, it begins by discussing how the promulgation of the housewife ideology by the Park Chung Hee regime induced the institutionalization of the definition of urban housewives' work in productive and domestic labor. It was achieved by considering women's work as "side work" and identifying household work as women's unpaid responsibility. Accordingly, this section discusses how the logic for domesticating women's labor in urban areas was also applied to the productive and domestic labor of rural women, despite the growing significance of rural women's labor in rural society.

Development of the Ideology of Housewife

Paek Misuk (2015) defines the development of the housewife ideology in South Korea as occurring in three phases: the 1950s, 1960s, and 1970s. During the 1950s, coinciding with the Korean War, many women had become breadwinners for their families, but they were expected to help rebuild the ruined masculinity of Korean society by leaving the labor market and returning to the private sphere when the war ended.[2] In the 1950s, the re-establishment of "traditional women" who could act as supporters and caregivers for families and were scattered and ruined by the war was a high priority within the modern housewife ideology (Kim Ŭn'gyŏng 2009). In this sense, Paek Misuk (2015) characterizes the housewife ideology in the 1950s as the period of national reconstruction after the Korean War, where women were summoned as housewives to reconstruct families and masculinities dismantled by the war and restructure values regarding "home" as a place to which women should belong.

During the second stage in the 1960s, Korean society witnessed the gradual emergence of "full-time housewives" (*chŏnŏpchubu*), and the housewife ideology was systematically promoted by the developmental state. Along with the gradual proliferation of the discourses on stay-at-home housewives, economic participation for urban middle-class women was depicted as out of step with the ideal woman, who was meant to focus on mothering and childcare during this early industrialization period. Accordingly, discourses about urban working mothers in major newspapers expressed the view that the proper social place was the home, even describing the economic agency of working mothers as harmful to children. For instance, an article from *Donga Ilbo* (February 11, 1975) notes that "the absence of mothers will negatively affect children's emotional and intellectual development".

During the third phase in the 1970s, Korea witnessed a mixed period when urban housewives from the middle class gradually became socially visible and prevalent. In this connection, women were expected to fulfill the role of a "professional" housewife who manages housework with "modern" knowledge and makes the home a comfortable sanctuary for family members. Meanwhile, women's economic activities increased in this period. By the late 1970s, positive discourses on the economic activities of women began to emerge. However, it did not necessarily mean women's work outside the home could surpass their socially ordained work as housewives (Paek Misuk 2015). The economic activities of urban middle-class women were still considered "additional" and "supportive", where their income supplemented that of their husbands, who were perceived as the primary breadwinners (Chang Migyŏng 2007, 158–159). This thinking was well presented in discourses on "side jobs" (*puŏp*), which began to be proliferated intensively in the 1970s. The creation of a new ideology on productive labor pushed housewives to engage in side economic activities for additional household income, such as selling pieces of embroidery and knitting and temporal wage labor through sewing. Such activities could be conducted in the domestic sphere and were not considered to interrupt the "main" gender role as household managers. For instance, *Kyunghyang Shinmun* (May 14, 1970), one of the major daily newspapers, published an article titled "Side Jobs for Housewives". It noted that housewives, traditionally focused solely on domestic responsibilities, had begun to express an increased interest in pursuing additional employment. The newspaper acknowledged that this shift in behavior was attributed to social changes, including the transformation of family structures from extended to nuclear units, advancements in reducing gender disparities, and decreased gendered responsibilities in childrearing for women. It also suggested that homemakers should not view these "secondary" jobs solely as financial opportunities but as opportunities to contribute their skills to society. The newspaper further emphasized that homemakers should prioritize considering how they could make a meaningful societal impact with their "surplus time" dedicated to these "secondary" occupations. It also stressed that these "secondary" roles should not overshadow their "primary" responsibilities within the family, as the family remains their "central" priority.

As indicated in the analyses of the changing discourse in media, along with the increase in economic participation in the spheres of productive labor by married urban women, the discourse on working women changed from negative to positive by recognizing them as double earners in their households. However, in the media, the economic activities of married urban women were limited to those of "supportive" and "docile" housewives. Women's productive labor in urban areas was, thus, positioned as activities for extra income for the household.

The housewife ideology was applied to productive labor and in the domestic labor sphere for urban housewives. Considering news media reports that 2.2 out of 10 Seoul households in 1966 employed domestic helpers, Kang Isu (2007) explains how the housework of middle-class women in urban areas was overtaken by young rural–urban female domestic workers. This change is closely related to the massive migration of unskilled young female rural–urban migrants at the time (Kang Isu 2009). Regarding domestic houseworkers, it has often been suggested in the media since the 1960s that domestic labor should be tackled by housewives. For instance, a *Chosun Ilbo* article dated January 15, 1967, argued that the modernization of the family structure could only be achieved if housewives assumed the responsibilities of household work—a role traditionally fulfilled by domestic helpers. Clearly, household work was considered a fundamental responsibility of housewives. Similarly, a *Donga Ilbo* article titled "The Abolition of Bad Customs: Housework without Domestic Workers" (March 27, 1972) defined household work as a "natural duty" of housewives, and the employment of domestic helpers in urban areas was attributed to the "absence of housewives" at home. The article further emphasized that unless urban housewives fulfilled their roles as homemakers, the definition of "housewife" would become blurred.

In this context, household work was (re)defined as women's work, and urban women who were considered "stay-at-home housewives" but supported by domestic workers were subject to criticism, as they were not considered to be fully completing their responsibility as domestic household managers. Moreover, household work was considered a symbol of affection and devotion to family members rather than being hard and cumbersome (Yun Chŏngno 1999). As Mies (1998, ix) maintains, by redefining domestic work on an "emotional" level, a woman's work "was considered to be only supplementary to that of her husband, the so-called breadwinner, and thus devalued". Regarding the devaluation of productive labor by women and the depreciation of household work, Barber and Bryan (2014, 31) note that, under capitalism, women were renamed "as housewives, as carers, as nonproductive entities or labor reservists, not because they are those things, but because they have been constituted as such things".

Moreover, during the Park Chung Hee regime in South Korea, it is significant to note that the leisurely lives of urban housewives were interpreted within the context of the nation's industrialization. They were viewed as "unproductive", "overindulgent", and "aberrant", which contradicted "modern" work ethics and were perceived as not contributing to the economic development of the nation. *Kyunghyang Shinmun*, in its newspaper article released on December 8, 1976, noted that the widespread adoption of electric home appliances had resulted in increased free time for urban housewives. In this context, a growing concern highlighted in the article is the utilization of this "newfound" free time by urban housewives. The paper maintains that many urban housewives use their free time for "unproductive" or "aimless" pursuits, which is considered a "societal issue". According to a survey cited in the article, 18% of urban housewife respondents spend their free time watching television, while the remaining respondents admitted to engaging in activities such as casual chatting, knitting, pursuing handicrafts, taking naps, and reading. This survey data suggests that a significant portion of urban housewives may not be channeling their free time toward more "constructive" and "meaningful" endeavors, which the article implies is a missed opportunity for "self-development" and "national productivity".

As noted, discourses on the proliferation of modern home appliances among middle-class women in South Korea were loaded with negative connotations that differed from common discourses observed in other countries where home appliances were seen as "liberating" women from their workloads (Forty 1986), affording them more time to contribute to their family's well-being and happiness (Pérez 2012). Domestic labor by urban housewives was, thus, criticized relative to the laboring of rural women in South Korea. The newspaper *Donga Ilbo*, released on July 15, 1976, highlighted that most rural women actively engaged in productive labor. The newspaper further commented that rural women tend to experience comparatively lower levels of "emotional instability", despite facing time constraints in managing their households, unlike urban housewives. It maintained that this emotional stability is attributed to their sense of accomplishment through labor and the strong support system provided by extended families and tightly knit rural communities. In stark contrast, urban housewives were depicted as leading lives characterized by modern convenience, nuclear family structures, and a more isolated societal context. Therefore, this newspaper article portrayed urban housewives as lacking a distinct "work identity" and being surrounded by modern home appliances, which, as the article suggested, could induce different emotional and social dynamics relative to their rural counterparts.

This notion should be understood in the context of the socialization process of housewives in South Korea, where women were required to contribute to national economic development through labor at the traditional-modern gender role interaction. Overall, the development of the housewife ideology during the Park Chung Hee regime regarding labor was characterized by the systematic subordinate positioning of women's productive and domestic labor. The depreciation of urban housewives' labor was justified via the newly defined work ethics, positioned by the state as national values for the maximization of the nation's productivity.

The Housewife Ideology, Labor, and Work Ethics for Rural Women

In the modern Korean history of the 1960s and 1970s, women's participation in the labor force increased most rapidly – from 26.8% in 1960 to 45.7% in 1975. In this same period, men's participation in the labor force increased from 73.5% in 1960 to 77.8% in 1975. The increase in female workers is remarkable, tallying an increase of 70.5%, relative to an increase of 5.8% for male workers during the same period (Chang Migyŏng 2001). Female labor participation in this period would prove to be indispensable to the Korean economy's initial industrial take-off (Chang 2010; Kim 2011), as was recognized and encouraged in contemporary media: "The diligent, industrious and hardworking female rural labor force has made a great contribution to the industrialization of our country" (*Happy Home* March 5, 1974). In the 1960s and 1970s, this labor force was mainly led by young single female workers under 24 years old. For instance, the economic participation ratio of females from the 15–19 age group increased from 28.6% in 1960 to 44.5% in 1975. During the same period, the economic participation ratio of females aged 20–24 increased from 31.8% to 49.7% (Chang Migyŏng 2001).

Young female workers were concentrated in underpaid export-oriented light manufacturing industries and worked under harsh conditions. Indeed, 75% of total national exports were from the female-dominated light manufacturing sector until 1975 (Kim 2001). Moreover, 88% of the garment industry, 77% of the textile industry, and 68% of electronics were supported by young female factory workers in 1985 (Koo 2001). Although the female labor force mostly comprised young female workers until 1980, the share of married women who participated in economic activities also consistently increased, reaching 40% in 1980. Among married women in particular, most of the female working population comprised rural women (Chang Migyŏng 2001). However, despite rapid industrialization, 59.7% of women's labor participation still occurred in the agricultural industry in 1970 (Kim Hyegyŏng 2007).

The population exodus from rural areas that began in the early 1960s resulted in a noticeable decrease in the rural population by 1969. However, it did not necessarily mean a decrease in the number of rural households. Rather, it meant a decrease in the number of members in each household. Furthermore, most of the early rural exodus occurred among young working-age males. Hence, the burden of rural work fell on married rural women left behind in rural areas. For instance, the percentage of the economically active rural female population increased by 48.2% in 1960, a trend that would continue until the 1970s (Kim 2011). Moreover, the rural–urban migration of young daughters meant a decrease in support for their mothers regarding domestic labor, such as household chores, and caring for the elderly and younger siblings.

A survey by the Ministry of Health and Social Welfare in the 1960s and 1970s on the ratio of labor input for agricultural activities by gender in rural areas demonstrates that the working burden of rural women drastically increased across this period. It indicates that 71.9% of the agricultural work was conducted by male farmers and 28.1% by females. However, by 1979, the labor input of male farmers in agricultural work decreased to 57.6%, and the labor input by female farmers increased to 42.4% (Kim Chusuk 1981). Moreover, a survey on working hours and the labor input of female farmers during the farming season conducted by the Institute for Rural Development indicates an increase in total working hours for rural women and a dramatic shift in their participation in labor. First, the total daily working hours of rural women were 11.9 in 1965, but this figure increased to

14.24 hours in 1979. Second, female farmers' labor input in productive labor also increased. Rural female workers spent 3.42 hours farming and 8.48 hours per day on housework during the high farming season in 1965. Thus, female farmers spent a significant amount of time on housework in the 1960s. Nonetheless, the situation dramatically transformed by 1979, when working hours devoted to farming (housework) were 9.77 (4.47) hours per day. Of course, this change might partly reflect the decrease in working hours allotted to housework given the proliferation of electric home appliances in rural households. However, if considering the increase in the working hours of female farmers, the productive labor working burden for female farmers drastically increased from 3.42 hours in 1965 to 9.77 hours in 1979.

The increase in rural women's productive labor working hours was also perceived by rural women (Yokota 2002b, 149). In one study conducted based on fieldwork in eight rural villages in 1976, 74% of female farmer respondents replied that [they] felt their work burden had increased (Kim Chusuk 1994). In another study, over 90% answered that they supposed rural women worked much more than urban housewives (Kim Chusuk 1981). A German missionary dispatched to South Korea in the 1960s who implemented development activities in rural villages depicted the heavy working burden of rural women in those times in a personal letter she sent to the German church asking for financial support: "Disregarded by the male world, neither consulted nor heard, rural women have to carry a heavy workload in the house, in the field, in bearing and raising children without much help from their husbands".[3]

The significance of the rural female workforce to rural development became obvious to Park Chung Hee's regime, as noted in the document published by the Ministry of Health and Social Welfare regarding the New Community Movement: "Rural housewives should take part in production activities to increase the income of rural households. Rural housewives are responsible for farming labor" (Ministry of Health and Social Welfare 1981, 85).

Hence, the Rural Development Administration, a governmental organization established by the US military administration in the 1950s to promote the welfare of farmers, began conducting agricultural machinery operation training for rural women at the national, provincial, city, and county levels from the 1970s (Rural Development Administration 1979). Agricultural Cooperatives were also entrusted to the Rural Development Administration, and agricultural machinery education for rural women began in 1978.

Even so, despite the growing significance of rural women's labor in rural society, the logic of the housewife ideology for urban housewives – positioning women's productive and domestic labor as subordinate and docile under the name of "housewives" – was also applied to the productive and domestic labor of rural women who were in principle working women. Even though rural women became the main labor force in rural areas, the increase in the labor of rural women did not necessarily induce the recognition of rural women's labor nor the appreciation of rural women's contribution to farming activities. *Kyunghyang Shinmun*, in an article on October 25, 1965, described the increasing labor burden of rural women, citing the findings of a research study examining the rising work hours of urban and rural housewives conducted by the Rural Development Administration. According to the study, rural housewives spend an average of 13 hours and 19 minutes per day on various tasks, while urban housewives' daily work hours average 10 hours and 40 minutes. The Rural Development Administration offers several recommendations for rural women to reduce their workload. These include careful planning of working hours, implementing "gender-specific divisions of labor in agricultural tasks to maximize productivity", enhancing rural living conditions through the modernization of agricultural machinery and the reorganization of housing facilities, and active participation in government-led initiatives aimed at improving the quality of life for rural residents. Notably, the study states that the primary factor contributing to the heavier workload of rural women is attributed to the inefficiencies in their living arrangements.

First, from the expression "gender-specific divisions of labor in agricultural tasks to maximize productivity" in the newspaper article excerpt (*Kyunghyang Shinmun*, October 25, 1965), the increase in the workload of rural women did not induce the transformation of gender roles in agricultural activities. Rather, it induced the solidification of clearly defined gender roles. In particular, along with the transition to market-oriented agriculture given rapid urbanization, gender roles in agricultural activities were clearly divided.[4] That is, farm work regarding skilled labor in market-oriented crops was conducted by men, and simple and unskilled supportive work was done by women (Yokota 2002b, 151). Kim Chusuk (1981) maintains that even though the working burden of rural women had increased immensely given the introduction of market-oriented crops and sericulture and the concept of productivity maximization, rural women's subordinate role in farming had not changed. Men were involved in establishing greenhouses, fertilizer and pesticide spraying, and crop sales, while women were engaged in unskilled labor such as sowing, thinning, and growing vegetables. This gender segregation was closely related to the agriculture training program provided by the government. Rural men were allowed to learn specialized skills and knowledge about the cultivation of cash crops (Kim Chusuk 1994), while rural women engaged in the educational program, comprising training in supportive and subordinate jobs such as the usage of small-scaled agricultural machinery and engagement with small income-generating projects (Ministry of Health and Social Welfare 1981).[5] The clear gender division in the marketization of agricultural products in rural areas in South Korea empirically proves Mies' theory in that it demonstrates the close connectedness between the rise of capitalism and the separation of the public and private spheres in labor (Mies 1998).

More importantly, it is crucial to pay special attention to the fact that rural women began to be broadly "named" as "rural housewives (*nongch'onjubu*)", whereas women in urban areas were deemed "urban housewives (*toshijubu*)" by the media and in official governmental documents. Even though the term "rural housewives" was scarcely used in the 1930s, they were used often and consciously during the 1960s. This fact demonstrates that the capitalist system, the state, and other institutions such as the media played a primary role in shaping the marginalization of women's labor by strongly supporting the housewife ideology. The abovementioned media article by one of the major daily newspapers shows the prevalent usage of the term "rural housewives".

The clear division of the two social groups – "rural housewives" versus "urban housewives" – hence denotes rapid urbanization and the emergence of a Korean middle class and full-time housewives, whose only work was domestic. Meanwhile, special attention must be paid to the meaning behind renaming rural women as "rural housewives". In fact, rural women could not be categorized as housewives in a classic sense, as a significant number of them participated in productive labor. Rural sociologist Kim Chusuk (1981) provides data indicating the difference in the economic participation rate between rural and urban women in 1970. Indeed, 55.3% of the rural female population aged 25–54 participated in productive labor relative to 20.8% of the urban female population. Furthermore, 29.5% of rural women over 55 remained active in productive labor, while merely 9.1% of urban women in the same age group participated in the labor market. Such data demonstrate rural women's high rate of participation in productive labor, even the elderly. Rural women must become involved in productive subsistence activities such as farming and seasonal wage labor, following the rural–urban exodus of much of the male labor force. Given that a rural exodus generally meant proletarianization for rural laborers, rural women's contributions somewhat allowed men to migrate to urban areas without threatening the whole farming economy (Chang 2010). Nevertheless, renaming "rural women" as "rural housewives" meant the blurring of the boundaries of female farmers' productive labor.

Moreover, the idea of "side work" of urban housewives discussed in the earlier section notably penetrated rural society at the time. In a 1976 survey, 63% of the rural women respondents replied that they wanted to engage in "side work" such as sericulture, poultry farming, and beekeeping, even though they were already fully involved with farming work (*Chosun Ilbo* July 15, 1976). In fact, given the "Low Grain Pricing Policy", rural women were expected to supplement their household income through seasonal wage labor (Chang 2010). However, as such small-scale income-generating activities in the informal sector present no clear distinction between remunerated and non-remunerated work, it is challenging for them to be perceived as proper work (Moser 1993).

On domestic labor in rural areas, while household work and the employment of domestic workers were at the center of discussions in the media regarding the definition of work for urban housewives, rural women's household chores were rarely discussed. Though household work was partly overtaken by members of the extended family given the continuation of the large family systems commonly found in rural areas, relative to the proliferation of nuclear families in urban areas (Shin Kyŏnga 2007), rural women remained responsible for most of the domestic work of households. Yi Jiŭn (1979) illustrates that rural women's domestic labor was simplified regarding washing given the change in textiles from natural to chemical products, the increasing number of households equipped with rice cookers, improvements in water supply and electricity, and the distribution of refrigerators at a rate of 1 in 26.3 households. However, a survey in 1976 reveals that only approximately 10% of households had basic facilities such as drainage and oil stoves in their kitchens (Yi Hyojae and Kim Chusuk 1976).

The housewife ideology regarding the positioning of household work as women's work further legitimized "traditional" gender roles in housework in rural areas by resummoning the preexisting patriarchal orders. Tilly and Scott (1989) analyzed women's economic participation during industrialization in the United Kingdom and France and demonstrated that women's economic participation did not necessarily induce improvements in women's rights or changes in gender norms within the labor market or household. Despite women's participation in the labor market, the public–private sphere division remained unclear, and women's perceived responsibility to conduct a household was not "problematized", as it occurred as a continuation of "tradition".

In fact, contrary to urban housewives, rural women's work ethics were highly praised in public discourse. For instance, the *Donga Ilbo* newspaper article (December 15, 1975) entitled "The Traditional Values of Korean Women" emphasized that traditional values, such as endurance, sacrifice, and diligence, are prominently exemplified through the active involvement of rural women in the New Community Movement. Hence, previous research clarifies that the Park Chung Hee regime enacted a "feminization" of rural women's labor, applying traditional "feminine'" values such as "self-sacrifice", "endurance", and "devotion". The endowment of the "traditional" and "feminine" values to rural women's labor has led to the justification of the labor burdens by rural women under the name of rural mothers' nature and virtue, leading to the "invisibility" of rural women's economic contribution (Kang Isu 2007; Kim Suyŏng 2001). Moreover, not only the recollection of such traditional cultural values and the gendered nature of capitalism but also the housewife ideology actively promoted during the Park Chung Hee regime, which positioned women's labor in productive and domestic spheres as subordinate to that of males, further systematized the "invisibility" and "depreciation" of rural women's labor by situating all of their labor within the domain of the "modern" term of "housewives".

Embrace of Work Ethics and the Housewife Ideology by Rural Women

As noted, state-sponsored nationalism contributed to the creation of a nationwide work ethic. As the general populace shared common experiences of hunger, poverty, and war, there was a widespread social consensus at the time that "today" is better than "yesterday", and "tomorrow" would even be better than "today". Abelmann (2002) maintains in her anthropological study on Korea that "the idea of an era of shared struggle has also been publicly promoted by the developmentalist state's calibration of its own economic achievements" (29). Critically, rather than social welfare, people's willingness to work hard was the key to the developmentalist Park Chung Hee and his successors in the mobilization of the grassroots toward industrialization in South Korea. As economic resources were concentrated on national economic development, individuals must work to ensure their social welfare on the private level. It was especially the case for the underprivileged; without work, they would face total social alienation (Chang 2002).

Beyond state promotion, rural women's aspirations to join the national modernization project also functioned as a strong driving force for the acceptance of the new national work ethic. In particular, the so-called *jalsarabose* ("Let us work for a better life") spirit was internalized by rural women at the individual level via the economic advancement of the village communities to which they belonged. Many interviews in the daily newspapers on "successful" stories of rural villages reveal that rural women believed that hard work could alleviate poverty (Chang Migyŏng 2008). That is, rural women believed hard work to be a chance for social mobility, reflecting the democratic ideology that everyone can achieve equal opportunities through hard work (Sewell 1985). Thus, values such as diligence and being hard-working and industriousness were relevant at the individual level, as they were reinterpreted in "modern" terms by rural women. Rural women appearing in the media repetitively emphasized the importance of a strong work ethic to their success in rural development projects. Rural mothers were depicted as figures who "struggle to get out of poverty and live better" (*Happy Home* April 5, 1971), and successful stories of rural women were repeatedly introduced, narrating that hard work is the path to abundance for themselves, their family members, and the village to which they belong (*Happy Home* May 5, 1969).

The link between the betterment of the village as a whole and abundance on the individual level was strategically promoted by the Park Chung Hee regime. Through the New Community Movement, every rural village was categorized into one of three categories – "basic", "self-help", and "self-reliance", with villages upgraded to higher levels per project results, as elaborated in the previous chapter. Davis (2004) maintains that the classification of villages itself reflects "an eminently middle-class sense of attaining self-sufficiency and increased production" (130–131) by endowing the rural population with a specific aspiration toward upward social mobility through the achievement of reaching a higher stage of classification. Such an achievement was considered to stem from modern abilities such as "self-help" and "self-management" and was a step toward the transition from the traditional to the modern middle class. Further, the village became a space in which "long-standing middle-class ideologies about personal success, hard work, and competition and their impact on productivity, capital accumulation, and thus overall development" were rendered (ibid., 131).

Even social reformers believed that social mobility could be realized through self-discipline by rural women. Kwon (2007, 75) notes that "the sense of time, punctuality and time-thrift" was emphasized as "modern" thinking during industrialization. In those times, Korea definitely accepted its place on the development scale as determined by the West. Hence, an emphasis on work ethic and the acceptance of a "modern" mindset was associated with an aspiration for economic achievement at the individual level. In this context, it was generally accepted that the adoption of "modern" ideas such as "efficiency", "time-saving", and "proficiency" was a personal responsibility in the pursuit of upward social mobility. Nolan (1990) also maintains in her study on housewives in Germany that management of time in everyday lives was "a slogan for productivity and efficiency, for science and prosperity, for ill-defined visions of modernity" (ibid., 549).

The Korean Catholic Peasant Women's Organization is a grassroots peasant group founded in 1976 to establish an autonomous organization to improve rural women's work and livelihood.[6] When considering the harsh political environment of the times, the establishment of the peasant organization can be considered "progressive". However, in a magazine published by female intellectuals, the editors also shared that rural poverty is rooted in the lack of a "modern" mindset and working practices of the rural populace. It was assumed that rural Korean women spent most of their working hours without a clear plan, and poor time management led to inefficient labor. In one magazine published in the early stages of the organization's establishment, rural Korean women were compared with rural women in Europe, who were described as working and resting according to concrete timetables, and whose practice of taking time for leisure on the weekends maximized productivity (*Rural Women* October 15, 1975).[7]

Paradoxically, rural women's acceptance of the values of diligence and hard work did not necessarily signify strong aspirations to continue working as farmers – the very profession in which these values were rooted. However, "stay-at-home-housewife" was interpreted by rural women as a "modern" and "ideal" form of womanhood. Chang Migyŏng (2007) maintains that the rapid economic development of the 1970s meant a "liberation" from labor for most women, leading to an increase in full-time housewives. Therefore, middle-class urban housewives in the 1960s and 1970s were pleased to identify as "stay-at-home-housewives" and differentiate themselves from working women who must juggle productive labor and housework. "Labor" was socially perceived as representative of the lower working class, at least until the mid-1970s, as many working women were married in rural villages or had young daughters who migrated to work low-end jobs in the manufacturing and domestic sectors. The preference of women to be full-time housewives is also reflected in a survey by a national newspaper: 52% of urban housewife respondents replied that they agreed it was challenging to gain recognition in society if they stayed at home as housewives. However, 71% of the respondents among them answered that they wished their daughters would stay at home as "stay-at-home housewives" caring for their family members (*Donga Ilbo* June 1, 1981). Thus, the housewife ideology was accepted by middle-class and working-class women as an "ideal" and "modern" womanhood in addition to being propagated by the developmental state as part of modern nation-state building.[8]

Conclusions

This chapter examined the "ironical" coexistence between the increasing work burden on rural women as primary laborers in rural villages given the rural migration and the general acceptance of the housewife ideology by such women. It demonstrates that the productive and domestic labor of urban middle-class women and the labor of rural women were subsumed under the "housewife" mantle by the state in its promotion of the housewife ideology. It also discusses the issue that the newly defined work ethic was interconnected with the definition of labor by urban and rural women. Furthermore, the chapter clarifies that rural women attempted to interpret the state-promoted work ethics in the context of becoming middle-class.

Notes

1 Vincent Brandt, an anthropologist who has published significant work based on fieldwork in rural areas in South Korea in the 1960s and 1970s, observed that "in addition to a pervasive work ethic, [the Korean population] embodies strong traditions of cooperation and solidarity at the village level" (Brandt 1980, 185). Similarly, Davis (2004) suggests that the work ethos of small farmers in South Korea, based on hard work and self-discipline, provided the mindset required of urban-based industrial workers, thereby laying the foundation for South Korea's economic development.

2 The return of traditional gender roles for women after wars has been well-observed in countries such as in France, America, and the United Kingdom (Duchen 1991).

3 The exact date of the letter is not clear. The interviewee stated that it might have been written in the early 1970s (personal interview on September 21, 2007). She was involved in the Korean peasant movements for 30 years after coming to Korea from Germany in 1965.

4 Grain (in particular, rice) was the main agricultural product for farming households until the 1960s, accounting for 80% of all production in farming households; such agricultural products were partly consumed by the farm households. However, the market-oriented agricultural product (e.g., fruits, vegetables, and livestock) share increased to 42.5% alongside the rapid expansion of the urban population (Yi Mankap 1981; Yokota 2002a, 140–141). Unlike rice, which was partly consumed by the farm households, the increase in market-oriented agricultural products means that the contribution of the labor by rural women could be measured and visualized as remunerated labor.

5 The Rural Development Administration started agriculture training programs for rural women in 1975. Moreover, the Rural Co-operative Institute offered rural women education programs concerning the usage of agricultural machines starting in 1978.

6 For further discussion on the emergence of the Korean Catholic Peasant Women's Organization, see Kwon (2011).

7 The perceptions of the Korean Catholic Peasant Women's Organization regarding the structural causes of poverty in rural villages changed dramatically after the late 1970s when it became clear that rapid industrialization in South Korea was based on the sacrifices of farmers and paid for with a cheap rural labor force and the low-priced grain policy.

8 Regarding Japan, Garon (2010, 331) argues that "the status of the 'housewife' had become the aspiration of those who engaged in wage labor or household production" and that the spread of this idea was through the mass media via the circulation of women's magazines.

Bibliography

Abelmann, Nancy. 2002. "Women, Mobility, and Desire: Narrating Class and Gender in South Korea." In *Under Construction: The Gendering of Modernity, Class, and Consumption in the Republic of Korea*, edited by Laurel Kendall, 25–53. Honolulu: University of Hawai'i Press.

Barber, Pauline Gardiner, and Catherine Bryan. 2014. "'Value plus plus': Housewifization and History in Philippine Care Migration." In *When Care Work Goes Global: Locating the Social Relations of Domestic Work*, edited by Mary Romero, Valerie Preston, and Wenona Giles, 29–44. London and New York: Routledge.

Brandt, Vincent S. R. 1980. "The Agricultural Sector in Contemporary South Korea." *Asian Affairs: An American Review* 7, no. 3: 182–194.
Chang, Kyung-sup. 2002. "South Korean Society in the IMF Era: Compressed Capitalist Development and Social Sustainability." In *Rethinking Development in East Asia: From Illusory Miracle to Economic Crisis*, edited by Pietro P. Masina, 189–222. London: Curzon.
Chang, Kyung-sup. 2010. *South Korea under Compressed Modernity: Familial Political Economy in Transition*. London and New York: Routledge.
Chang Migyŏng. 2001. "Kŭllo yŏsŏng 50nyŏnsa ŭi chŏngni wa p'yŏngga (50 Years of History of Working Women)." In *21segi kŭllo yŏsŏng jŏngch'aek ŭi kibon banghyang e kwanhan t'oronhoe (A Discussion of Policy on Working Women in the 21st Century)*, edited by Korea Labor Institute, 75–125. Seoul: Korea Labor Institute.
Chang Migyŏng. 2007. "1960-70nyŏndae kajŏngjubu (anae) ŭi hyŏngsŏng gwa chendŏ jŏngch'i": 'yŏwŏn', 'chubu saenghwal' japchi tamnon ŭl chungshim ŭro (The Formation of Housewives and Institutional Politics: Focusing on Magazine Discourse, 'yŏwŏn' and 'chubu saenghwal')." *Sahoe gwahak yŏn'gu (Social Science Research)* 15, no. 1: 142–180.
Chang Migyŏng. 2008. "Kaebal kukka shigi, saemaŭl undong punyŏ chidoja ŭi chŏngch'esŏng ŭi hyŏngsŏng kwa pyŏnhwa: punyŏ chidojaŭi sŏnggongsarye, sugirŭl chungshimŭro (Formulation and Transformation of Female Leadership Identity in the New Community Movement within the Developmental State: Examining Successful Cases and Essays of Female Leaders)." *Sahoe kwahak yŏn'gu (Social Science Research)* 16, no. 1: 426–660.
Chosun Ilbo. 1967. "Shin kajŏng kyŏngyŏnghak: shingmo ŏmnŭn sallim (Modern Home Management: Housework without Domestic Workers)." January 15.
Chosun Ilbo. 1976. "Nongch'on chubu ŭi saenghwal kwa ŭishik (The Life and Perception of Rural Women)." July 15.
Davis, Diane E. 2004. "An Introduction to Middle Classes, Discipline, and Development." In *Discipline and Development: Middle Classes and Prosperity in East Asia and Latin America*, edited by Diana E. Davis, 1–25. New York: Cambridge University Press.
Donga Ilbo. 1972. "P'yesŭp shingmo sallim (The Abolition of Bad Customs: Housework without Domestic Workers)." March 27.
Donga Ilbo. 1975. "Matpŏri nŭn chanyŏ sŏnggyŏk hyŏngsŏng e chijang (Dual Income Families Harm Personality Development for Children)." February 11.
Donga Ilbo. 1975. "Han'guk yŏsŏngŭi chŏngshinjŏk chŏnt'ong ŭn innae pongsa chŏngsuk i k'ŭn chiju (The Traditional Values of Korean Women: Endurance, Sacrifice, and Resilience)." December 15.
Donga Ilbo. 1976. "Nongch'on chubu ŭi saenghwal kwa ŭishik (The Life and Perceptions of Rural Women)." July 15.
Donga Ilbo. 1981. "Toshi chubu ŭi kajŏng kwalli ŭishik (Household Management of Urban Housewives)." June 1.
Duchen, Claire. 1991. "Occupation Housewife: The Domestic Ideal in 1950s France." *French Cultural Studies* 2: 1–11. https://doi.org/10.1177/095715589100200401
Forty, Adrian. 1986. *Objects of Desire. Design and Society, 1750–1980*. London: Cameron Books.
Garon, Sheldon. 2010. "State and Family in Modern Japan: A Historical Perspective." *Economy and Society* 39, no. 3: 317–336. https://doi.org/10.1080/03085147.2010.486214
Happy Home. 1969. "Ponbogi kajok kyehoek ŏmŏnihoe rŭl ch'ajasŏ (Examining Successful Mothers' Clubs: A Case Study)." May 5.
Happy Home. 1971. "Kanan ŭl ch'ubang hayŏ chom tŏ chal saraboja (Improving Our Lives by Combating Poverty)." April 5.
Happy Home. 1974. "Ponbogi ŏmŏnihoe: kanan ŭi kulle rŭl pŏtkoja momburim (A Successful Mothers' Club Case: The Struggle to Escape Poverty)." March 5.

Kang Isu. 2007. "Sanŏp'wa ihu yŏsŏng nodong shijang ŭi pyŏnhwa wa ilgajok kwan'gye (Changes in the Labor Market for Female Workers and Work-Family Relations after Industrialization)." *P'eminijŭm yŏn'gu (Feminist Studies)* 7, no. 2: 1–35.

Kang Isu. 2009. "Kasa sŏbisŭ nodong ŭi pyŏnhwa ŭi maengnak kwa shilt'ae (A Study on the Changing Work Structure of Domestic Service in Korea)." *Sahoe wa yŏksa (Society and History)* 82: 213–247.

Kim, Andrew Eungi, and Gil-Sung Park. 2003. "Nationalism, Confucianism, Work Ethic and Industrialization in South Korea." *Journal of Contemporary Asia* 33, no. 1: 37–49. https://doi.org/10.1080/00472330380000041

Kim Chusuk. 1981. "Nongch'on yŏsŏng munje sogo (A Study on the Socioeconomic Situation of Rural Women)." *Han'guk sahoehak (Korean Sociology)* 15: 49–60.

Kim Chusuk. 1994. *Han'guk nongch'on ŭi yŏsŏng kwa kajok (Women and Family in Rural Villages in Korea)*. Seoul: Hanul Academy.

Kim Hyegyŏng. 2007. "Yŏsŏng ŭi nodongsa rŭl t'onghae pon il kwa kajok ŭi chŏp'ap: 60 nyŏndae sanŏp'wa ihu ch'injok kwan'gye ŭi pyŏnhwa rŭl chungshim ŭro (The Relationship between Women's Work and Family: A Historical Perspective since 1960s Industrialization)." *P'eminijŭm yŏn'gu (Feminist Studies)* 7, no. 2: 37–82.

Kim, Hyun Mee. 2001. "Work, Nation and Hypermasculinity: The 'Woman' Question in the Economic Miracle and Crisis in South Korea." *Inter-Asia Cultural Studies* 2, no. 1: 53–68. https://doi.org/10.1080/14649370120039452

Kim, Mikyoung. 2011. "Gender, Work and Resistance: South Korean Textile Industry in the 1970s." *Journal of Contemporary Asia* 41, no. 3: 411–430. https://doi.org/10.1080/00472336.2011.582711

Kim Suyŏng. 2001. "Han'guk ŭi sanŏp'wa gwajŏng gwa kajok, yŏsŏng (The Impact of Industrialization on Family Roles and Women's Lives)." *Chinbo p'yŏngnon (Progressive Critique)* 7: 57–75.

Kim Ŭn'gyŏng. 2009. "1950nyŏndae shinsaenghwarundong yŏn'gu: kajŏnggaeryangnon gwa sobit'ongje rŭl chungshimŭro (The New Life Movement in the 1950s: The Reform of Domestic Spheres and Consumption Control)." *Yŏsŏngg wa yŏksa (Women and History)* 11, no. 12: 203–240.

Koo, Hagen. 2001. *Korean Workers: The Culture and Politics of Class Formation*. Ithaca and London: Cornell University Press.

Kwon, Jaok. 2011. "Forging Discursive Space for Women in Social Movements in South Korea." *RIM*, 12–29.

Kwon, Keedon. 2007. "Economic Development in East Asia and a Critique of the Post-Confucian Thesis." *Theory and Society* 36, no. 1: 55–83.

Kyunghyang Shinmun. 1965. "Chubu ŭi saenghwal shigan: Ilgŏri ka nŏmu manayo (Challenges Faced by Rural Housewives: Heavy Workload)." October 25.

Kyunghyang Shinmun. 1970. "Chajo hanŭn chubu son'gil almajŭn puŏp ŭl (Side Jobs for Housewives)." May 14.

Kyunghyang Shinmun. 1976. "Yŏga saenghwal ŭl muŭimihage ponaenŭn (How Urban Women Utilize their Free Time)." December 8.

Mies, Maria. 1998. *Patriarchy and Accumulation on a World Scale: Women in the International Division of Labour*. London: Zed Books.

Ministry of Health and Social Welfare. 1981. *Yŏsŏng kwa saemaŭl undong (Women and the New Community Movement)*. Seoul: Ministry of Health and Social Welfare.

Moon, Seungsook. 2005. *Militarized Modernity and Gendered Citizenship in South Korea*. Durham and London: Duke University Press.

Moser, Caroline O. N. 1993. *Gender Planning and Development: Theory, Practice & Training*. London and New York: Routledge.

Nolan, Mary. 1990. "'Housework Made Easy': The Taylorized Housewife in Weimar Germany's Rationalized Economy." *Feminist Studies* 16, no. 3: 549–577. https://doi.org/10.2307/3178019

Paek Misuk. 2015. "1960–70 Nyŏndae chubu kyoyang p'ŭrogŭraem gwa t'ellebijŏn ŭi chendŏ chŏngch'i (The Housewife Culture and Gender Politics of Television in the 1960s–1970s)." *Ŏllon gwa sahoe (Media and Society)* 23, no. 4: 120–185.
Pérez, Inés. 2012. "Comfort for the People and Liberation for the Housewife: Gender, Consumption and Refrigerators in Argentina (1930–60)." *Journal of Consumer Culture* 12, no. 2: 156–174. https://doi.org/10.1177/1469540512446876
Rural Development Administration. 1979. *Han'guk ŭi nongch'on chido saŏp ŭi palchŏn kwajŏng (Development Process of Korean Rural Guidance Projects)*. Seoul: Rural Development Administration.
Rural Women. 1975. "Nongch'on yŏsŏngŭi shigan kwalli (Time Management of Rural Women)." October 15.
Sewell, William H. 1985. *Structure and Mobility: The Men and Women of Marseille, 1820–1970*. Cambridge: Cambridge University Press.
Shin Kyŏnga. 2007. "Sanŏp'wa ihu il-kajok munje ŭi tamnonjŏk chihyŏng kwa pyŏnhwa (The Discourse on Work-Family Relations and its Changes after Industrialization)." *Han'guk yŏsŏng hak'oe (Korean Women's Studies Association)*, 5–45.
Thompson, Edward P. 1967. "Time, Work-Discipline, and Industrial Capitalism." *Past & Present* 38: 56–97.
Tilly, Louise, and Joan W. Scott. 1989. *Women, Work, and Family*. Abingdon: Routledge.
Yi Hyojae, and Kim Chusuk. 1976. "Yŏsŏng kyŏngje hwaltong mit ch'wiŏp e kwanhan yŏn'gu-1960-70nyŏndae ŭi ch'ui (A Study on the Economic Activities and Employment of Women in the 1960s and 1970s in South Korea)." *Ihwanonjip (Ewha Journal)* 27: 267–293.
Yi Jiŭn. 1979. "Onŭl ŭi nongch'on yŏsŏng (Challenges and Opportunities for Today's Rural Women)." *Ch'angjak kwa pip'yŏng (Creation and Critique)* 14, no. 2: 53–67.
Yi Mankap. 1981. *Han'guk nongch'on sahoe yŏn'gu (A Socioeconomic Study of Korean Rural Society)*. Seoul: Taragwŏn.
Yokota, Nobuko. 2002a. "Kankoku ni okeru nōmin dōin to semauru undo (Mobilization of the Rural Population and the New Community Movement in South Korea)." In *Hendō no higashi ajia shakai (Changing East Asian Society)*, edited by Kitahara Atsushi, 131–160. Tokyo: Aokishoten.
Yokota, Nobuko. 2002b. "Kankoku ni okeru semauru undō to nōson josei no soshikika to dōin (Organizing and Mobilizing Rural Women in the New Community Movement in South Korea)." In *Kōhatsu Kōgyōkoku ni okeru josei rōdō to shakai seisaku (Women's Labor and Social Policy in Late-Industrializing Countries)*, edited by Murakami Kaoru, 129–157. Tokyo: Ajia Keizai kenkyūjo.
Yun Chŏngno. 1999. "Kasa kisul kwa han'guk yŏsŏng ŭi sam (Development of Household Technology and the Life of Korean Women)." In *Mosŏng ŭi Tamnon kwa Hyŏnshil (Discourses on Motherhood and Reality)*, edited by Shim Yŏnghŭi, 343–360. Chŏng Chinsŏng, Yun Chŏngno, Seoul: Nanam.
Weber, Max. 1968. *The Protestant Ethic and the Spirit of Capitalism*. New York: Scribner.

3 Family Planning, Nation Building, and Rural Motherhood

Of the various rural development projects of the New Community Movement that affected rural South Korean women in the domestic sphere, the family planning program was among the programs most earnestly and enthusiastically accepted by rural women. Starting with the 1974 World Population Conference for integrating population policies into development policy in Bucharest, Romania, and the International Conference on Population in Mexico City in 1984, a growing number of developing countries adopted family planning as part of their national development projects (Amin et al. 1994). Among such countries, the family planning program in South Korea has been considered to be among the most "successful" cases regarding its rapid reduction of the fertility rate over a short period (DiMoia 2008). Given family planning, the total fertility rate of 6.0 in 1960 decreased to 4.53 in 1970, and, since 1983, it has remained below the population replacement level (Lee 2009).

This chapter discusses the aspirations of rural women toward the middle class, as reflected in the family planning project. It begins with a description that family planning was implemented for nation building to achieve economic growth, enhance nationalism and collective identity, and establish a modern notion of motherhood within the modern housewife ideology. However, rural women responded differently to economic achievement and family planning discourses by associating family planning with educational opportunities and responded to the demand for a highly educated workforce during the industrialization process. They actively responded to the discourses of family planning while embracing the modern motherhood promoted within the housewife ideology, which positioned mothers as educational guides and caregivers. This analysis indicates that rural women's agency in family planning is important to understand the widespread educational fever and background of nurturing highly educated skilled workers in South Korea.

Implementation of the Family Planning Program

The necessity for a family planning program in South Korea has been addressed by American missionaries, domestic women's movement groups, and foreign private organizations since the 1950s. However, terms such as "family planning" or "childbirth control" remained unfamiliar to the ordinary population in South Korea (Korea Development Institute 1983), which, at the start of the Korean War,

DOI: 10.4324/9781003110538-4

remained primarily rural and agricultural.[1] Moreover, there was a deeply rooted Confucian belief in pronatalist ideology. Under these circumstances, the total fertility rate exceeded six children per woman at the time (Health and Society Research Institute 1991). Following the end of World War II, international organizations tried to reduce overpopulation in developing countries; starting in the early 1960s, the United States Agency for International Development began to address the necessity of a family planning program in South Korea. It was against this backdrop that the Five-Year Economic and Social Development Plan emerged after Park Chung Hee's May 16 military coup in 1961. Economists, demographers, public health officers, and policymakers argued that family planning should be incorporated into the national development project as a component of development planning (ibid.).

The Park Chung Hee regime determined a national family planning program at the Supreme Council for National Reconstruction in November 1961 to promote national economic development and improve maternal and child health via population control. Beyond the family planning institutionalization at the national level, the Park Chung Hee regime attempted to institutionalize it at the village level by establishing mothers' clubs for family planning (*kajok kyehoek ŏmŏnihoe*) in each administrative village. Apparently, participation at the grassroots level was as important as top-down policies such as administrative power mobilization and medical technology distribution. In 1961, the Planned Parenthood Federation of Korea (PPFK) was established, and charged with public enlightenment, information-sharing, and education. On July 31, 1968, chapters of the family planning mothers' club were organized in 16,652 South Korean villages, representing 98.7% of villages nationwide.[2] Such clubs aimed to improve the preparedness of new mothers for childcare, systematically promote family planning, foster a spirit of cooperation among members, and actively contribute to the creation of a prosperous community (Health and Society Research Institute 1991).[3] Each mothers' club had around 12 members, and the membership age ranged between 20 and 47 years old. Until 1977, more than 27,292 mothers' clubs were organized nationwide, and the number of members exceeded 750,000 (Ministry of Health and Social Welfare 1981). Beyond the establishment of mothers' clubs, family planning fieldworkers were assigned to health centers in each village to instruct rural women to practice family planning, starting in 1964.[4] Other developments included the establishment of the Korean Institute for Family Planning in 1970, which was responsible for research, monitoring, training those responsible for implementing the national program, and training field workers. Later, the 1973 "Mother-Child Protection Law" was enacted to expand the scope of permissions for abortion and revitalize the family planning program.

The establishment of mothers' clubs in rural villages provided social legitimacy for the previously secretive use of contraceptives by rural women. In the early stages of the family planning program, family planning fieldworkers who were dispatched by local governments to investigate project progress could not distinguish between those interested and those not interested in using contraceptives, as nobody was willing to talk on the theme openly in public (Kincaid et al. 1975).

According to a 1973 survey conducted by the Korea Family Planning Association, 57.4% of respondents replied that they took contraceptive pills without telling their husbands, 55.4% of women kept it secret from their in-laws, and 52.2% of respondents kept it secret from their parents. Therefore, one motivation for organizing mothers' clubs in rural villages was to give social legitimacy to contraception at the individual level with the aid of the establishment of government-led organizations dedicated to this task.

The mothers' clubs held the obvious goal of legitimizing the use of contraception and expanding it. In particular, during the first stage of family planning, when oral contraceptive pills were promoted as a primary contraceptive method, it was challenging for the governmental agencies of the family planning program to ensure rural women took the pills regularly. Thus, the mutual control of peer groups within the mothers' clubs was pivotal in the proliferation of oral contraceptive pills. Indeed, in an analysis of family planning projects in China, Indonesia, and Bangladesh, McNicoll (1980) notes that family planning institutionalization at the village level through group formation and group interaction provided women with social legitimization and peer-group support for reproductive practices. The Ministry of Health and Social Welfare (1981, 201) also promoted the activities of mothers' clubs, believing that "collective activities would promote mutual controls and foster an atmosphere of adopting the family planning program".

However, the implementation of family planning was met with initial resistance. A case study of a mothers' club in a village in South Korea (Kincaid et al. 1975) illustrates that rural women hesitated to practice family planning and participate in organizational activities at the beginning of the establishment of the organization, as they were afraid of breaking the conventional gender norms that existed in rural villages. More specifically, research illustrates that they were afraid of opposition from their husbands and in-laws. Resistance to family planning was persistent among rural women, elderly people who valued fertility, and, in particular, the informal leaders of villages, who were usually clan leaders. Thus, it is not surprising that, in many reported cases, family planning fieldworkers were reproached by the elderly and expelled from rural villages (Planned Parenthood Federation of Korea 1987).[5] Moreover, the female leaders of the mothers' clubs were criticized by the elderly for "leaving home and gathering outside" (ibid., 30) and discontinuing family lineages.

A further stumbling block to family planning was the fact that the economic value of children within agrarian households was different from that of urban children. As children in rural areas provided labor and served as future caregivers for the elderly, they were often indispensable to a household's survival (Screenivas 2021). For instance, with the examples of rural China, Guo (2014) demonstrates that multiple children in rural areas are closely associated with the late-life well-being of the parents by providing monetary support. The following interview from a rural mother was a common response to the implementation of family planning: "The more children I have, I feel much safer, since more children means more assets. [I] am not interested in family planning at all" (*Happy Home*, January 5, 1969). It was in this social context of traditional gender norms that the Park Chung

Hee regime emphasized family planning as a shortcut to achieving the national goal of modernization, "a way to national economic growth" and "modern nation-state building" at the national level.

Family Planning for Modern Nation Building

As with other postcolonial societies, South Korea saw family planning as part of modern nation-building (see Ahn et al. 1998; Ashford 2020; Screenivas 2021). The institutionalization of the family planning program must therefore be understood in the context of this modern nation-building in a broader sense. It is not surprising that the family planning program became central to the national development project in South Korea, as policies on population control for the economic welfare of the nation-state were a global issue at the UN among recently independent Third World countries (Newland 2001). Similarly, the implementation of the family planning program also contributed to the enhancement of nationalism and collective identity through economic development.

During the early stages of implementing family planning, it was considered part of population policy and referred to as "family planning for economic development" and "family planning for poverty alleviation" in media and governmental documents. The idea that linked it with being essential to poverty alleviation and a shortcut to achieving an independent economy was clearly reflected in the fact that the family planning program was incorporated into the first Five-Year Economic and Social Development Plan. While mobilizing administrative capacity and medical technology to control the fertility of women, the regime promoted the idea that family planning was directly linked to national economic growth and the modernization of the motherland (DiMoia 2008, 2013). Apparently, economic development through the implementation of the family planning program would contribute to enhancing social stability and national power. *Maeil Kyungje*, one of the daily newspapers, maintains in a newspaper article (January 24, 1972) that there is a direct correlation between population growth and the overall economic growth rate of the nation. The article underscores the functional relationship between national development levels and birth rates, emphasizing that population growth significantly influences government spending and is intricately linked to concerns such as food security, housing, and national defense. Slogans such as "the family planning program is a fundamental step toward achieving economic development" were propagated through government-issue posters displayed in public spaces, such as railway stations, hospitals, community centers, and cinemas. Radio programs on the family planning program were aired daily. These slogans permeated daily life on stamps, cigarette packages, cinema admission tickets, bank account books, lottery tickets, and clock towers (Ministry of Health and Social Welfare 1981).

Motherhood is a socially constructed idea developed in a specific sociocultural and historical context (Collins 1994). During the Park Chung Hee regime, women were (re)imagined as mothers who supported national development. Modern motherhood and modern housewife ideals were measured by a reduction in the number of children. Rural areas were the first to be transformed, as they were seen as highly "traditional" regarding reproductive practices. The "population control policy" was eventually rebranded as "modern family-building" when it was disseminated to rural societies. By bringing the "modern" value of planning to the forefront, the Park regime attempted to reduce the negative views associated with terms such as "population control", "fertility reduction", and "contraception" by emphasizing that "traditional" ideas such as the preference for sons and large families were detrimental to national growth. Modern motherhood was, thus, restructured to support giving birth in a "planned", rather than "disorderly", manner (Hwang Chŏngmi 1999). The magazine *Happy Home*, a monthly magazine for rural women published by the PPFK for the modernization of rural villages and the promotion of modern housewife ideals, consistently advocated for the essential modernization of all households in rural areas, emphasizing its significance for the progress of communities and the nation. In this context, the implementation of family planning was promoted as a crucial step toward achieving the nation's modernization goals. The magazine asserts that maintaining an "appropriate" number of children, which a family can adequately support, not only promotes the well-being of children but also contributes to the economic prosperity of households (*Happy Home* August 5, 1969). In short, it positions the practice of family planning as a virtue of modern "rural housewives" in their everyday lives.

Interpretation of the Family Planning by Rural Women

Given how rural women in South Korea initially perceived family planning, how rural women's attitudes toward family planning shifted from strong resistance to active acceptance should be examined. Discourses regarding family planning were closely related to "liberation from hunger" and the achievement of "abundance" at the household level in rural villages. Such discourses were propagated to rural women by family planning field workers. In the essay written by former family planning field workers, one describes attempting to persuade rural women that family planning is a faster way to achieve prosperity than buying fields (*Happy Home* March 5, 1974). Another emphasizes the importance of rural women having two children before the age of 30, reassuring them that having daughters alone does not pose inheritance and family registration problems. Additionally, she attempted to persuade rural mothers that daughters can have the same rights as sons.[6] She assured them that family planning can lead to a "rich" and "comfortable" life and better educational opportunities, instead of poverty (*Happy Home* April 5, 1972).

As the remarks from the family planning fieldworkers indicate, though family planning was originally established to support "national construction" and the creation of modern motherhood within the housewife ideology, as discussed in the previous section, it was presented as directly related to salient issues at the individual level, such as "rich modern and affordable life", "opportunities for modern education for children", and "a shortcut to the modern life of the urban population". Thus, the PPFK eventually reported that rural women's perceptions of family planning gradually changed from simply involving contraception to a consideration of economic factors (*Chosun Ilbo* December 14, 1972).

The idea of family planning for economic achievement was rapidly disseminated to rural women through discourse in mothers' clubs and opportunities to gain financial resources by joining organizational activities. In other developing countries, incentivizing rural women's participation by setting up income-generating projects through collective economic activities was among the objectives of family planning.[7]

Kincaid et al. (1975) demonstrate that the ancillary activities of mothers' clubs in rural villages were a driving force for participation in the family planning project. Kincaid et al. (ibid.) explain that the activities of mothers' clubs were limited to encouraging the practice of contraception in the early stages. The family planning scope was then broadened to cover income-generating projects to attract rural women to the project. PPFK introduced a savings project and various small-scale income-generating projects, such as collective labor, livestock breeding, and collective sales activities. Given the success of the livestock breeding project, rural women in the village extended their income-generating projects to making children's uniforms, harvesting rice, and funding activities. Thus, mothers' clubs became promoters of modern family planning and were instrumental in encouraging rural women to perceive family planning as an economic concern and a means to realize their aspirations for social mobility.

Family planning organizations offered subsidies to each mothers' club every three months to cover organizational operating costs and attract rural women to the monthly family planning assemblies. The subsidies supported the mothers' clubs and the monthly membership fees paid by the members functioned as financial seed resources for rural women; additional capital was distributed to select rural villages where family planning was successful (Kincaid et al. 1975). From the monthly magazine – *Happy Home* – reports based on an interview with family planning-related governmental health care officers, there were even discussions on distributing subsidies to rural women among the governmental officials: In the discussion, one participant notes that it is a cause for concern that rural women seem to prioritize financial assistance over the concept of family planning. The government officer expressed his worry that it appears rural mothers view family planning organizations merely as a means to accumulate capital. Another raised the question of whether individual rural mothers would continue to participate in the monthly regular meetings for family planning if there were no financial benefits from the family planning organization (*Happy Home*, April 5, 1969).

The promise of capital, though insignificant, was immensely appealing to rural women, as they had few personal assets and little access to formal banking institutions. Mothers' clubs were also home to mutual credit groups through which few women invested money and shared profits and savings projects. As interviews in *Happy Home* demonstrate, these credit groups could be financially invaluable to rural women. One rural woman noted the advantages of the mothers' clubs' savings, highlighting the easy geographical access opportunity given confined transportation facilities in rural villages (*Happy Home* August 5, 1971) and access to loan opportunities (*Happy Home* July 5, 1973).[8] In Kincaid et al.'s (1975) case study, rural women explain that the profits from participating in mothers' clubs were often used to provide their children with educational opportunities. One rural mother expressed that she started family planning "to give birth to one child properly and raise my child well" (*Happy Home*, July 5, 1971). Another mentioned that she wants "to educate her children well, as children these days cannot get a decent job without education" (*Happy Home*, December 5, 1974). As can be gleaned from these statements by rural women, discourses on the benefits children stood to gain through family planning were particularly powerful. As Kincaid et al. (1975) describe, interest in family planning projects increased "as the long range benefits, especially *their children's education* became more and more feasible" (ibid., 47, italics in original).

Some articles in *Happy Home* introduce "successful" stories of rural women who saved money through the initiation of collaborative community-based rural development projects and used the financial resources to support their children's education. One female leader of the New Community Movement comments that she could actively participate in rural development projects despite resistance from her in-laws and elderly people in the village because she could successfully save money for village children's education. Following her success, those who opposed her began to acknowledge the contributions of the rural development project, which was mainly led by rural women.[9]

Economic theorists have asserted a direct "resource effect" of family planning, as it increases parental incomes and children's opportunities (Johnson 1966; Nixon 1969). This idea has been further promoted through the development of the human capital theory, strongly supported by developmentalists in academia (Becker and Lewis 1973). Considerable research has focused on the negative association between the number of children and education (see Lloyd 1994). In particular, a strong correlation between low fertility and educational aspiration is a common, observable phenomenon in many East Asian countries (Anderson and Kohler 2013). Given that Confucian values place a high priority on education for children as the best means of achieving upward social mobility and economic prosperity, South Korea has witnessed "education fever" (Seth 2002). Therefore, it may not be surprising that rural women in South Korea responded earnestly to discourses on better educational opportunities for their children via family planning. Beyond the existent Confucian values, rural women's interpretations of family planning as a chance to provide educational opportunities should be understood within the context of the educational policies of the Park Chung Hee regime, as the rapid proliferation of educational opportunities for *anyone*, including the rural population, was strongly promoted during his rule.

Increasing Educational Opportunities and Rural Women's Aspiration for Children's Education

The 1948 Constitution noted that all citizens were equal in education and guaranteed the right to receive mandatory and free primary education (Kim Chongch'ŏl 1985). In the "Education Act" of 1949, every citizen had the right to receive six years of elementary education. Under this law, the state and local public administrations must provide educational facilities, and the guardians of school-age children must send their children to primary schools. Accordingly, a six-year compulsory education plan was established and set to begin in June 1950. However, it was not carried out given the outbreak of the Korean War in the same year. Thus, compulsory education at the primary level only began after the armistice with the establishment of the "Six-Year Plan for the Completion of Compulsory Education (1954–1959)" in 1954. As over 80% of the total population was rural in the 1950s, the education completion policy eventually induced the expansion of rural primary educational opportunities (Im Yŏn'gi 2006). Access to education expanded widely such that the national entrance rate for elementary schools was recorded as 100% until the late 1970s (Yi Mijŏng 1998). Based on fieldwork conducted in rural villages, Hwang (1973) notes the emergence of problems such as a lack of teaching staff and classrooms and poor management given the drastic increase in primary schools in rural areas.

The rapid expansion of primary school enrolment in the 1950s also induced fierce competition on the middle and high school entrance exams. In particular, within an education system in which entrance to a limited number of elite middle and high schools guaranteed upward social mobility, the middle class became active participants in the private education market (Park 2010, 582). Indeed, 90% of the sixth graders in primary schools, 50% of the fifth graders, and 20% of the rest of the students in Seoul were estimated to take private lessons (*Chosun Ilbo* October 22, 1967). The problems of competition and the financial burden of private education on parents motivated the Park regime to implement the "Middle School Equalization Policy" in 1969 and the "High School Equalization Policy" in 1974. The latter was originally enacted to standardize educational quality in high schools nationwide and prevent overinvestment in the preparatory education needed to enter elite high schools. However, despite the original intention of the government, the enactment of the law led to an increase in private educational institutions and mistrust of public education (*Donga Ilbo* February 8, 1978). A survey by the Ministry of Education, with data on 1,800 students, revealed that 15% of respondents from elementary school, 8% from middle school, and 23% from high school were taking private lessons after school (*Donga Ilbo* February 8, 1978).

At any rate, the introduction of the Middle and High School Equalization Policies meant entrance to school without an exam. The biggest "beneficiary" of the abolishment of the school entrance examinations was the rural population (Im Yŏn'gi 2006). Until these policies came into place, most middle schools were located in larger administrative units. Following the implementation of the Middle School Equalization Policy, a significant number of middle schools were newly established in smaller administrative units in rural areas. For instance, the number of middle schools nationwide in 1966 was 1,251, but it increased to 1,977 in 1976. Following these changes, the national middle school enrolment rate, which was only 41.4% in 1965, increased sharply to 95.1% in 1980. The national high school enrolment rate was 25.4% in 1965 but increased to 63.5% in 1980 and reached 94.6% in 1997 (Yi Hyeyŏng 1998).

Rural households responded actively to the increased educational opportunities. In a survey on saving conducted in 1973, 35.2% of rural households responded that they saved money for their children's education, followed by saving to stabilize the quality of living (22.6%), to improve agricultural facilities (8.8%), and for ceremonial occasions such as weddings, funerals, and ancestral rites (2.5%) (*Maeil Kyungje* August 16, 1973). Further, the expenditure for children's education increased from 5.0% in 1964 to 7.2% in urban areas in 1971 but increased from 3.8% to 7.6% in rural areas during the same period (*Maeil Kyungje* April 27, 1973).

Under the import of egalitarian ideas from the West, along with the collapse of traditional social classes, education became "the most powerful means to achieve upward social mobility and economic prosperity, and many Korean parents believe that they [could] help their children succeed by emphasizing, and even imposing, education for their children" (Park 2009, 51–51). The strong desire of rural parents to provide education for their children was clearly reflected in a survey on children's future occupations. In a 1958 survey, in response to "what kind of profession do you want your children to have in the future?", 23.8% of the respondents answered agriculture. However, in a 1968 survey, only 4.9% answered agriculture, indicating that their attitudes toward agriculture as a profession had changed drastically. Engineering (17.6%), commerce (11%), civil service, and other professional occupations (8.6%) occupied the top choices (Yi Mankap 1981). Yi Mankap commented that this shift signaled a change in the aspirations of rural women to build modern homes and send children to good schools for better education (*Donga Ilbo* February 6, 1978). Regarding educational aspirations and desirable occupations for the next generation in rural society, Chang (2010) explains that most resources and opportunities were concentrated in cities. The continuous reproduction of public and media discourses on rural areas as a symbol for underdeveloped and outmoded places induced the spread of a defeatist mindset and dissatisfaction with agricultural work. Meanwhile, with the development of media, images of urban life spread to rural areas. These images inspired positive views of city life and the educational opportunities available there. Parents in rural areas judged the educational environment in rural villages to be undesirable for their children's education; therefore, they attempted to either send their children to schools in urban areas or move as families to cities, despite the unbearably high expenses (Chang 2010).

A farmer explained in an interview that the costs of the rental fee for sending his children to school in an urban area were high such that it could only be covered by a lifetime of work by five family members. Given the fact that the allocation system for schools was based on registered address, it was not uncommon for some rural households to register under an address in the city with the help of relatives and acquaintances to send their children to schools in urban areas, even if their real residences were rural villages (*Chosun Ilbo* June 14, 1979). A governmental survey in 1985 indicates that the expenses for children's education in rural areas exceeded the expenditure for education in urban areas. This difference could be explained by the fact that there were, on average, more children per rural household than per urban household. Moreover, aspirations for children's education had been rising in rural areas since the 1970s (*Chungang Ilbo* June 3, 1985). According to a survey by a rural sociologist, Yi Mankap, in 1979 in a rural village, 90% of elementary graduates went on to middle school, with affluent rural households often sending their children to Seoul in pursuit of better educational opportunities (*Donga Ilbo* February 14, 1979).

Rural households had begun to recognize education as a chance for social upward mobility and orienting toward "modern" occupational opportunities. Education had been accessible to only a limited segment of the upper class until the 1950s, and upward social mobility had been extremely challenging for lower social classes under Korea's hierarchical and rigid social class system to reach (Lee 2011). An interviewee who attended an elementary school in the mid-1970s reminisced on the days of changing attitudes toward education in rural areas:

> My classroom teacher told us every day that the agricultural society was coming to an end and we were the first generation to enter the industrialized society. He insisted that we had to give our best in study in order not to remain in rural areas as farmers, but to have a decent job.[10]

While strong educational aspirations had always vaguely existed in Korea under its Confucian value system (Chang 2008), aspirations for higher education in the 1970s were based on a clear rationale that higher education would guarantee a higher income (Kim Yŏnghwa 1993). The salary increase available to middle school graduates was only 2.08% between 1972 and 1980, but that of university graduates rose to 25.3% over the same period (Kim Yŏnghwa 1993, 44). Thus, as the demand for highly educated workers increased with rapid economic development, parental desires for better educational opportunities for their children were reinforced and popularized (Kim and Bang 2017).

The middle school non-examination admission system and the High School Equalization Policy were important steps to resolving entrance exam issues and achieving equal educational opportunities for the general populous. The abolition of first-tier schools, bridging the gap in educational conditions between schools, and students' assignment to schools by lottery were also measures to achieve such goals. Park (2010) argues that, as economic inequality broadened dramatically since the 1970s along with a sense of relative deprivation among working-class and lower middle-class citizens, the Park regime endeavored to prevent social stratification by ensuring equal access to education. He maintains that the equalization policies were aimed at social integration and political stability. Deeming the relationship between the state and society a "social egalitarian contract", Park concludes that "the Korean developmental state maintained a broad societal base through strong egalitarian social policies – for example, in its educational policymaking … in order to maintain a high degree of mobilizational capacity as well as political legitimacy" (ibid., 596).

Despite a state–society "social egalitarian contract" in the educational sector, growing aspirations for children's education in rural villages did not necessarily match the original intentions of the educational equalization policies of the Park Chung Hee regime. Given a shortage of specialized workers in the heavy-industry and chemical-centered industrialization context (Kim 2013), the regime's education planning largely focused on vocational and technical schools (ibid.; Park 2010). As noted, one intention of Park Chung Hee's equalization policy was to suppress education fever, symbolized by parents' overinvestment in private tutoring and extreme competition among students. The Park Chung Hee regime attempted to systematically repress the aspirations fueling these issues, defining educational fever as "a waste of national resources".[11] The stance of the government was indicated in educational policy and emergent statistics. For instance, middle school teachers were instructed by the state to advise students to abandon entering high school and enter the labor market instead (Chŏng Yŏngsu et al. 1986). Given such measures, and the various educational policies hindering entrance to university, the ratio of high school graduates who directly entered the labor market increased from 21.5% in 1968 to 30.8% in 1979 (Kim Yŏnghwa 1993). Moreover, the increase in university entrance at the national level between 1962 and 1980 was only 7.9%, relative to 29.2% between 1945 and 1961, and 9.5% between 1981 and 1990 (Yi Hyeyŏng 1998).

"Modern" Motherhood among Urban and Rural Mothers

Under South Korea's Confucian patriarchal social order, mothers were considered caregivers and managers for children's educational achievement and tasked with helping children develop sound minds, healthy bodies, and academic success. Motherhood under the Confucian system could, therefore, be said to have been measured by a woman's ability to provide care for the physical development and education of children (Cho Sŏngsuk 2002), strongly impacting mothers' roles in contemporary Korea (Kim 2005). The role of mothers as advocators for children's educational success within a Confucian social order was further strengthened through the state-led proliferation of the housewife ideology during the Park Chung Hee regime. Under the notion of "intensive mothering", where "the methods of appropriate child rearing are constructed as child-centered, expert-guided, emotionally absorbing, labor intensive, and financially expensive" (Hays 1996, 8), mothers came to be expected to assume "their duty to provide their children with the proper educational resources and support in order to produce successful and competitive children" (Anderson and Kohler 2013, 203).

The idea of "modern" motherhood as accompanied by a strong emotional attachment between mother and child was promoted as part of the housewife ideology among urban middle-class women in South Korea. Despite criticism toward the educational fever of the middle class (Park 2010), discourses on urban housewives regarding their roles as mothers focused on becoming "modern" educational guides responsible for "planned time and study plans" (*Maeil Kyungje* July 24, 1971), "disciplined study planning" (*Maeil Kyungje* July 23, 1977), and "sharing emotions and experiences with children" (*Maeil Kyungje* July 25, 1977). Articles in such nationwide major daily newspapers demonstrated intensive mothering (Hays 1996) as being characterized by "mothers' role as the central caregivers for children" and "mothering as an energy- and time-consuming job".[12] Lee (2008, 164) clarifies how mothering in Korea changed after the 1980s "from a style of mothering, which focuses on biological safety and the provision of educational opportunities, to intensive mothering, which demands a high degree of emotional concentration and a strong level of attachment between the mother and her children". Intensive mothering developed into mothers' roles in supporting children's academic achievement and sending children to good universities (Yi Chaegyŏng 2003; Yun T'aengnim 1996).

However, rural motherhood was considered apart from intensive mothering, which had begun to emerge as a modern concept among middle-class women at the time. As Lee (2008, 142) notes, the case study of the mothering practices of rural mothers in South Korea indicates that "motherhood is not a universal and innate quality of women but instead created out of the socio-economic and discursive conditions of the current age"; it varies per social class, educational level, and time. Rural women attempted to practice modern motherhood by actively responding to the governmental campaign slogans of family planning – "quality over quantity" to pursue better educational opportunities for their children (Anderson and Kohler 2013). As Hays (1996) suggests, the intensive mothering ideology proliferated in urban areas among middle-class women was dispersed through cultural media such as books, radio, and TV shows, affecting working mothers and lower-class women. However, the modern motherhood of rural mothers could not include a full emotional attachment to children and intensive mothering. Rather, mothers focused on allocating resources among family members for social mobility for themselves and the whole family (see Chapter 6 for an in-depth discussion).

State expectations of rural mothers were limited to the reduction of fertility rate and devotion to children's physical welfare and sanitation. Moreover, newspapers hardly dealt with rural women's mothering practices in the context of children's education. Instead, rural mothers were expected to manage rural youth's desire to leave rural villages, and this responsibility was connected with the emergence of discourses on "dangerous" rural youth who "impulsively" leave their homes, as inspired by "urban life" under the rapid increase in young rural–-urban migrants (Kwon 2020). Similarly, the educational fever of rural villagers was often problematized by the media in the context of the rapidly urbanizing, crowded cities. Concerns about the migration of the rural population to urban areas were partly fueled by the rural parents' drive for education. *Donga Ilbo* (February 14, 1979) expressed concerns that the biggest interest among farmers is children's education. It commented on the negative influences of the mobility of children from rural areas given rapid urbanization and the rising educational fever in rural villages. In the same vein, *Chosun Ilbo* (June 10, 1975) also expressed deep concern that the educational fever from urban areas had broadened into rural villages, consequently accelerating the migration of rural populations to Seoul.

Regardless of public and state concerns regarding education fever in rural areas, mothers' aspirations for children's education in rural areas were high. Moreover, rural mothers' desires for higher education for their children were higher than the educational aspirations fathers held for their children. A 1980 study with 821 rural residents in eight regions indicates that 74.7% of male respondents were willing to educate their children to the university level, even if they would need to sell entire rice fields (the main income sources for farmers), while 80.7% of female respondents replied that they were willing to do the same (*Donga Ilbo* January 21, 1981).

Conclusions

This chapter explores how rural mothers perceived family planning in the context of prevalent "intensive mothering" ideologies and practices, presenting it, as portrayed in the media, as a component of "modern motherhood" within the housewife ideology. The chapter reveals that rural women actively responded to societal expectations of being good mothers" by embracing family planning. However, their response did not necessarily imply passive acceptance of the state's agenda to position family planning as a tool for modern nation building or the promotion of the housewife ideology, which considered reducing the number of children as an ideal characteristic of "modern" housewives. Instead, rural women interpreted family planning as an opportunity to access educational resources provided by the state and fulfill the demand for a highly educated workforce during the process of industrialization.

Notes

1 The rural population accounted for 81.6% of the whole population in 1950 (Pak Chindo 2003).
2 These organizations could be established nationwide over a short period because the family planning program started as part of the National Reconstruction Movement in the early 1960s, and Family Planning and Child Health Classes had been established within the women's association (Hwang Chŏngmi 2001).
3 There were five specific aims for small, village-based family planning groups and mothers' clubs: Modernizing rural women through education, improving children's education by training rural women to be educators, improving the financial situation of rural villages through small income projects led by rural housewives, promoting family planning and health education, and general rural development (Planned Population Federation of Korea 1987, 32).
4 The main duties of the family planning fieldworker were education and enlightenment activities in rural villages. The preconditions for becoming a family planning fieldworker were to be a local woman aged 25–40 with a qualification as a nursing assistant.
5 Resistance to the implementation of family planning from the elderly is commonly seen in other sociocultural contexts. In research on family planning in Ghana, Ashford (2020) describes "grandmothers" as representing the elderly generation and "tradition", hindering the embrace of "modern" ideas. For the elderly generation with a strong belief in pronatalist ideas, an acceptance of family planning was considered as being against conventional social orders.
6 Since the enactment of the new Civil Code in 1960, the concept of gender equality has been widely introduced in law, including women's right to inherit property.
7 See Amin et al. (1994) on the impact of women's participation in income-generating projects and family planning in other developing countries.
8 Limited access to bank loans for rural women can be explained as a consequence of class and gender and by the socioeconomic situation of Korean society after the Korean War. Given the continuing inflation since the outbreak of the Korean War, banks lost

their function, with people investing money in speculative domains such as purchasing real estate rather than saving with banks. Thus, banks' profit and lending ability were extremely limited. Hence, it became challenging for ordinary people to access bank loans (Han 1965).

9 J. Kim was actively involved with the activities of the New Community Movement in the 1970s and 1980s after she was selected as a female leader in the village. She was one of the few women who **were educated at the high school level in the village. Personal communication on August 28, 2007.

10 C. Yi, born in 1970 and raised in a small rural village, moved to an urban area given the strong desire of her mother for better educational opportunities for her children. Interviewed on September 3, 2007.

11 Expenditure for children's education was often considered among the major factors reducing the savings rate in Korea, as schooling expenses were usually disproportionately high considering Korea's income level (Han 1965).

12 This situation was also the case for Japan, in which "the growing cult of motherhood created the post-war norm that held mothers responsible for the educational success of their children" (Garon 2010, 332).

Bibliography

Amin, Ruhul, A. U. Ahmed, J. Chowdhury, and M. Ahmed. 1994. "Poor Women's Participation in Income-Generating Projects and their Fertility Regulation in Rural Bangladesh: Evidence from a Recent Survey." *World Development* 22, no. 4: 555–565.

Anderson, Thomas, and Hans-Peter Kohler. 2013. "Education Fever and the East Asian Fertility Puzzle: A Case Study of Low Fertility in South Korea." *Asian Population Studies* 9, no. 2: 196–215. https://doi.org/10.1080/17441730.2013.797293

Anh, Truong Si, John Knodel, David Lam, and Jed Friedman. 1998. "Family Size and Children's Education in Vietnam." *Demography* 35, no. 1: 57–70. https://doi.org/10.2307/3004027

Ashford, Holly Rose. 2020. "Modern Motherhood, Masculinity, and Family Planning in Ghana, 1960–75." *Journal of West African History* 6, no. 2: 61–91. https://doi.org/10.14321/jwestafrihist.6.2.0061

Becker, Gary S., and H. Gregg Lewis. 1973. "On the Interaction between the Quantity and Quality of Children." *Journal of Political Economy* 81, no. 2: 279–288.

Cho, Sŏngsuk. 2021. *Ŏmŏni ranŭn ideollogi: ŏmŏni ŭi kyŏnghŏm segye wa chaa ch'atki.* (The Ideology of Motherhood: The Mother's World of Experience and Self-Exploration) Seoul: Hanul.

Chang, Kyung-sup. 2010. *South Korea under Compressed Modernity: Familial Political Economy in Transition*. London and New York: Routledge.

Chang, S. J. 2008. "A Cultural and Philosophical Perspective on Korea's Education Reform: A Critical Way to Maintain Korea's Economic Momentum." *Academic Paper Series* 3: 157–178.

Chŏng Yŏngsu, Chŏng Chin'gon, Han Man'gil, and Chŏng Chaegŏl. 1986. *Han'guk kyoyuk chŏngch'aek ŭi Inyŏm: kukka palchŏn kwa kyoyuk (Korean Educational Policy: Driving National Development through Education)*. Seoul: Korean Educational Development Institute.

Chosun Ilbo. 1967. "Kwaoe kongbu shibi (Exploring Private Tutoring)." October 22.

Chosun Ilbo. 1972. "Kajok kyehoek ŭi hyŏnjang (Exploring Family Planning)." December 14.

Chosun Ilbo. 1975. "Nongch'on kwa toshi (A Comparative Landscape of Rural and Urban Communities)." June 10.

Chosun Ilbo. 1979. "Panghwang hanŭn nongch'on (Rural Society at Risk)." June 14.

Chungang Ilbo. 1985. "Nongch'on kyoyukpi toshi nŭngga (Higher Education Costs in Rural versus Urban Areas)." June 3.
Collins, Hill. 1994. "Shifting the Centre: Race, Class, and Feminist Theorising Motherhood." In *Mothering: Ideology, Experience, and Agency*, edited by Evelyn Nakano Glenn, Grace Chang, and Linda Rennie Forcey, 45–65. London: Routledge.
DiMoia, Paul John. 2008. "(Let's Have the Proper Number of Children and Raise Them Well!): Family Planning and Nation-Building in South Korea, 1961–1968." *East Asian Science, Technology and Society: An International Journal* 2, no. 3: 361–379. https://doi.org/10.1215/s12280-008-9054-5
DiMoia, Paul John. 2013. *Reconstructing Bodies: Biomedicine, Health, and Nation-Building in South Korea since 1945*. Stanford: Stanford University Press.
Donga Ilbo. 1978. "Kyoyukyŏl (Education Fever)." February 6.
Donga Ilbo. 1978. "Kogyo p'yŏngjunhwa 5nyŏn kwaoe yŏlp'ung (5 Years after the Introduction of the High School Equalization Policy)." February 8.
Donga Ilbo. 1979. "Kyoyukyŏl (Education Fever)." February 14.
Donga Ilbo. 1981. "Nongmindŭl chanyŏ kyoyuk e hŏnshinjŏk (Championing Children's Education in Rural Communities)." January 21.
Garon, Sheldon. 2010. "State and Family in Modern Japan: A Historical Perspective." *Economy and Society* 39, no. 3: 317–336. https://doi.org/10.1080/03085147.2010.486214
Guo, Man. 2014. "Parental Status and Late-life ell-being in Rural China: The Benefits of Having Multiple Children." *Aging & Mental Health* 18, no. 1: 19–29.
Han, Naebok. 1965. "'Kye' – One Aspect of Korean Savings." *Korea Journal* 1: 25–31.
Happy Home. 1969. "Chidowŏn sugi: on'gat pukkŭrŏum ŭl murŭpssŭgo (Diary of the Family Planning Fieldworkers: A Struggle with Difficulties)." January 5.
Happy Home. 1969. "Kajok kyehoek ŏmŏnihoe ŭi 1nyŏn (Looking Back at 1 Year of Mothers' Clubs)." April 5.
Happy Home. 1971. "Saenghwal kiban takki wihae kyŏrhon ch'o put'ŏ yak pokyong (The Introduction of Contraception for a Better Household Economy)." July 5.
Happy Home. 1971. "Ŏmŏni kŭmgo unyŏng ŭi shilche (The Current Situation of the Savings Programs of the Mothers' Clubs)." August 5.
Happy Home. 1972. "Ilsŏn yowŏn sugi ch'ŏngnyŏndŭl ŭi kajok kyehoek sangdam to matko (Diary of the Family Planning Fieldworkers: Advice for Young Mothers and Youth for Family Planning)." April 5.
Happy Home. 1973. "Ponbogi ŏmŏnihoe: kaim yŏsŏng 89myŏngi nŏdo nado kajok kyehoek shilch'ŏnhae (A Successful Mothers' Club Case: Contraceptive Practice among 89 Village Women)." July 5.
Happy Home. 1974. "Ponbogi ŏmŏnihoe: kanan ŭi kulle rŭl pŏtkoja momburim (A Successful Mothers' Club Case: The Struggle to Escape Poverty)." March 5.
Happy Home. 1974. "Ponbogi ŏmŏnihoe: imshin ch'ulsan haji ank'ettago kyŏrŭi hagi kkaji (A Successful Mothers' Club Case: Towards the Decision for Contraception and the Reduction of Childbirth)." July 5.
Happy Home. 1974. "Ponbogi ŏmŏnihoe: namp'yŏn tŭlto anae tŭlto ch'ŏngnyŏn tŭlto sonŭl matchapko (A Successful Mothers' Club Case: A Cooperation between Husbands, Wives, and Young People)." December 5.
Hays, Sharon. 1996. *The Cultural Contradictions of Motherhood*. New Haven: Yale University Press.
Health and Society Research Institute. 1991. *In'gu Chŏngch'aek 30nyŏn (30 Years of Population Policy in Korea)*. Seoul: Health and Society Research Institute.
Hwang Chŏngmi. 1999. "Palchŏn kukka wa mosŏng: 1960–70nyŏndae punyŏ haengjŏng ŭl chungshimŭro (The Developmental State and Motherhood: Policy on Women and Children in the 1960s and 1970s)." In *Mosŏng ŭi tamnon kwa hyŏnshil (Discourses on Motherhood versus Reality)*, edited by Shin Yŏnghŭi, Chŏng Chinsŏng, and Yun Chŏngno, 167–195. Seoul: Nanam ch'ulp'ansa.

Hwang Chŏngmi. 2001. "Kaebal kukka ŭi yŏsŏng chŏngch'aek e kwanhan yŏn'gu: 1960–70 nyŏndae han'guk punyŏ haengjŏng ŭl chungshimŭro (Women and the Developmental State: State Policy on Women in Korea in the 1960s and 1970s)." Doctoral diss., Seoul National University.

Hwang, Jong-Gon. 1973. "Social Change and Education in Rural Communities." *Korea Journal* 13, no. 8: 4–20.

Im Yŏn'gi. 2006. "Han'guk nongch'on kyoyuk chŏngch'aek ŭi pyŏnch'ŏn kwa kŭ t'ŭksŏng mit kwaje (Features of the Rural Education Policy in Korea and its Future Directions)." *Kyoyuk haengjŏnghak yŏn'gu (Educational Administration Research)* 24, no. 4: 27–50.

Johnson, Lyndon B. March, 1966. Special Message to the Congress on Domestic Health and Education. March 1.

Kim Chongch'ŏl. 1985. *Kyoyuk kwa palchŏn (Education and Development)*. Seoul: Seoul National University Press.

Kim, Hyung-A. 2013. "Industrial Warriors: South Korea's First Generation of Industrial Workers in Post-Developmental Korea." *Asian Studies Review* 37, no. 4: 577–595. https://doi.org/10.1080/10357823.2013.790341

Kim, Jin-Sook, and Hyeyoung Bang. 2017. "Education Fever: Korean Parents' Aspirations for their Children's Schooling and Future Career." *Pedagogy, Culture and Society* 25, no. 2: 207–224. https://doi.org/10.1080/14681366.2016.1252419

Kim Yŏnghwa. 1993. *Han'gugin ŭi kyoyukyŏl yŏn'gu (Research on Education Fever in Korea)*. Seoul: Korean Educational Development Institute.

Kim, Yun-Jung. 2005. "Reconciling Work and Motherhood: The Experiences of Korean Working Mothers." Doctoral diss., University of Bath.

Kincaid, D. Lawrence, Hyung-Jong Park, Kyung-Kyoon Chung, and Chin-Chuan Lee. 1975. *Mothers' Clubs and Family Planning in Rural Korea: The Case of Oryu Li*. Honolulu: East-West Communication Institute.

Korea Development Institute. 1983. *Han'guk ŭi kyŏngje kaebal kwa in'gu chŏngch'aek (Economic Development and Demographic Policy in South Korea)*. Seoul: Chŏnghwa inswae munhwasa.

Kwon, Jaok. 2020. "Modern Womanhood, the Ideology of Housewife, and Young Female Rural-Urban Migrants in the 1960s–1970s in South Korea." *European Journal of Korean Studies* 19, no. 1: 171–194. https://doi.org/10.1080/0023656X.2018.1470142

Lee, Jae-In. 2008. "Changes in Mothering of Korean Women: Based on Narrative Interview Data." *Development and Society* 37, no. 2: 141–168.

Lee, Jihye. 2011. "Education and Family in Conflict." *Journal of Studies in International Education* 15, no. 4: 395–401. https://doi.org/10.1177/1028315310385462

Lee, Sam-Sik. 2009. "Low Fertility and Policy Responses in South Korea." *The Japanese Journal of Population* 7, no. 1: 57–70.

Lloyd, Cynthia B. 1994. "Investing in the Next Generation: The Implications of High Fertility at the Level of the Family." In *Population and Development: Old Debates, New Conclusions*, edited by Robert Cassen, 181–202. Washington, DC: Overseas Development Council.

Maeil Kyungje. 1971. "Panghak chung ŭi chanyŏ kyoyuk (Education for Children during the Summer Holidays)." July 24.

Maeil Kyungje. 1972. "Kajok kyehoek saŏp amhŭk e (Family Planning in Danger)." January 24.

Maeil Kyungje. 1973. "Kyoyukpi wa kajŏng kyŏngje (Expenditures in Education and Home Economics)." April 27.

Maeil Kyungje. 1973. "Nongch'on saenghwal sujun hyangsang (The Improvement of Life Quality in Rural Areas)." August 16.

Maeil Kyungje. 1977. "Chanyŏ panghak chido nŭn irŏk'e: ilsang saenghwal (Guidelines for Children's Education during the Summer Holidays: Discipline in Daily Life)." July 23.

Maeil Kyungje. 1977. "Chanyŏ panghak chido nŭn irŏk'e: ch'uŏk ŭl shimŏ chuja (Guidelines for Children's Education during the Summer Holidays: Making Memories with Parents)." July 25.

McNicoll, Geroffrey. 1980. "Institutional Determinants of Fertility Change." *Population and Development Review* 6, no. 3: 441–462. https://doi.org/10.2307/1972410

Ministry of Health and Social Welfare. 1981. *Yŏsŏng kwa saemaŭl undong (Women and the New Community Movement)*.Seoul: Ministry of Health and Social Welfare.

Newland, Lynda. 2001. "The Deployment of the Prosperous Family: Family Planning in West Java." *NWSA Journal* 13, no. 3: 22–48.

Nixon, Richard. 1969. Special Message to the Congress on Problems of Population Growth.

Pak Chindo. 2003. "Inong ŭi chŏn'gae kwajŏng kwa kŭ ŭimi (The Process of Rural-Urban Migration and its Meaning)." In *Han'guk nongch'on sahoe ŭi pyŏnhwa wa palchŏn (Changes and Development of Rural Society in Korea)*, edited by Korea Rural Economic Institute, 79–101. Seoul: Korea Rural Economic Institute.

Park, Jin-Kyu. 2009. "'English Fever' in South Korea: its History and Symptoms." *English Today* 25, no. 1: 50–57. https://doi.org/10.1017/S026607840900008X

Park, Sang-Young. 2010. "Crafting and Dismantling the Egalitarian Social Contract: The Changing State-Society Relations in Globalizing Korea." *The Pacific Review* 23, no. 5: 579–601. https://doi.org/10.1080/09512748.2010.522247

Planned Parenthood Federation of Korea. 1987. *Kajok kyehoek ŏmŏnihoe yŏn'gu (Research on Mothers' Clubs)*. Seoul: Planned Parenthood Federation of Korea.

Screenivas, Mytheli. 2021. "Feminism, Family Planning and National Planning." *South Asia: Journal of South Asian Studies* 44, no. 2: 313–328. https://doi.org/10.1080/00856401.2021.1886731

Seth, Michael J. 2002. *Education Fever: Society, Politics, and the Pursuit of Schooling in South Korea*. Honolulu: University of Hawaii Press.

Yi Chaegyŏng. 2003. *Kajok ŭi irŭmŭro: han'guk kŭndae kajok kwa p'eminijŭm (In the Name of Family: Feminism and Modern Family in Korea)*. Seoul: Tto Hana ŭi Munhwa.

Yi Hyeyŏng. 1998. *Han'guk kŭndae hakkyo kyoyuk 100nyŏnsa yŏn'gu(III): haebang ihu ŭi hakkyo Kkoyuk (100 Years of Education in Korea: The Education System after Independence from Colonialism)*. Seoul: Korean Educational Development Institute.

Yi Mankap. 1981. *Han'guk nongch'on sahoe yŏn'gu (A Study of Korean Rural Society)*. Seoul: Taragwŏn.

Yi Mijŏng. 1998. "Kajok nae ŭi sŏngch'abyŏlchŏk kyoyuk T'uja (Gender-segregated Educational Investment in Family)." *Han'guk sahoehak (Korean Sociology)* 3: 63–97.

Yun T'aengnim. 1996. "Saenghwal munhwa sok ŭi ilsangsŏng ŭi ŭimi (The Meaning of Everyday Life in Culture)." *Han'guk yŏsŏnghak (Korean Women's Studies)* 12, no. 2: 79–117.

4 Rural Women as Saving Agents

The Morals of Frugality, Thriftiness, and Saving

The Tokyo Organizing Committee of the Olympic and Paralympic Games awarded athletes medals salvaged from discarded mobile phones and other small electronic devices at the Tokyo 2020 Olympic Games. Responding to a shortage of precious metals, the Japanese government initiated a collection drive for metals from home electronic gadgets, which could be donated toward the creation of Olympic medals at post offices and schools. This so-called "urban mining" was criticized by the general public and critics as "reminiscent of a World War II government having the public donate metal items to make aircraft and bullets" (*The Mainichi* September 2, 2018). During World War II, the government mobilized Japanese housewives to participate in savings drives and collection activities to support the war at a grassroots level (Wakakawa 1995). These saving campaigns financed military costs, targeting women by repositioning them as the managers of household economies and their families' consumption (Garon 2000).

Saving activities and collection drives "to save our nation" have also been undertaken in Korea at specific historical moments, such as during the Japanese colonialization in the early 20th century, the military threat from North Korea in the 1980s, and economic crises at the end of the 1990s. As early as 1907, the Movement of Compensation of National Debt in Korea was initiated by housewives to donate money to pay off a national debt to Japan. Nationwide collective action for the building of the "Peace Dam" in the 1986–1987 period was initiated by the Chun Doo-hwan military regime to allegedly prevent catastrophic flooding caused by the collapse of the North Korean dam. The Gold Drive Campaign after the Asian financial crisis in the 1997–1998 period aimed to pay back the national debt through the donation of private gold (Cho 2008). Beyond such collection drives, an emphasis on saving and frugality became a national agenda in Korea during the colonial period when the Japanese imperial government urged the colonized Korean public to save to finance the costs of its military expansion. State-led emphasis on frugality continued until the post-Asian financial crisis when American-style consumption began to become a social norm (Nelson 2006; Yi 2016).

Saving campaigns and collection drives represented a national agenda and legitimized the state's intervention in people's everyday lives. By appealing to nationalistic sentiments, saving campaigns and collection drives urged people to scale back personal consumption and practice saving for the sake of the nation. These campaigns and initiatives were also gendered. As women were now considered

DOI: 10.4324/9781003110538-5

housewives regardless of age, class, and employment, and as housewives were considered to be in charge of household economies and consumption, women were expected to save (Nelson 2000). In an analysis of the women's participation in the savings drives during wartime Japan, Garon (2000, 70) notes that "with the men away at the front or the workplace, even humble women became 'housewives', totally responsible for household finances" and introduces how savings drives by rural women at the lowest grassroots levels were a strong driving force for saving activities nationwide.

This chapter explores the intersection of the role of rural women in governmental savings initiatives within the context of the economic development that occurred in the 1960s and 1970s and rural women's aspirations toward social mobility. It maintains that savings drives were a national agenda through which women, in their roles as housewives, were expected to save financially for their households and the motherland. This idea was promoted nationwide through different regulations for the urban middle and rural working class and intertwined with the historical legacy of colonialism, acceptance, and denial of Westernized modernity; discourses on postcolonialism; and the geopolitical situation of the Cold War. Furthermore, they were strongly gendered in their positioning of women as financial managers of the home and nation. The chapter also underscores that rural women actively responded to governmental interventions and programs by interpreting state-led saving initiatives as an opportunity to realize middle-class virtues by integrating urban lifestyles such as purchasing modern home appliances.

Saving for Our Nation: Monitoring Everyday Life

Unlike the US, where consumption has long been considered virtuous by the general population, capital accumulation through the restraint of consumption and the encouragement of saving was actively promoted in East Asia, where it proved vital to national economic growth (Garon 2006). In Korea, regulations regarding savings and consumption have existed under different names since modernization began during the colonial period. Saving initiatives were conducted under the "Life Improvement Movement" during the colonial period and the "New Life Movement" in the 1950s. They continued through the "People's Movement for National Reconstruction" initiated in 1961 and the "New Community Movement" in the 1970s.[1]

Savings promotion, initially encouraged by the Japanese colonial government during wartime in the 1940s, which continued until the 1950s through the New Life Movement (Kim Ŭn'gyŏng 2009), was accelerated under the authoritarian rule of Park Chung Hee. Unlike the savings campaigns of previous years, saving and collection drives under the Park Chung Hee regime were more systematic, detailed, and intrusive. In 1962, the Park Chung Hee regime urged firms and regions to fill savings quotas assigned by the government under the "National Savings Cooperative Law". Starting in 1964, the "Day of Savings" became an annual celebration, promoting savings with presidential recognition for successful savings stories. The national savings champions were announced as the "King/

Queen of Savings of the Year" and were highly praised and given interviews with major daily newspapers (Yi 2016). A 22% interest rate in 1965 helped to further increase the savings rate despite high inflation at the time. The "Savings Promotion Plan of 1966" specified methods to stimulate a saving-oriented mindset through posters, stamps, ceremonies, memorial towers, and film advertisements. As part of the "Savings Promotion Plan" of 1966, it was encouraged that high-positioned public officers receive their monthly payments through bank accounts that automatically placed 10% of their salaries into savings. Students from elementary, middle-, and high-school levels were supervised in their savings monthly. Housewives and women's organizations were the first social actors to be mobilized for saving programs on household finances and the national economy. In the 1970s, Park Chung Hee strengthened saving promotion campaigns and emphasized the significance of household savings. In 1970, the "Saving Promotion Law" was introduced to accumulate capital for investments for economic development. Thus, the savings rate within the GDP rapidly increased from 8% in 1960 to 25% in 1980 – a more than fourfold increase.[2]

Given its lack of political legitimacy, the Park Chung Hee regime was very sensitive to growing social inequalities among the general population (Park 2010). Savings initiatives were key to reducing social gaps. People were mobilized to save, which allowed the state to regulate people's everyday lives, from eating practices to celebrations and personal consumption. Savings drives were accompanied by a series of laws and controls regarding people's everyday lives. First, the "Law on the Simplification of Family Ceremonies" was enacted in 1969 to discourage excessive expenditure of the upper class on family ceremonies. The law was revised in 1973 to regulate ritual-related customs. For instance, the distribution of invitation cards for wedding ceremonies and funerals, ceremonial decorations with more than two flower bouquets, and presents to ceremony participants were forbidden (Han Hyŏngsŏng 2017; Ko Wŏn 2006). The law defined products such as imported alcohol, automobiles, jewelry, gold, and electric appliances (e.g., televisions, refrigerators, vacuum cleaners, and washing machines) as luxury goods, and imposed high consumer taxes on them. Moreover, luxury goods were criticized as immoral and unpatriotic (Yi 2002). Thus, despite income disparities among the populous, the suppression of consumption induced conformity by giving people a commonly shared feeling, "as though they were in the same boat during the Park's years" (Nelson 2006, 193).

The year 1966 was designated as the year of work. It was also the year of savings. The New Year presidential speech in 1966 demonstrates how the Park Chung Hee regime viewed the savings campaigns and attempted to position them as integral to national economic growth. He proclaimed that the increase in savings demonstrates that national capital, previously stagnant and unproductive, has transitioned toward capital dedicated to the industrialization of our motherland (Park Chung Hee, *Donga Ilbo* January 18, 1966).

Moreover, government saving initiatives occurred against the backdrop of growing threats from communist states, in particular from North Korea. Economic development was positioned as a means of competing with communist threats. As

Nelson notes, "Park believed that South Korea needed a strong industrial base and a healthy citizenry" to compete against North Korea (2006, 191). Nelson (ibid.) discusses the "healthy citizenry" in the context of "consumer nationalism", which represents frugality, saving, and rational consumption of the general populous for national economic growth. The perspective that connects saving activities for economic development with the alleviation of communist threats is clearly expressed in a national daily newspaper. An article in *Donga Ilbo*, dated August 15, 1970, demonstrated that the efforts to eliminate poverty and achieve economic development had contributed to minimizing the threats from communism.

Consequently, domestic and foreign capital was concentrated, not on consumption, but on production. Several large chaebol companies, which are family based conglomerate structures in South Korea, stood at the center of state-led industrial policy, focused on the export-oriented industry. For the developmental state, this chaebol-centered export-oriented industrial policy was the key to establishing the industrial base. Meanwhile, responsible consumption and frugality came to symbolize a "healthy" citizenry with rational consumption practices. As the basis for the economic development of the motherland, savings were not simply for prosperity at the individual level but for the nation. This logic justified strong governmental intervention, regulation, and supervision of the everyday lives of the common people (Ko Wŏn 2006).

Positioning Housewives as Savers

Notably, all women were labeled as housewives and summoned for the savings initiatives during the Park Chung Hee regime, regardless of their economic situation. Women-centered savings drives were closely associated with the historical legacy of colonialism. Park Chung Hee was convinced of the centralized capital-controlling methods of the Japanese imperial government during the colonial period and the "Japanese economic model" of the postwar period. He believed that the most efficient way to modernize the nation was for the central government to focus on maximizing productivity and improving the national economy (Yi Sangnok 2013). Park's embrace of frugality echoed similar discourses from Japan, and many of his saving policies and programs were inspired by Japanese efforts (see Garon 2006).

From the daily newspaper excerpts below, colonial memories were mobilized to promote thrift campaigns in a complicated, contradictory, and multifaceted way. While some intellectuals saw the extravagant consumption of Korea's affluent class as a legacy of colonialism and criticized them as "anti-patriotists" eroding national economic development (Yi Sangnok 2013), Korean women's consumption habits were negatively compared with those of Japanese women. For instance, a newspaper article in *Kyunghyang Shinmun* (September 1, 1978) depicted Japanese housewives as figures "who are willing to drive thousands of miles for a chance to purchase cheaper products to save one cent", contrasting them with Korean housewives who make "impulse decisions" when purchasing products. Savings drives were associated with postcolonialism and promoted "patriotism" through saving.

In this context, saving became a path to liberation from the "old" and "premodern" historical legacies of colonialism and was a way to establish a "new" and "modern" nation through saving for national economic development. However, savings initiatives sometimes intermingled with colonial memories with Japanese women appearing in discourse as the "colonizing Others" who were more "advanced" and "modern" in their frugality and thrift. Thus, Koreans' consumption was portrayed in terms of the "colonized Self", positioned as "uncivilized" and "traditional".

Campaigns for frugality were promoted by civic organizations, such as a women's organization; the Central Committee for Promotion of Savings by Women, established in 1967; and the Central Committee for Promotion of Savings, established in 1969.[3] These Central Committees encouraged housewives to save through campaigns and discourses on frugality by creating a "Frugal Housewife of the Year Award" and distributing household account books (*kakebu*) (Han Hyŏngsŏng 2017). The concept of household account books was introduced by the Japanese colonial government during the 1920s and 1930s and further encouraged in the early 1970s and beyond in South Korea (Garon 2006).

Saving and frugality were considered the path to the large-scale consumption observable in the "West". In this sense, the "West" was suggested as an ideal model and the goal Koreans should eventually reach. However, even though consumption was considered a symbol of modernization and material prosperity, luxury and waste were also considered "premodern". "Frugality' and saving were seen as "modern" ways of thinking and living (Ko Wŏn 2006). Consumption was anticipated to be realized in the future only through today's hard work and saving, as indicated in a presidential speech. In a speech in 1966 (*Donga Ilbo*, January 18, 1966), Park proclaimed that an abundant new era with massive production and consumption would come when their Five-Year Economic and Social Development Plans ended. Consumption would be positioned as a beautiful virtue because of modernization.

Consumption was likened to "untouchable fruits which are expected to be harvested in the future" (Yi Sangnok 2013, 142). Housewives with extravagant consumption habits were depicted as immoral, irrational, and hasty in the discourse of consumption as "untouchable fruit". In particular, as global inflation occurred in the aftermath of the oil crisis in the 1970s, women's magazines promoted the necessity of mobilizing the home economy to overcome the national economic crisis. Housewives emerged as household managers who must respond sensitively to government economic policies and practice rational consumption and saving (Ch'oe Kyŏnghi 2016). Therefore, the discourse on frugality and thriftiness was closely associated with women, and women deviant from the "ideal woman" in terms of thriftiness were to be regulated, controlled, and monitored.

Molding the Spirits of Frugality and Class

The saving ideology was different for urban and rural women. Urban middle-class women were expected to control their husband's monthly incomes by keeping household account books and saving with official banking institutions. Therefore, it was an urgent assignment for the Central Committee for the Promotion of Savings by Women to transform women's conventional and informal saving methods in urban areas. Conventionally, Korean women saved money through a mutual aid system called *kye*, which was an informal financial saving system used by women who had no official access to financial institutions. This system was usually used for capital-consuming familial events, such as children's weddings, funerals, and other ceremonies.

However, *kye* began to be seen as problematic in the mid-1950s. The inflation triggered by the outbreak of the Korean War continued even until after the end of the Syngman Rhee regime. *Kye* was actively organized among women in urban areas, particularly through the 1950s and 1960s, as the wives of men with social status and reputation could easily earn each other's trust and women usually had more time to organize and maintain *kye* activities than their husbands. Savings attained using a *kye* were not channeled into productive investments but consumption or speculative investments (Han 1965). Women involved with *kye* were called "*kye*-madams" and were seen as a deviant social group violating the ideals of the housewife ideology. In short, such women were considered to be irresponsible with household finances. *Kye* was further seen as a social problem post-1960s when the government attempted to systematize savings initiatives. Discourses on *kye* were about the role of housewives as savers and also expressed worry about women's involvement in economic activities in general (Yi Imha 2005, 249–256). The negative image of the "*kye*-madam" was repeatedly reproduced throughout the 1960s and 1970s as a symbol of extravagance, intemperance, and depravity. The *Kyunghyang* daily newspaper had a special column "*yŏjŏk*" that constantly problematized "*kye*-madam". For instance, a newspaper article in *Kyunghyang Shinmun* (September 15, 1971) depicted "*kye*-madam" as "'free madam', 'luxury madam' who ruins the beauty of the morals and order of women".

Kye came to be considered a social evil symbolic of urban housewives' vanity and selfish desires. While urban housewives were expected to shift their savings from this informal mutual aid system to official banking institutions, *kye* in rural areas were seen as representing the "beauty" of old customs and tradition and were actively promoted as a saving method for rural housewives. *Kye* for rural women was recommended under the limited financial source and restricted access to formal financial institutions (*Happy Home* May 5, 1969). Saving with a group or mothers' club or establishing a *kye*-group were recommended, as it was believed that such measures would strengthen mutual control effects such that rural women would encourage each other in their saving practices.[4] This disparity is also further evidence that the modernization project of the Park Chung Hee regime was contradictory, inconsistent, and incongruous – a mixture of "tradition" and "modernity", "new" and "old", and "desirable" and "undesirable" (Kwon 2020).

The importance of the role of housewives in savings drives and practices of thriftiness was equally emphasized for urban and rural women. However, urban and rural housewives were regulated in different ways and were often juxtaposed.

Beyond different regulations in the informal saving practices of middle-/upper class women in urban areas and rural women, differences in official governance of the two social groups could be seen in national rice-saving initiatives. Beyond land improvement, land reclamation projects, and the modernization of agricultural machines, the rice-saving initiative became one of the most important projects assigned to women in everyday life. The movement was originally initiated by the government in the 1950s to respond to the shortage of rice. Park's government still faced the shortage of rice and the surplus of wheat gained with aid from the American government, introduced in the mid-1950s. Thus, Park's government tried to oppress the consumption of rice by encouraging the general public to eat meals with more grains rather than white rice (Kong Cheuk 2008). The rice-saving campaign was continued until a new rice variety – "unification rice" – was developed in 1971 and distributed nationwide starting in 1976. During the campaign, housewives and restaurants were recommended to mix white rice with other grains, such as brown rice and barley.[5] In 1964, all restaurants nationwide were suggested to sell barley and noodles up to 25% out of their whole gross profit. Restaurants were made to observe Wednesdays and Saturdays as "days of no rice" and sell no food, including rice, from 11 AM to 5 PM from 1969 until 1975. Further, in 1973, it was forbidden for food manufacturers to produce snacks made from rice. Farmers were forced to cultivate a highly productive species of rice known as *t'ongilbyŏ* — a measure farmers strongly resisted, as the species was not tasteful and did not hold up well against insects. Through strong governmental intervention, the Park Chung Hee regime achieved a high level of rice productivity in 1977. The "day of no rice" was abolished, and a ban on rice alcohol was lifted in the same year.

While the general population and restaurants in urban areas were mobilized to mix grains with white rice, the rural population could not afford to cook with pure white rice in the first place. Despite the scarcity of rice in rural villages, rice-saving initiatives in rural areas were further accelerated after the New Community Movement commenced in 1971. Successful cases were actively appreciated by the president, Park Chung Hee. Such success stories were introduced as important topics in well-known newspapers.

Reflecting the realities in rural areas, rural women were entreated to save rice in everyday life by depositing a handful of rice in a jar every time they cooked rice for the family. The rice collected by each household could be exchanged for cash or savings in the village's collective banking account for community projects, such as street repair, improving sanitary systems, and purchasing kitchen goods for the community. The pattern of the successful savings initiative story was similar and constantly introduced in daily newspapers and women's magazines for rural women. The first notable point is that rice-saving activities further strengthened the gender-segregated division of labor by clearly defining household work as women's labor. Rural women were seen as the main actors responsible for the savings initiatives, as they were in urban areas. However, the difference with urban areas was that rural housewives were responsible for their personal households and the whole village community.

Rural Women's Interpretations of Savings Initiatives

Even though the Park Chung Hee regime promoted savings drives to support the national economy, rural women interpreted this governmental intervention as a chance to improve their financial situations at the individual level. As Garon (2000) demonstrates in the case of Japan, the government did not merely invoke values of frugality and self-denial but also the middle-class virtues of cities. Under these circumstances, the Japanese populace vigorously complied with the government's saving initiatives to finance the costs of battle during World War II, as "people often understood official exhortations to save in more self-interested terms" (41). Governmental initiatives, thus, actually accorded with the strong desire for becoming middle-class and achieving the virtues of the cities, which were gradually emerging alongside rapid economic growth. This congruity helps explain why rural women in South Korea responded actively to savings drives, as they attempted to ride the tide of material prosperity.

Korean society in the 1960s and 1970s was in the midst of rapid changes in lifestyle and rapid industrial growth. Through the establishment of Fordist mass production systems, consumption rose sharply, and the ideology of "let us have a better and prosperous life" (*jalsarabose*) became prevalent in society (Kim Jonghŭi and Kim Yŏngch'an 2008). Rural women attempted to realize an imagined middle-class status by purchasing home appliances via the economic opportunities provided through organizational activities and saving initiatives. Just as product advertisements published in women's magazines in the 1920s and 1930s in the US guided and encouraged American consumers not to fall behind in modern consumer life (Marchand 1985), Korean women's magazines played a significant role in informing readers of new technologies and "modern" consumption patterns (Sŏ Yŏnju 2007).

In particular, the "American lifestyle", in which consumption was focused on home and family, suggested an ideal form of domesticity (De Grazia 2005; Scrivano 2005). Along with the spread of a modern image of the middle class, the number of farming households with home appliances and technical goods such as televisions, fans, and record players was increasing significantly. According to a sample survey by the Ministry of Agriculture and Fisheries of 3,375 households in 225 rural districts nationwide, as of the end of 1978, each household had one radio (the same numbers as at the end of the previous year). However, there were 62 television sets per 100 households, an increase of 44% from 43 television sets per 100 households at the end of 1977. The survey also revealed that one in four households owned a fan, one in six owned electric fans, one in nine owned gramophones, and one in 25 owned refrigerators (*Chosun Ilbo* March 1, 1979). The statistics on home appliances were often released in the media and governmental documents on the New Community Movement. As in other countries, modernity was measured by the number of home appliances in the household (see France Duchen 1991). As could be seen during the reform era in China, people were encouraged to pursue new "social norms of middle-class identity often defined around consumer practices" (Anagnost 2008, 498). Similarly, as Pérez (2012) illustrates in her study on refrigerator purchases in Argentina in the 1930s through the 1960s, the purchase of electronic home appliances meant the achievement of a middle-class status where male breadwinners provided modern technological gadgets and women were liberated from domestic work. In short, consumption promised a middle-class life for the rural population and was, therefore, an act toward the construction of a middle-class identity (Miller 1987, 1994; Peiss 1996).[6]

As indicated in the following report by a rural woman, it seemed rural Korean women also perceived the purchase of modern technical home appliances as a measurement of modernity, which was equated with urban life: "We have successfully increased our income through collective savings drives. We have 24 sets of television, 28 radios, seven telephones, and one refrigerator in total for 27 households. Each household has a bicycle. We believe that this is almost the level of consumption the urban population has" (*Happy Home,* October 5, 1978).

Consumer purchases rural women made through savings activities were often a means for achieving upward social mobility and, thus, stood in opposition to the developmental state's original intentions. "Success stories" of the organizational activities of rural women demonstrate that the decision-making power of women regarding controlling savings and consumer purchasing increased in rural areas in South Korea. A study based on fieldwork in 296 rural households in 1988 showed that women were often heavily involved in decision-making for the purchase of clothing for family members (75.3%), followed by materials for household interiors, such as wallpaper (54.6%), furniture (51.9%), and home appliances (25.8%) (Pak Hyein 1991). This involvement could be evaluated as a positive development, considering that domestic decision-making in the 1960s depended heavily on male heads of household (Ch'oe Chaesŏk 1975). Moreover, the purchasing of rice cookers or electric irons, for instance, was considered an abandonment of one's responsibility as a daughter-in-law and demonstrated a lack of sincerity and respect for the elderly, as rural women were expected to cook warm meals three times per day for elderly family members and prepare well-ironed clothes for parents-in-law (*Kyunghyang Shinmun* July 7, 1977). Therefore, women's decision-making power to purchase home electric appliances was perceived by rural women as a means to go against the expected social role as daughters-in-law in large families.

Conclusions

This chapter examined the role of rural women as economic actors within the context of the housewife ideology promoted by the state. It investigated how rural women were positioned as savers and consumers and how they interpreted the state-led saving initiatives. Notably, the Park Chung Hee regime relied on rural women, who were referred to as "housewives" regardless of their social class, economic situation, or economic activities, to accumulate the capital necessary for central state-led economic development. Moreover, the chapter highlights that state-led initiatives were perceived by rural women as a means to fulfill their aspirations toward middle-class virtues. It argues that this interpretation of state-led saving initiatives can be attributed to the desire among rural women to transcend their current social and economic status. In summary, this chapter sheds light on the complex interplay between the housewife ideology, state-led saving initiatives, and the aspirations of rural women in South Korea.

Notes

1 These initiatives were called "movements" if they were carried out at the grassroots level; however, most were initiated by the central government and were promoted through support from women's organizations, intellectuals, and local governments.

2 Korean Statistical Information Service, www.kosis.kr (accessed on January 11, 2022).

3 Civic organizations were actively involved seemingly because the government was actively trying to downplay views that savings drives were government initiatives (Han Hyŏngsŏng 2017).

4 Access to banking loans for rural households was extremely restricted, but *kye* was easily accessible. Thus, rural households had from two to three *kye* for various reasons, such as expenses for children's marriages, children's education, and the purchase of home appliances. However, as *kye* was used for purchasing electric appliances and kitchen utilities on credit (Kim Yŏnhŭi 2011), it accounted for much of the debt in rural society since the mid-1970s. Hence, the *kye* of rural villages were eventually seen in a negative light by the government and the media. Saving via formal banking institutions was recommended after the establishment of the banking system by the National Agricultural Cooperative Federation, and *kye* came to be considered a hindrance to the enhancement of the saving rates (*Maeil Kyungje* February 2, 1976). *Kye* was perceived as a supporting impulse for extravagant consumption practices by the rural population by the end of the 1970s (*Kyunghyang Shinmun* July 12, 1977).

5 In Korea, cooked rice (*bap*) with other grains was considered imperfect and unclean, which is why the best quality white rice was traditionally offered to the elderly and male family members, while mixed grain rice was provided to women and children (Hahm 2005).

6 *Donga Ilbo* (November 19, 1974) reports on the rural population's attempts to pursue the image of modern urban life through the purchase of electronic home appliances using a monthly installment system. In fact, as most rural households could not financially afford to purchase pricey home appliances, approximately 90% of the purchases were via a monthly installment loan method (Kim Yŏnhŭi 2011). Most households purchased electronic appliances by organizing *kye*, with rural households often having more than two *kye* organizations to purchase electric gadgets (*Kyunghyang Shinmun* July 12, 1977).

Bibliography

Anagnost, Ann. 2008. "From 'Class' to 'Social Strata': Grasping the Social Totality in Reform-Era China." *Third World Quarterly* 29: 497–519. https://doi.org/10.1080/01436590801931488

Cho, Younghan. 2008. "The National Crisis and De/reconstructing Nationalism in South Korea during the IMF Intervention." *Inter-Asia Cultural Studies* 9, no. 1: 82–96. https://doi.org/10.1080/14649370701789666

Ch'oe Chaesŏk. 1975. *Han'guk nongch'on sahoe yŏn'gu (Research on Rural Society in Korea)*. Seoul: Ilchisa.

Ch'oe Kyŏnghŭi. 2016. "1960–70 nyŏndae yŏsŏngji rŭl t'onghae pon kŭndaehwa ŭi chendŏ yangsang yŏn'gu (Research on Gendered Modernization through the Lens of Women's Magazines in the 1960s–1970s)." *Han'guk munhwa iron kwa pip'yŏng (Korean Cultural Theory and Critique)* 20, no. 4: 313–331.

Chosun Ilbo. 1979. "Kajŏn chep'um pogŭbyul (Penetration Rate of Electronic Home Appliances)." March 1.
De Grazia, Victoria. 2005. *Irresistible Empire: America's Advance through Twentieth-Century Europe*. Cambridge: Belknap Press of Harvard University Press.
Donga Ilbo. 1966. "Pak taet'ongnyŏng yŏndu kyosŏ (Park Chung Hee's New Year's Presidential Speech)." January 18.
Donga Ilbo. 1970. "Pin'gon kwa kongsan chuŭi (Poverty and Communism)." August 15.
Donga Ilbo. 1974. "Sach'i p'ungjo toshi esŏ nongch'on ŭro (Extravagant Consumption Practices: From Urban to Rural)." November 19.
Duchen, Claire. 1991. "Occupation Housewife: The Domestic Ideal in 1950s France." *French Cultural Studies* 2: 1–11. https://doi.org/10.1177/095715589100200401
Garon, Sheldon. 2000. "Luxury is the Enemy: Mobilizing Savings and Popularizing Thrift in Wartime Japan." *The Journal of Japanese Studies* 26, no. 1: 41–78. https://doi.org/10.2307/133391
Garon, Sheldon. 2006. "The Transnational Promotion of Saving in Asia: 'Asian Value' or the 'Japanese Model'?" In *Ambivalent Consumer: Questioning Consumption in East Asia and the West*, edited by Sheldon Garon and Patricia L. Maclachlan, 163–187. Ithaca: Cornell University Press.
Hahm, Hanhee. 2005. "Rice and Koreans: Three Identities and Meanings." *Korea Journal* 45, no. 2: 89–106.
Han Hyŏngsŏng. 2017. "1970nyŏndae pakchŏnghŭi ch'ejeesŏ ŭi kagyebujŏkki undong (The Home Accounting Movement during the Park Chung Hee Regime in the 1970s)." *Kyŏngyŏngsahak (Business History)* 32, no. 2: 203–230.
Han, Naebok. 1965. "'Kye' – One Aspect of Korean Savings." *Korea Journal* 1: 25–31.
Happy Home. 1969. "Ponbogi kajok kyehoek ŏmŏnihoe rŭl ch'ajasŏ (Looking for a Successful Case of Mothers' Club)." May 5.
Happy Home. 1978. "Yŏllyŏ chŏngssi ŭi ch'ungjŏngshim i huson ege iŏjyŏ (Continuity of the Commitment to Family Planning of the Next Generation)." October 5.
Kim, Jonghŭi, and Kim Yŏngch'an. 2008. "1960–70nyŏndae yŏsŏngji e nat'anan kŭndaejŏk chugŏ konggan mit chugŏ munhwa tamnon e kwanhan yŏn'gu (Formation of Cultural Discourses of 'Modern' Homes and Residences in Women's Magazines in the 1960s and 1970s)." *Midiŏ, chendŏ & munhwa (Media, Institution, and Culture)* 10: 109–155.
Kim Sŏnghwan. 2017. "1960–70 nyŏndae nodong kwa sobi ŭi chuch'ehwa yŏn'gu (A Study on the Subject of Labor and Consumption in the 1960s and 1970s)." *K'ogit'o (Kogito)* 81: 544–585.
Kim Ŭn'gyŏng. 2009. "1950nyŏndae shinsaenghwarundong yŏn'gu: kajŏnggaeryangnon gwa sobit'ongje rŭl chungshimŭro (The New Life Movement in the 1950s: The Reform of Domestic Spheres and Consumption Control)." *Yŏsŏnggwa yŏksa (Women and History)* 11, no. 12: 203–240.
Kim Yŏnhŭi. 2011. "Nongch'on chŏn'gi konggŭp saŏp kwa saemaŭl undong (Electricity Projects in Rural Villages and the Saemaul Movement)." *Yŏksabip'yŏng (Historical Critique)* 97: 397–425.
Ko Wŏn. 2006. "Pakchŏnghŭi jŏnggwŏn shigi kajŏng ŭirye junch'ik kwa kŭndaehwa ŭi pyŏnyong e kwanhan yŏn'gu (Development, Acculturation, and Modernization in South Korea during the Park Chung Hee Regime with a Focus on Simplified Family Ritual Standards)." *Tamnon (Discourse)* 9, no. 3: 191–223.
Kong Cheuk. 2008. "Honbunshik changnyŏundong kwa shiksaenghwal ŭi pyŏnhwa ('Honbunshik Changnyŏ Undong' and Changes in Diet during the Period of State-Mobilization)." In *Kukka wa ilsang (The State and Everyday Life: The Park Chung Hee Era)*, edited by Kong Cheuk, 141–189. Seoul: Hanwool Academy.
Kyunghyang Shinmun. 1971. "Yŏjŏk (Opinion Column)." September 15.
Kyunghyang Shinmun. 1977. "Puŏk sallim ŭi sae igi (The New Modern Home Appliances in the Kitchen)." July 7.

Kyunghyang Shinmun. 1977. "Nongch'on changnong sok kyŏnyang ch'iyŏrhan p'anmaejŏn (Sales Competition among Companies in Rural Villages)." July 12.
Kyunghyang Shinmun. 1978. "Sodŭk apchirŭnŭn sobi p'ungjo (Income and Consumption)." September 1.
Kwon, Jaok. 2020. "Modern Womanhood, the Ideology of Housewife, and Young Female Rural-Urban Migrants in the 1960s–1970s in South Korea." *European Journal of Korean Studies* 19, no. 1: 171–194. https://doi.org/10.1080/0023656X.2018.1470142
Maeil Kyungje. 1976. "Nongch'on chŏch'uk yuin ŭi chedohwa (Institutionalization of Savings in Rural Villages)." February 2.
Marchand, Roland. 1985. *Advertising the American Dream: Making Way for Modernity, 1920–1940*. Berkeley: University of California Press.
Miller, Daniel. 1987. *Material Culture and Mass Consumption*. Oxford: Basil Blackwell.
Miller, Daniel. 1994. *Modernity: An Ethnographic Approach: Dualism and Mass Consumption in Trinidad*. Oxford: Berg.
Nelson, Laura C. 2000. *Measured Excess: Status, Gender, and Consumer Nationalism in South Korea*. New York: Columbia University Press.
Nelson, Laura C. 2006. "South Korean Consumer Nationalism: Women, Children, Credit, and other Perils." In *Ambivalent Consumer: Questioning Consumption in East Asia and the West*, edited by Sheldon Garon and Patricia L.Maclachlan, 188–207. Ithaca: Cornell University Press.
Pak Hyein. 1991. "Han'guk nongch'on kajok ŭi pubu kwan'gye e taehan kajok paldaljŏk chŏpkŭn (Understanding Husband-Wife Dynamics in Korean Families)." *Han'guk nongch'on saehwal kwahak hŏji (Korean Journal of Rural Life Science)* 2: 109–123.
Park, Sang-Young. 2010. "Crafting and Dismantling the Egalitarian Social Contract: The Changing State-Society Relations in Globalizing Korea." *The Pacific Review* 23, no. 5: 579–601. https://doi.org/10.1080/09512748.2010.522247
Peiss, Kathy. 1996. "Making Up, Making Over: Consumer Culture, and Women's Identity." In *The Sex of Things: Gender and Consumption in Historical Perspective*, edited by Victoria de Grazia and Ellen Furlough, 311–336. Berkeley: University of California Press.
Pérez, Inés. 2012. "Comfort for the People and Liberation for the Housewife: Gender, Consumption and Refrigerators in Argentina (1930–60)." *Journal of Consumer Culture* 12, no. 2: 156–174. https://doi.org/10.1177/1469540512446876
Scrivano, Paolo. 2005. "Signs of Americanization in Italian Domestic Life: Italy's Postwar Conversion to Consumerism." *Journal of Contemporary History* 40, no. 2: 317–340. https://doi.org/10.1177/0022009405051555
Sŏ Yŏnju. 2007. "Yŏsŏng sooe kyech'ŭng e taehan tamnon hyŏngsŏng yangsang yŏn'gu: yŏwŏn e nat'anan sahoe hyŏnshil inshik ŭl chungshim ŭro (How the Discourse on Marginalized Females Formed: Examining Social Reality Awareness in Yŏwŏn)." *Yŏsŏng munhak yŏn'gu (Women's Literature Studies)* 18, no. 18: 93–130.
The Mainichi. 2018. "Criticism Grows against Government 'Urban Mines' Plan to Tokyo 2020 Medals." September 2.
Wakakawa, Midori. 1995. *Sensō ga tsukuru joseizō (How War Regulates Womanhood)*. Tokyo: Chikuma shobō.
Yi Imha. 2005. *Yŏsŏng, Chŏnjaeng ŭl nŏmŏ irŏsŏda (Women, Standing Up and Overcoming War)*. Seoul: Sŏhaemunjip.
Yi, Jeong Duk. 2002. "Globalization and Recent Changes to Daily Life in the Republic of Korea." In *Korea and Globalization: Politics, Economics and Culture*, edited by James Lewis and Amadu Sesay, 10–35. New York: Routledge.
Yi, Jong-Hyun. 2016. *History of Korean Modern Retailing: Repressed Consumption and Retain Industry, Perceived Equality and Economic Growth*. Leiden and Boston: Brill.
Yi Sangnok. 2013. "1970nyŏndae Sobi ŏkche jŏngch'aek kwa sobi munhwa ŭi ilsang jŏngch'ihak (The Consumption Control Policy and the Politics of Everyday Consumer Culture in the 1970s)." *Yŏksa yŏn'gu (History Research)* 29: 137–182.

5 State-led Rural Women's Organizations and the Making of Rural "Housewives"

Before the commencement of the New Community Movement, there were several state-led rural women's organizations. Beginning with Life Improvement Movement Clubs, established in 1958 by the Rural Development Administration under the motto of "rationalization of rural life", rural women's classrooms (*punyŏgyoshil*) were organized by the Ministry of Health and Social Welfare in 1967. Mothers' clubs (*ŏmŏnihoe*) were set up in 1968 by the Planned Parenthood Federation of Korea for the proliferation of family planning. Women's associations, originally founded in each village in 1961 as part of the People's Movement for Nation Reconstruction, were revived in 1973 after the commencement of the New Community Movement (Korean Women's Development Institute 1985, 386). Organizational activities varied from improving the sanitation and nutrition of children to caring for children and the elderly, promoting savings activities, community management, and family planning.

Different women's organizations were integrated into the New Community Movement's women's associations (*saemaul punyŏhoe*) in 1977 to implement the Movement more efficiently and consistently. Even after the commencement of the New Community Movement, there remained different organizations and, in some cases, multiple organizations per village. However, the proliferation of different women's organizations under different names induced neither confusion nor dissent among rural women, as most rural women's organizations comprised members aged 20–60 years, except for the mothers' clubs, whose membership was limited to the 20–47 years age group (Kincaid et al. 1975). Another reason various women's organizations could coexist without confusion was that the female leader for each organization was the same in most villages. Following the initiation of the New Community Movement, a female leader for each village was officially appointed as a saemaul leader. However, most of these female saemaul leaders had already been involved in rural development activities in various forms before the implementation of the New Community Movement (Chang Migyŏng 2008). Therefore, there was functionally only one women's group in most villages, even though the name and functions of each group varied along with the main theme and the content of their organizational activities (Kincaid et al. 1975). Despite their different names, the state-sponsored organizations for rural women aimed to reshape them as modern housewives and position them as responsible for the modernization of their households.

DOI: 10.4324/9781003110538-6

Mies (1998) maintains that the restriction of women to the "domestic" sphere legitimize the loss of women's political and bargaining power through atomization and individualization. This chapter sheds light on the fact that "becoming a housewife" was systemically organized and led by the state, which also, contrarily, supported rural women's organizational activities. It discusses that the Park administration newly positioned rural women, who had hitherto been considered to be mainly in charge of domestic spheres, as the primary local agents responsible for rural development projects such as saving initiatives, family planning, and the management of community matters. The chapter also clarifies that this state intervention in organizational activities was not always passively adopted by rural women but was used as a means to achieve the "modernization" they envisioned, transform their rural environments, and, partly, bargain with the patriarchal order upheld within their families and communities.

The Background of Rural Women's Organizations: Before the Commencement of the New Community Movement

The so-called "natural village (*chayŏnburak*)" was a naturally and spontaneously organized group; it was a basic unit of rural society in South Korea. As of 1975, there were approximately 48,000 naturally established rural villages nationwide in South Korea (Kincaid et al. 1975).[1] Each village had its customs and traditions and was a basic community unit (Ch'oe Chaesŏk 1975). Moreover, it was a place where community members shared a collective consciousness, voluntarily and cooperatively participating in agricultural production and daily life. A natural village was a space where social norms were shared by community members. Meanwhile, it was a unit where invisible mutual control and social sanctions among village members existed. Labor groups such as *ture*, a joint labor organization for agricultural work in rural areas, existed based on the village unit. Villages also had *p'umashi*, a form of unpaid labor exchanged among villagers that function based on trust.

The natural village was a territorial entity within which common social norms were maintained and shared by community members who often shared blood ties and the same paternal lineage. Family clans were formed through the process of settling in a certain place for a long time (Kim Chusuk 1994). Regarding a family clan village, ancestral rituals that support patrilineal relatives and the operation and management of common assets were carried out by *munjung*, a patriarchal group of descendants with common ancestors. Leaders of family clans, *ŏrŭn*, played a primary role as informal leaders of villages. The clan leader was usually the eldest son of the oldest generation of the family. Even though the role and authority of clan leaders varied per village (Ch'oe Chaesŏk 1975), clan leaders were responsible for managing the common property of the family and holding ceremonies to honor clan ancestors. A family clan had about 100 households on average, where "cooperation, social sanctions, and information transmission, some key ingredients of social capital" (Yang 2019, 34) coexisted.

According to the "Temporary Measures Law concerning Local Autonomy" enacted in 1961, as part of the strengthening of local administration, administrative units were established in place of natural villages. These administrative units, named "legal villages (*pŏpchŏngburak*)", were the smallest governmental administrative unit and comprised two or three natural villages (Kincaid et al. 1975). As per the shift of the village unit from a natural to a legal village, each legal village established a village chief system where a leader called an *ijang* was appointed by the head of the government for administrative management as a formal leader for the village. The main roles of the administrative leaders were to convey instructions from the government to village residents and collect taxes. Further, they were responsible for filing birth, marriage, and death reports, and managing villages' joint funds on behalf of farmers who could not go to the office during the farming season. That is, the chiefs of the legal villages served a dual position as a messenger for the administrative agency and spokesperson for the residents (Ch'oe Chaesŏk 1988). The average age of the chief of a legal village ranged between the 30s and 40s. They were in charge of the administration of the villages and were promoters of rural development projects. However, the chief of the villages often asked villages' informal leaders (*ŏrŭn*) for advice when implementing important projects. Therefore, *ŏrŭn* were villages' opinion leaders, and the chiefs of villages were not completely independent from the informal leaders (Ch'oe Chaesŏk 1975; Yi Mankap 1973). This leadership structure in which informal leaders strongly influence the decision-making process for village-related matters was also applied to new government-appointed leaders and affected the promotion of rural development projects. For instance, mothers' clubs for family planning and male and female saemaul village leaders were in close contact with the informal leaders in the decision-making process during the implementation of the New Community Movement.

In 1961, the "Temporary Measures Law concerning Local Autonomy" induced many changes in local administrative units under the charge of the Ministry of Home Affairs. Among the various changes, the major difference with the previous administrative system was the establishment of specific forms of village units: "*ri*" (village) and "*dong*" (subdivision of the village). The administrative village system further segmented existing villages and was intended to extend central administrative power to every corner of rural areas.

Following these changes, in 1965 the administrative organizations of each village were rearranged following the enactment of the "Basic Administration Development Plan", with many abolished or integrated. Before this reorganization, village administrative organizations could be roughly divided along informal and formal lines. Regarding formal organizations, there were "legal organizations" stipulated by national law and "administrative organizations" guided by the local governments. Legal organizations included Agricultural Cooperatives, committees for forestry and irrigation, committees for agricultural land, and committees for savings. Administrative organizations regarded food production, committees for epidemic prevention, committees for the survey of agricultural land, and associations for women and youth (Ministry of the Home Affairs 1987, 2382–2383). However, as most of the legal organizations and administrative organizations restricted admission to heads of household and village representatives, opportunities for rural women to participate in organizational activities on formal occasions were rare (Shin Hyŏnok 1999, 72). Official channels available for rural women to participate in organizational activities included women's associations organized as part of the National Reconstruction Movement between 1961 and 1964, which continued during the New Community Movement. The Park Chung Hee regime organized women's associations in each village nationwide to convey medical information primarily related to family planning. Women's associations for rural women nationwide later became the governing bodies for the family-planning-focused mothers' club organized by the Korean Family Planning Association (Kim et al. 1972). However, as the National Reconstruction Movement was not successful, its women's associations were not particularly active in the 1960s.

Further, 1965 saw the establishment of the "ri/dong Development Committee", a comprehensive residents' cooperative governing village organizations. The ri/dong Development Committee comprised up to 15 members representing each village. However, even after this rearrangement, rural women's organizations such as the Life Improvement Movement Club, which existed as an informal organization at the time, were not formalized. That is, while male farmers were allowed to participate in formal venues through legal organizations such as Committees for the Improvement of Forests and Farmland, rural women were confined to informal venues and were excluded from decision-making processes in the public sphere (Shin Hyŏnok 1999, 76). From a 1968 survey of 491 rural households conducted by rural sociologist Ch'oe Chaesŏk, male household heads represented the family in most formal scenes, including community meetings (92%), sending money for familial ceremonies such as weddings and funerals (82%), and meeting with governmental officials (82%) (*Kyunghyang Shinmun* May 17, 1969).

While not institutionalized, gender-segregation was readily apparent in organizational activity content. The Park Chung Hee regime established the Rural Development Administration to oversee its agricultural policy under the "Rural Development Law" in 1962. The Administration was a unified version of the Agricultural Institute and the Agricultural Teaching Center, which were established by the US military administration in the 1950s. The Rural Development Administration aimed to promote the welfare of farmers via research, guidance, dissemination of technology, and the training of leaders toward the development of rural areas (Central Association for Agricultural Cooperatives 1965, 445–447). While developing farming techniques and training programs for civil servants, the Rural Development Administration managed Agricultural and Livelihood Improvement Clubs in each village. The Agricultural Improvement Clubs primarily provided education for agricultural management and machinery; they were organizations for male farmers to disseminate and practice new farming techniques, cultivate spirits of self-help and cooperation through organizational activities, and nurture diligence among farmers. The Life Improvement Clubs primarily provided guidance for improving clothing, food, housing, health and hygiene, childcare, and farmers' part-time jobs. They aimed to help members learn the significance of democracy through independent learning activities of rural women and girls, foster spirits of cooperation through independent group life, and disseminate information on the improvement of living standards (Rural Development Administration 1970).

Agricultural Cooperatives had been established to improve the rural economy by recognizing existing informal cooperatives in 1961. Agricultural banks and Agricultural Cooperatives were later integrated through the revision of the "Agricultural Cooperatives Law" in 1973, thus founding general Agricultural Cooperatives for the first time. The government was widely involved in the overall operation of Agricultural Cooperatives and the introduction of the pre-approval system for Agricultural Cooperative business plans, management, personnel management, and financial management (Central Association for Agricultural Cooperatives 1965, 21–22). The president could even appoint the chairman of the Central Agricultural Cooperative under the "Temporary Measures Law concerning the Appointment of Officers" (Chang Sanghwan 2006, 30). As of 1962, the number of Agricultural Cooperatives in administrative villages exceeded 20,000, and the number of union members accounted for more than 90% of the farmers. Agricultural Cooperatives introduced new farming techniques, ran life improvement projects, purchased agricultural products, provided daily necessities through a retail system, and funded lending and savings projects. Within the Agricultural Cooperatives, cooperative associations and crop groups were organized for male farmers, and women's associations were organized for female farmers starting in 1971. These associations and groups were given lessons on how to use agricultural machinery and farming techniques, and the women's associations were instructed in family planning, preparing family rituals, keeping household account books, and general life improvement activities. Furthermore, by assigning the chairwomen of the women's association to the savings projects, a system was established to incorporate rural women into savings initiatives (Kim Chusuk 1994).

As noted, before the commencement of the New Community Movement in 1971, farmers were organized based on gender roles. That is, male farmers, as the bearers of production, acquired "scientific" and "modern" farming techniques through state-sponsored organizational activities such as Agricultural Improvement Clubs, cooperatives, and crop groups, while female farmers were encouraged to focus on improving the lives of their families. This clear division of labor by gender in organizational activities was shown in the content of instruction for the rural development projects. Agricultural guidance projects for men included agricultural knowledge based on science, the development of science and technology in agriculture and crop cultivation, and animal science on breeding livestock, forestry, and silkworm farming. However, life improvement projects for women were based on home economics and addressed issues of consumption, savings, clothing, food and housing, nutrition, health and hygiene, family relations, childcare, and home management (Shin Hyŏnok 1999, 64).

New Community Movement and the Redefinition of Housewives: From Family Managers to Community Managers

The Life Improvement Movement, which was mainly carried out by the Rural Development Administration, starting in the 1960s to improve clothing, food, and living conditions, continued to be promoted even after the commencement of the New Community Movement in 1971. The state's intention to position women as agents in charge of the domestic sphere was well-reflected in a speech by Park Chung Hee in 1965 entitled "A Message to Housewives". Park emphasized that it was a traditional virtue for women to take charge of the modernization of the domestic sphere, as represented by the "modernization of the kitchen": "I send the message of 'wise mother and good wife' to all housewives this New Year. Women of our nation have long been wearing white clothes, which symbolize chastity, and have acquired the wisdom of sacrifice, patience, and silence. These virtues for women still survive in our lives as a tradition. I think that the most important thing for housewives in our country is the 'modernization of the kitchen'" (President's Office 1965, 382).

Rural women were organized into mothers' clubs concentrated on various domestic activities to realize the modernization of the domestic domain, including enhancing public sanitation and family health, improving nutrition, vegetable cultivation, food storage, housing improvement, simplification of rituals, keeping household account books, practicing scientific child-rearing methods, and financial saving (Ministry of Health and Social Welfare 1981, 83–91). Until the early stages of the New Community Movement, the participation of rural women in the rural development project was confined to "activities that can only be done by women" (Ministry of Home Affairs 1977, 56); that is, rural women were expected to enact their roles as modern mothers and housewives solely within the private sphere.

Rural women's roles were redefined with the progress of the New Community Movement, following the rural–urban migration of the young labor force given urban-centered industrialization in the latter half of the 1960s. Under these circumstances, the Park Chung Hee regime faced challenges in identifying the main agents of the New Community Movement. By redefining rural women as the carriers of the New Community Movement, the Park Chung Hee regime tried to maximize the outcomes of its rural development projects. Rural women and girls were positioned from "potential power" of rural village development to "authentic power" in leading the New Community Movement (Ministry of Home Affairs 1975, 83).

Consequently, the boundaries of the domestic sphere expanded from the household to the rural community level (Yokota 2002). It was first apparent in the establishment of common wells, common laundry and kitchen facilities, joint cooking during the farming season, the operation of daycare centers, and the joint cooking of school lunches for children. Such a consortium meant shifting rural women's duties as family managers to duties as community managers (Shin Hyŏnok 1999, 103). The state's intention to do so is indicated in, for instance, the following statement by the Ministry of Home Affairs (1977, 263): "It is important to free women and girls from the kitchen and let them carry out rural development projects with collaborative support at the community level to produce the potential labor force of women and girls in rural areas". Moreover, the Ministry of Health and Social Welfare (1981, 45) noted that "women's associations have naturally participated in projects such as road expansion, bridge construction, and sanitation improvement projects, as rural societies are currently lacking manpower".

Notably, the New Community Movement's living environment improvement project shifted work typically defined as men's work, such as road expansion, roof improvement, and the construction of community buildings, to women. Sewerage ditch maintenance, which was conducted by the government as part of the infrastructure improvement project, also became the responsibility of rural women. It meant that the content and scope of activities rural women were involved in expanded with the progress of the New Community Movement. Further, some rural women even represented their rural village communities, negotiated with local governments, and were involved in decision-making processes for local community agendas (Chang Migyŏng 2008).

Rural Women's Interpretation of Organizational Activities and Challenges for the Shift of Gender Roles

Organizational activities in rural villages were seen by rural women as an opportunity to share in the growth-oriented ideology of the Park Chung Hee regime. The organizational activities of rural women were also perceived as a channel to negotiate with the local patriarchal system of rural villages. "Success stories" of women's associations frequently appeared in regional daily newspapers during the New Community Movement and provided rural women a space for sharing in growth ideologies.

As discussed in Chapter 1, the New Community Movement was focused on the demonstration effect. Results were visibly "quantified" through such projects. The New Community Movement was accepted by rural women for its visible results and the feeling that their daily lives had been improved. Female saemaul leaders illustrated positive reactions from the village residents when they successfully negotiated with the local administration for water supply (*Jeonbuk Ilbo*, May 26, 1978) and a road expansion (*Jeonbuk Ilbo*, September 5, 1978).[2]

Rural women showed positive attitudes toward the New Community Movement when physical aspects of their daily lives, such as kitchens and water supply, improved. Moreover, after electronic appliances, recognized as symbols of "urban life", began to proliferate in rural areas, rural women more readily accepted the discourses of "liberation from hunger" and "abundance" that the Park Chung Hee regime propagated through the New Community Movement, contributing to the perception that a life similar to that of urban areas would be realized.

Pérez (2012) maintains that the "democratization" of home electronic appliances among newly middle-class and working-class homes in Argentina from the 1930s to the 1960s provided women with a shared feeling of "democratization of welfare" symbolizing the "growth of the middle class and the search for new signs of distinction" (ibid., 158). Moreover, it seemed rural women in South Korea shared a feeling of "democratization of welfare" from the prevalence of modern electronic home appliances and the improvement of their living environments through the extension of water and electricity, which were closely connected with women's everyday lives and domestic labor. According to a survey by the Ministry of Agriculture and Fishery in 1978 conducted among 3,300 rural households nationwide, one out of 2.6 households had water facilities, and the extension rate of electricity was 98% (*Kyunghyang Shinmun* February 28, 1979). The rural electrification rate surged from 24% in 1970 to 98% in 1979 given the Agricultural and Fishing Village Electrification Project, which was promoted as part of the New Community Movement (Ministry of Home Affairs 1980, 53). Kim Yŏnhŭi (2011) maintains that the extension of fundamental infrastructure such as drinking water and electricity was among the most favored projects of the rural population, as they recognized the project as an opportunity to plant commodity crops, improve children's educational outcomes, gain easy access to information regarding urban life, and realize a comfortable living standard.

Under a village structure in which hierarchies of age, gender, and family relations were firmly established, the organizational activities of rural development projects were perceived by rural women as an opportunity to overcome opposition from the elderly. Elderly people, represented by *ŏrŭn*, were reluctant to allow young rural women to get involved in family planning and community development projects, as they considered such activities as destructive to patrilineal society and gender roles. A rural woman explained that they were recognized by the elderly when they installed electricity in the village with funds from the women's association, even though they were criticized with the old saying, "if a hen sings, the house will be destroyed" (*Happy Home* June 5, 1976).

Rural women took state intervention and the legitimization of their organizational opportunities as opportunities to negotiate patriarchal relations within the family. For instance, in the context of the state-led saving initiatives, husbands' drinking and gambling during the nonfarming season were depicted as "vices". As the New Community Movement aimed for a new life, and rural women were named "renovators" and "reformers" by the state, rural women attempted to use this governmental intervention to negotiate with their husbands at the household level. In a newspaper article in *Jeonbuk Ilbo* (September 3, 1977), a female saemaul leader explained that the first project they worked on after organizing the women's association was to eliminate the bar from the village to fight against alcohol drinking culture and gambling practices of male farmers.

From this interview with a female saemaul leader, rural women sometimes strategically used the women's association as a means of resisting the patriarchal order that existed in villages and the gender roles and customs expected of rural women in the home and within the rural community. Similarly, rural women's participation in state-supported organizational activities led to increased negotiating power, sharing of housework by husbands, and more egalitarianism in domestic relations (Chang Mikyŏng 2008):

> I was very busy at that time with the governmental developmental projects within the New Community Movement. It was a very dramatic change for

> rural women to become leaders at that time. During the first stage, the elderly and males in the village laughed at me and the rural housewives about the things we tried to achieve. My husband was angry at me whenever I tried to go outside for village projects. However, since we had achieved visible results with saving accounts, they began to be interested in our achievements. In addition, I had an opportunity to visit Taiwan to learn about the experiences of rural development projects during the 1970s. The 1970s were when travel abroad for ordinary people was forbidden.[3] To work as a female saemaul leader was actually not easy because of the balance of overwork and the pressure from the government. However, it is also undeniable that the governmental pressure helped us women to avoid pressure from husbands and mothers-in-law and *ŏrŭn*, who were against the activities organized by women in rural villages, as the governmental order was considered irresistible. Since my status had been changed in local society, my husband began to help with housework and my mother-in-law began to cease blaming me for my frequent "going outside".
>
> (Interview with a female saemaul leader)[4]

Regarding husband–wife relations, Kim Hyegyŏng (2009) suggests the active response of rural women to "reforming" husbands can be understood in the context of the gradual proliferation of the nuclear family in rural society and the intention of rural women to build husband–wife-centered relations within this ideology by integrating husbands "into" family boundaries. Regarding mothers-in-law, rural women tried to strengthen decision-making power within households by actively participating in the rural development project. As for their social positions relative to the *ŏrŭn*, they attempted not to be constrained within the limited social networks by broadening the scope of their activities through public activities. Bargaining by rural women in relationships with their mothers-in-law and *ŏrŭn*, thus, reflects the aspirations of women to be independent of the control of the patrilineal society and "traditional" kinship of the local patriarchal order (see Kandiyoti 1988).

Conclusions

The process of becoming a housewife in rural areas of South Korea differs significantly from the Western context, as it was largely driven by the state in the context of modern nation-state building. Unlike in the West, rural women's daily lives were not confined solely to domestic spheres but were subject to regulation, guidance, and monitoring through various organizational activities. State intervention positioned rural women, previously seen as primarily responsible for the domestic sphere, as central figures in community development and management. However, state intervention was not always passively adopted, and rural women used it as a means of achieving the "modernization" they envisioned and negotiating with the patriarchal order in the local society. It included taking advantage of the resources and opportunities provided by the state to gain access to education, training, and other forms of support that would help them participate more fully in the broader project of national development. Overall, this chapter highlights the unique and complex ways in which the housewife ideology intersected with state-led development initiatives in rural areas of South Korea and emphasizes the need to recognize the agency and experiences of rural women in shaping their own lives and communities within this context.

Notes

1 The village (*maŭl*) was a basic unit of Korean rural society and was usually consistent with a natural village. The term *maŭl* is more commonly used in daily life than "natural village".

2 *Jeonbuk Ilbo* reinterviewed male and female saemaul leaders, releasing a "success story" from the New Community Movement every week from 1977 to 1978.

3 Travel abroad has been open to ordinary people since 1989. Until the 1980s, the Korean government restricted travel abroad for ordinary people for reasons of preventing foreign currency outflow and contact with residents from communist countries (especially North Korea), making it difficult for the general public to issue passports without stating the purpose of study, overseas employment, business trips, or immigration. The situation explains why, in those days, being issued a passport was considered a privilege.

4 H. Lee was the female saemaul leader I interviewed in person on September 27, 2008.

Bibliography

Central Association for Agricultural Cooperatives. 1965. *Han'guk nongjŏng 20nyŏn (20 Years History of Agricultural Policy)*. Seoul: Central Association for Agricultural Cooperatives.

Chang Migyŏng. 2008. "Kaebal kukka shigi, saemaŭl undong punyŏ chidoja ŭi chŏngch'esŏng ŭi hyŏngsŏng kwa pyŏnhwa: punyŏ chidojaŭi sŏnggongsarye, sugirŭl chungshimŭro (Formulation and Transformation of Female Leadership Identity in the New Community Movement within the Developmental State: Examining Successful Cases and Essays of Female Leaders). *Sahoe kwahak yŏn'gu (Social Science Research)* 16, no. 1: 426–660.

Chang Sanghwan. 2006. "Onŭl ŭi hyŏnshil esŏ tashi pon han'guk ŭi nongŏp chŏngch'aek (Looking Back on Korea's Agricultural Policy from Today's Perspective)." *Yŏksa (History)* 23: 24–42.

Ch'oe Chaesŏk. 1975. *Han'guk nongch'on sahoe yŏn'gu (Research on Rural Society in Korea)*. Seoul: Ilchisa.

Ch'oe Chaesŏk. 1988. *Han'guk nongch'on sahoe pyŏndong yŏn'gu (Research on Changes in Rural Society in Korea)*. Seoul: Ilchisa.

Happy Home. 1976. "Ponbogi ŏmŏnihoe: Kajok kyehoek kwa kajŏng ŭirye chunch'ik shilch'ŏnhayŏ 1paek manwŏn chŏlgamshik'in isaek ŏmŏnihoe (A Successful Mother's Club Case: An Achievement by a Mothers' Club through Family Planning and Savings Initiatives)." June 5.

Jeonbuk Ilbo. 1977. "Successful Stories of Female Saemaul Leaders." September 3.

Jeonbuk Ilbo. 1978. "Successful Stories of Female Saemaul Leaders." May 26.

Jeonbuk Ilbo. 1978. "Successful Stories of Female Saemaul Leaders." September 5.

Kandiyoti, Deniz. 1988. "Bargaining with Patriarchy." *Gender and Society* 2, no. 3: 274–290.

Kim Chusuk. 1994. *Han'guk nongch'on ŭi yŏsŏng kwa kajok (Women and Family in Rural Villages in Korea)*. Seoul: Hanul Academy.

Kim Hyegyŏng. 2009. "Pak chŏnghŭi ch'eje ha 'haekkajok tamnon ŭi pyŏnhwa gwajŏng gwa iwŏn gujo yŏn'gu (Discourses on the Nuclear Family and the Double Structure during the Park Chung Hee Era)." *Sahoe wa yŏksa (Society and History)* 82: 169–212.

Kim, Taek Il, Tagil Kim, John A. Ross, and George C. Worth. 1972. *The Korean National Family Planning Program*. New York: The Population Council.

Kim Yŏnhŭi. 2011. "Nongch'on chŏn'gi konggŭp saŏp kwa saemaŭl undong (Electricity Projects in Rural Villages and the Saemaul Movement)." *Yŏksabip'yŏng (Historical Critique)* 97: 397–425.

Kincaid, D. Lawrence, Hyung-Jong Park, Kyung-Kyoon Chung, and Chin-Chuan Lee. 1975. *Mothers' Clubs and Family Planning in Rural Korea: The Case of Oryu Li*. Honolulu: East-West Communication Institute.

Korean Women's Development Institute. 1985. *Yŏsŏng paeksŏ (Yearbook on Women's Issues)*. Seoul: Korean Women's Development Institute.

Kyunghyang Shinmun. 1969. "Han'guk nongga ŭi kwŏllyŏk kujo (The Power Structure of Rural Society in South Korea)." May 17.

Kyunghyang Shinmun. 1979. "Naengjanggo set'akki shidae majŭn nongch'on (Introduction of Refrigerators and Washing Machines into Rural Society)." February 28.

Mies, Maria. 1998. *Patriarchy and Accumulation on a World Scale: Women in the International Division of Labour*. London: Zed Books.

Ministry of Health and Social Welfare. 1981. *Yŏsŏng kwa saemaŭl undong (Women and the New Community Movement)*. Seoul: Ministry of Health and Social Welfare.

Ministry of Home Affairs. 1975. *The New Community Movement*. Seoul: Ministry of Home Affairs.

Ministry of Home Affairs. 1977. *The New Community Movement*. Seoul: Ministry of Home Affairs.

Ministry of Home Affairs. 1980. *Saemaŭl undong 10nyŏnsa: charyop'yŏn (10 Years of History of the Saemaul Undong: Documents)*. Seoul: Ministry of Home Affairs.

Ministry of Home Affairs. 1987. *Han'guk chibang haengjŏngsa (The History of Rural Prefectures in Korea)*.

Pérez, Inés. 2012. "Comfort for the People and Liberation for the Housewife: Gender, Consumption and Refrigerators in Argentina (1930–60)." *Journal of Consumer Culture* 12, no. 2: 156–174. https://doi.org/10.1177/1469540512446876

President's Office. 1965. *Pakchŏnghŭi taet'ongnyŏng yŏnsŏlmun (Speech of Park Chung Hee)*. Seoul: President's Office.

Rural Development Administration. 1970. *Nonghyŏp yŏn'gam (Yearbook of Agricultural Cooperation)*. Seoul: Rural Development Administration.

Shin Hyŏnok. 1999. "Kukka kaebal chŏngch'aek kwa nongch'on chiyŏk ŭi yŏsŏng chojik e kwanhan yŏn'gu (National Development Policy and Women's Organizations in Rural Areas)." Doctoral diss., Yonsei University.

Yang, Hyunjoo. 2019. "Family Clans and Public Goods: Evidence from the New Village Beautification Project in South Korea." *Journal of Development Economics* 136: 34–50. https://doi.org/10.1016/j.jdeveco.2018.09.001

Yi Mankap. 1973. *Han'guk nongch'on sahoe ŭi kujo wa pyŏnhwa (The Structure of Rural Society and the Changes in Korea)*. Seoul: Seoul National University Press.

Yokota, Nobuko. 2002. "Kankoku ni okeru semauru undō to nōson josei no soshikika to dōin (Organizing and Mobilizing Rural Women in the New Community Movement in South Korea)." In *Kōhatsu Kōgyōkoku ni okeru josei rōdō to shakai seisaku (Women's Labor and Social Policy in Late-industrializing Countries)*, edited by Murakami Kaoru, 129–157. Tokyo: Ajia Keizai kenkyūjo.

6 Gendered Social Mobility Strategies and Limited Negotiation

The previous chapters discussed that the scope of "labor" by rural women had been extended from productive and reproductive labor to participation in family planning, rural development and saving initiatives, and organizational activities, redefined under the housewife ideology by the Park Chung Hee regime. The examination also considered how rural women interpreted and engaged in this series of everyday developments as opportunities to pursue middle-class aspirations and negotiate with patriarchal orders. However, whether these efforts by rural women influenced the transformation of the patriarchal system in rural society and induced significant changes in gender relations within the household and the community is a separate issue worthy of discussion.

This chapter attempts to discuss the gendered nature of rural women's social mobility strategy and the limited sociocultural conditions for the shift from the patriarchal system at the time. It maintains that, even though the broadening of the scope of the labor and rural development activities by rural women laid a foundation for the formation of the middle class in Korea during industrialization, rural women's future-oriented social mobility via the gendered allocation of resources for children eventually contributed to the (re)construction of gender relations.

Rural Women's Gendered Social Mobility Strategies

Rural women's economic autonomy was somewhat achieved through organizational activities such as mothers' clubs and women's associations of the New Community Movement and national savings drives. However, rural women did not see access to the household economy and control of the financial sector at home as especially liberatory but as an opportunity for resource allocation for family members (Pae Ŭn'kyŏng 2008). It could be interpreted that, for rural women, savings activities and access to financial resources did not necessarily lead either to the "empowerment" of rural women or the erosion of the local patriarchal power in rural society, as savings and consumer practices remained strongly family-oriented, despite their increased autonomy in decision-making power in the household economy sector.

In fact, to understand the aspirations of rural women toward achieving middle-class status, it is essential to pay special attention to the fact that the social mobility strategy by rural women was gender-segregated. Rural mothers who could not

DOI: 10.4324/9781003110538-7

easily achieve the status of a middle-class housewife marked by "liberation from labor" often attempted to pursue upward mobility through the economic and social success of their family members. For rural mothers who did not have enough financial resources to care equally for multiple children, gender-segregated selective strategies of intensive educational investments for sons and the achievement of "professional" housewife status for daughters by promoting marriage to urban salaried men were "rational" investments. This tendency was much stronger among the lower working class. When the whole household faced financial difficulties, daughters were the first to be forced to drop out of school, leave the family to join the labor market as unskilled workers, or postpone marriage to support family members (Kim Yŏnchu and Yi Chaekyŏng 2013); intensive educational investments were reserved for sons.

Regarding the strong educational aspirations of rural parents, Kim Suyŏng (2001) explains that the sustenance and upward mobility strategy of the low-working class was generally based on gender-segregated roles among family members. This thinking was more pronounced in families with few financial resources, inducing a selective investment in sons, as is commonly observed in the Asian context (see Brinton 1988; Greenhalgh 1985; Parish and Willis 1993; Salaff 1981). In rural families with many children, competition among siblings for educational opportunities was common. Educational investments in children were widely considered to be a measure to establish a social security system for parents, given no concrete governmental social welfare system in the early industrialization period. In general, the family members who were financially supported were sons and male relatives (Yi Mijŏng 1998).

> I still feel bad about my eldest sister. In fact, her academic performance was much better than mine at school. However, only because she is the eldest out of five children and I am the only son in my family, I was sent to the home of a relative who lived in a city for education in a middle school, and she had to work in a factory after graduating from elementary school. This pattern – sending sons to schools and girls to factories – was quite common at that time. Therefore, some would say that I do not have to feel bad about it. But I have tried to repay the favor to my eldest sister by financially supporting the education of her children. I have so far paid all of the university tuition fees for her children.[1]

In a male-centered labor market, limited occupational chances were given to young semi-skilled female workers, who usually left the labor market for marriage, childbearing, and childrearing. For instance, a study by Kim (1997) in 1987 of 718 young female factory workers demonstrates that women's motivations for starting factory work were family related: "main support for family (2%)", "partial support for family (13%)", "siblings education (4%)", and "dowry savings (11%)". Kim (ibid.) demonstrates that most workers put a higher priority on saving than consuming. Moreover, she notes that the reinvestment of the income of traditionally structured families is a sign of interaction between patriarchal gender ideology and capitalist systems of domination. Moreover, daughters were considered members of their husband's families after marriage under the patrilineal society at that time (Gelb and Palley 1994; Kim 2005). Hence, in family communities where financial resources were limited, daughters were required to concede educational chances to male siblings, as parents expected investment in a son's education to lead to future social security, for sons would remain part of their parents' households (Brinton 1988). Thus, the idea of gender-segregated investment in children was particularly strong for mothers (Hŏ Minsuk 2014).

Regarding the social mobility strategies for daughters, rural mothers attempted to marry their daughters to non-farmers in cities to realize their unfulfilled aspirations, given their experience of unbalanced rural–urban growth and increasing labor burdens during industrialization. Even if this upward mobility strategy was passive relative to the active financial investment and emotional support given to sons' education, it is key to understanding the rapidly changing family structure of rural society and the collapse of reproductive order in rural areas that began in the 1980s (Yi Jŏngŭn 2010).

Of course, young rural–urban female migrants' aspirations for becoming housewives were also closely connected with a widespread informal institution under which married women were expected to drop out of the labor market or continue to work under poor working conditions. However, it should be interpreted as a strategy of mothers in rural villages to pursue upward mobility. Major daily newspapers in Korea began to "problematize" married rural women's willingness to have their daughters get married to salaried workers in urban areas, not farmers, as it means more rural–urban migration and the gender quota imbalance in rural areas. A newspaper article in *Donga Ilbo* (February 28, 1977) criticized rural girls' aspiration to leave rural villages and rural mothers who try to send their daughters to the cities to find partners, highlighting the situation against the background of the collapse of rural society.

The following interview with a rural woman also reflects the marriage strategy of many rural women of those days.[2]

> Even though it was normal to get married to a man who lived in a rural village in my days, I spent my whole life working my fingers to the bone and successfully supported my children's education. I wanted my daughter to marry a salaryman or governmental officer who had a regular income and lived in an apartment in a city. How comfortable it is to live as a full-time housewife without hard work as we had.

Clearly, even though rural women perceived diligence and being hardworking as a means of upward mobility, their goals for their children were not the endowment of life based on hard work or farming. Furthermore, the interview excerpt clearly suggests that the rural aspiration toward "becoming a housewife" was based on a specific middle-class image of "salarymen" and "apartment complexes".[3] In short, we could imagine from the interview that the "visible" but not easily "touchable" aspiration to become a housewife was reflected through the marriage of their daughters to "modern" men with regular incomes.

The aspiration of "becoming a housewife" was not only that of rural mothers but also of their daughters. S. Sŏ, a female social movement activist,[4] reminisced in an interview about her attempts to organize rural–urban migrant workers in labor movements during Park Chung Hee's regime.

> Female factory workers actively engaged with the labor movement when they realized how they were working under bad working conditions through the education we offered. However, the biggest barrier to the sustainability of the female labor movement at that time was the marriage of female workers. To get married [to] a man and become a housewife was considered to be sort of the best solution for all of the problems of the factory workers at that time.

Regarding rural women's agency and upward mobility, the strategies of rural mothers for their daughters and their daughters' active acceptance of marriage strategies can be interpreted in various ways. Chang Migyŏng (2004) discusses how the primary aim of female rural–urban migrant workers was to become housewives, as labor was gendered and based on traditional gender norms. The marriage strategy for daughters in rural areas might, therefore, be interpreted as simply the "continuation" of Confucianism, under which women were expected to stay at home and conduct the duties of a "wise mother and good wife" (see Kim Suyŏng 2001). Still, women maintained a degree of agency in the decision-making process for marriage via the abandonment of rurality and farming; decisions interconnected with upward social mobility.

Chang (2010) characterizes Korean people's perceptions of social mobility relative to the boundaries of "middle classness". He argues that financial support by peasant families for their children, kin, and siblings was common during industrialization and was a rational calculation relative to perceptions of the scope of the South Korean middle class. Chang (2002, 198) maintains that "South Koreans' material and psychological attachments to adult education, parents, and siblings induced them to link their class status to those of their extended family members (in particular, successful ones)". Accordingly, daughters' upward mobility through marriage was connected with the extended perceptions Koreans held regarding the boundaries of the middle class and their family members. Meanwhile, even though it did not manifest in the form of financial support, the realization of the aspiration of "becoming housewives" via the marriage of daughters to "salarymen in cities" could be interpreted as a future-oriented and inter-generational class mobility strategy.

Of course, the social aspirations of rural mothers and their daughters were not necessarily always realized, even for successful marriage strategies. Chang (2010) shows that urban women were continuously engaged in casual and disguised wage labor and housework in informal and small-scale tertiary sectors, similar to how women in rural villages performed household and agricultural work and seasonal wage laborers. Meanwhile, some empirical studies conducted on the life histories of rural–urban female migrant workers have even revealed that a significant number of women achieved middle-class status via economic activities, even though marriage to "salarymen in cities" did not necessarily guarantee the automatic upward mobility at the earlier stage of the marriage (see Hŏ Minsuk 2014; Kim Yŏnchu and Yi Chaekyŏng 2013).

Limited Bargaining Power

Moreover, rural women's increasing autonomy in the household economy, rising social status in the local community, and growing negotiation power in gender relations through their position as local agents in rural development projects did not induce a drastic change in gender relations. Rural women achieved some degree of social recognition from their husbands, mothers-in-law, and community members. However, their negotiations reflected unchanging gender norms and orders. The *Oryu* village case demonstrates that the active participation of rural women in the New Community Movement did not necessarily mean a drastic change in gender relations in rural society, despite the visible accomplishment of rural women. *Oryu* village remains well-known nationwide as among the successful cases when it comes to the New Community Movement. Given the enormous success, the savings drives by rural women in *Oryu* village were filmed by a governmental body, the National Film Production Center, in 1974 to propagate the New Community Movement. Despite the great achievement by rural women through savings drives, the leader, Mrs. Kang, attempted to identify the rural women's activities not as "women's liberation" but as the continuation of protecting the conventional patriarchal orders within the households: "In the past, our husbands mistook the mothers' club for 'women's liberation'. But now they understand it. We persuaded them by serving them various delicious foods and entertainment" (Kincaid 1975, 31).

Regarding relations to mothers-in-law and *ŏrŭn*, rural women often avoided challenging the hierarchical order within the family and local community. A woman who had been involved in peasant movements for over 30 years reminisced about the bargaining process with her mother-in-law and the elderly in the community when young rural women first began organizational activities in her rural village.

> At first, it was very difficult for us to take over the management of the local community from elderly women, as organizational activities were managed by elderly women, and young women like us had been forbidden from participating in those meetings. Therefore, we very carefully asked them whether we may take over the assignments from them. We persuaded them that the hierarchical order would not be ruined, and we would follow their decisions for important issues for the village. Further, we tried to show our respect for them by regularly organizing banquets for mothers-in-law and *ŏrŭn*. We also organized bus tours for them.[5] As we had shown our respect, we could be accepted as part of the women's association, which had been led by elderly women until then.
>
> (Interview with a rural woman)[6]

As can be seen from the interview excerpt, rural women had to negotiate with members of the village community via community savings, building community centers, purchasing electronic and kitchen goods for the community, and organizing celebrations for the entertainment of elderly people to be recognized for their activities. This situation gave rural women the space to justify their savings activities as undertaken not for themselves but for the community within their roles as good mothers, wives, and daughters-in-law (Kincaid 1975, 31).

Such bargaining behavior by rural women should be understood in the context of the rapid social transitions in rural society at the time. Despite the rise of the nuclear family nationwide, rural societies remained "traditional" in family form, and the number of extended families was much higher in rural areas than in urban areas. For instance, as of 1970, only 1.8% of households in rural areas comprised one generation; 60.1% comprised two generations; 35.7% comprised three generations; and 2.5% comprised four generations. In Seoul, 4.8% of the households comprised one generation; 75.7% comprised two generations; 18.8% comprised three generations; and 0.8% comprised four generations (Yi Hyojae and Kim Chusuk 1976). Regarding care for the elderly, "traditional" social norms strongly remained existent. The late 1970s was the period when discourses on extended families in rural villages were actively disseminated by the government and media, alongside the promotion of nuclear families. Rural villages were highly praised as a place where the elderly remained supported by family members, unlike cities where the absence of family support was becoming a critical social issue. It contrasts with the prevalent public discourse of the 1960s where the ideal of the nuclear family was praised in family planning initiatives (Kim Hyegyŏng 2009).

Notably, the patrilineal social and gender order remained existent in South Korea despite the changing family structure from large to nuclear families nationwide (Kim Hyeyŏng 2016). According to a survey by the National Agricultural Cooperative Federation of 1,000 rural households in 1978, 46.4% of rural households responded that they wished to have a nuclear family. These responses reflected a changing value system in terms of family structure. Decision-making structures also shifted from the elderly to joint decisions by husbands and wives. Less than 10% of respondents replied that the eldest made decisions for familial matters such as farming, children's education, and household-related issues, while the spouses made decisions for approximately 70–80% of rural households in the study. Meanwhile, 50.4% of rural households replied that they planned to give most of their property to the eldest son, while merely 19.1% of respondents answered that they would grant property equally to all of their children or daughters. Further, 62.8% of the respondents answered that they had the responsibility to care for their parents, and 80.5% replied positively regarding filial piety and the necessity of traditional familial ceremonies (*Chosun Ilbo* April 11, 1978). Such data indicate that rural women had to bargain with the patriarchal order under constrained circumstances on gender roles despite their increasing autonomy in economic activities and their growing decision-making power through state-led organizational activities.

Conclusions

Rural women's economic autonomy was somewhat achieved through organizational activities and access to financial resources. However, their focus remained on resource allocation for family members rather than personal empowerment. Rural mothers prioritized education for sons and sought to secure their daughters' marriage to urban salaried men for upward mobility. Gender-segregated roles and limited resources induced unequal opportunities for education and employment for daughters. The aspiration for daughters to marry non-farmers in cities reflected rural women's desire for social and economic improvement. Becoming a housewife was seen as a middle-class aspiration tied to the image of salarymen and living in apartments in urban areas. Daughters' marriage to urban men was a strategy for inter-generational mobility. Despite some progress, gender norms and hierarchies within families and communities persisted, limiting rural women's bargaining power and ability to challenge existing orders. The negotiation process involved justifying their activities as serving the community and maintaining traditional roles. The persistence of extended families and caregiving norms further shaped rural women's decision-making and aspirations.

Notes

1 Personal communication with H. Kim, who was a high-ranking male manager of a large conglomerate in Korea on July 9, 2007. He studies at one of the elite universities in Seoul after studying in a middle school in the city.
2 J. Yun is a former rural resident who moved to the city in the late 1970s to educate her children (personal communication on July 9, 2006).
3 Ko Sŏnjŏng (2020) discusses the urban housing policy implemented by the Park Chung Hee regime as part of the modernization project. Through this governmental initiative, complex-style apartments were built for the first time and became a token of the middle class.
4 S. Sŏ majored in social welfare at university in the 1970s, after which she decided to work for the "weak", becoming a social movement activist for small farmers and workers (personal communication on November 18, 2006).
5 According to the gradual growth of the concept of leisure among the middle class in the late 1970s, a new trend of organizing one- or two-day bus tours for refreshment emerged in rural villages. One or two buses were rented for a collective trip by the residents of a rural village to visit touristic places near villages. For younger generations, organizing such bus tours came to be positioned as a way to express filial piety to one's parents, parents-in-law, and the elderly in the village (*Kyunghang Shinmun* May 23, 1977; *Kyunghang Shinmun* October 20, 1977), and such travels for the elderly in a rural village were usually organized by young rural mothers for parents-in-law. Given the insufficient financial situation, rural women often organized *kye* for the arrangement of bus tours for parents-in-law and the elderly (*Kyunghang Shinmun* October 28, 1977).
6 S. Lim started her organizational activity with the New Community Movement and later joined the peasant movements. Since then, she has worked as an activist for peasant movements for over 30 years (personal communication on August 4, 2008).

Bibliography

Brinton, Mary. 1988. "The Social-Institutional Bases of Gender Stratification: Japan as an Illustrative Case." *American Journal of Sociology* 94: 300–334.
Chang, Kyung-sup. 2002. "South Korean Society in the IMF Era: Compressed Capitalist Development and Social Sustainability." In *Rethinking Development in East Asia: From*

Illusory Miracle to Economic Crisis, edited by Pietro P. Masina, 189–222. London: Curzon.
Chang, Kyung-sup. 2010. *South Korea under Compressed Modernity: Familial Political Economy in Transition*. London and New York: Routledge.
Chang Migyŏng. 2004. "Kŭndaehwa wa 1960–70nyŏndae yŏsŏng nodongja (Modernization and Women Workers in the 1960s and 1970s)." *Kyŏngje wa sahoe (Economy and Society)* 61: 100–126.
Chosun Ilbo. 1978. "Nongch'on sŏdo taegajok chedo ka hŭndŭllinda (The Collapse of Large Families in Rural Society)." April 11.
Donga Ilbo. 1977. "Nongch'on ch'ŏnyŏ (Rural Women)." February 28.
Gelb, Joyce, and Marian Lief Palley. 1994. "Introduction." In *Women of Japan and Korea: Continuity and Change*, edited by Joyce Gelb and Marian Lief Palley, 1–22. Philadelphia: Temple University Press.
Greenhalgh, Susan. 1985. "Sexual Stratification: The Other Side of 'Growth with Equity' in East Asia." *Population and Development Review* 11, no. 2: 265–314. https://doi.org/10.2307/1973489
Hŏ Minsuk. 2014. "Yŏsŏng kusul saengaesa ro pon kaebal shigi toshi iju yŏsŏng ŭi kŭndae kyŏnghŏm kwa kach'i pyŏnhwa (The Experiences of Rural-urban Migrant Women during Industrialization and Changes in Social Values)." *Kajok kwa munhwa (Family and Culture)* 26, no. 3: 177–211.
Kim Hyegyŏng. 2009. "Pak chŏnghŭi ch'eje ha 'haekkajok tamnon ŭi pyŏnhwa gwajŏng gwa iwŏn gujo yŏn'gu (Discourses on the Nuclear Family and the Double Structure during the Park Chung Hee Era)." *Sahoe wa yŏksa (Society and History)* 82: 169–212.
Kim Hyeyŏng. 2016. "Tongwŏndoen kajok chuŭi ŭi shidae esŏ kajok wihŏm ŭi sahoero (From the Era of Mobilized Familism to Familism with Risk)." *Han'guk sahoe (Korean Society)* 17, no. 2: 3–44.
Kim, Seung-kyung. 1997. *Class Struggle or Family Struggle: The Lives of Women Factory Workers in South Korea*. New York: Cambridge University Press.
Kim Suyŏng. 2001. "Han'guk ŭi sanŏp'wa gwajŏng gwa kajok, yŏsŏng (Family and Women in Industrialization)." *Chinbo p'yŏngnon (Progressive Critique)* 7: 57–75.
Kim Yŏnchu, and Yi Chaekyŏng. 2013. "Kŭndae 'kajŏng jubu' doegi kkwajŏng gwa toshi chungsanch'ŭng kajog ŭi hyŏngsŏng (The Process of Becoming a Modern Housewife and the Construction of the Urban Middle-Class Family)." *Kajok gwa munhwa (Family and Culture)* 25, no. 2: 29–61.
Kim, Yun-Jung. 2005. "Reconciling Work and Motherhood: The Experiences of Korean Working Mothers." Doctoral diss., University of Bath.
Kincaid, D. Lawrence, Hyung-Jong Park, Kyung-Kyoon Chung, and Chin-Chuan Lee. 1975. *Mothers' Clubs and Family Planning in Rural Korea: The Case of Oryu Li*. Honolulu: East-West Communication Institute.
Ko Sŏnjŏng. 2020. "1960–70nyŏndae ap'at'ŭ ŭi saenghwal hyŏngmyŏng kwa mulchil munhwa e kwanhan yŏn'gu (Study of the Housing Revolution and the Material Culture of Apartments in the 1960s and 1970s)." *Sangp'um munhwa tijainhak yŏn'gu (Studies in Product Cultural Design)* 63: 253–262.
Kyunghyang Shinmun. 1977. "Porit kogae ch'ŏnnyŏn kanan pŏtko toshihwa param (Leisure: Escape from Poverty and the Modernization of the Rural Village)." May 23.
Kyunghyang Shinmun. 1977. "Kwan'gwang param yŏga param: hyodo ch'inmok kwan'gwang kye (Leisure: Kye for Filial Piety and Relationship-building)." October 20.
Kyunghyang Shinmun. 1977. "Kwan'gwang param yŏga param p'yŏngsaeng ch'ŏŭm nadŭri (Leisure: The First Leisure in Life)." October 28.
Pae Ŭnkyŏng. 2008. "Kusul saengaesa rŭl t'onghae pon sanŏp'wa shigi han'guk ŏmŏni ŭi mosŏng kyŏnghŏm kyŏngjejŏk kiyŏ wa tolbom nodong, ch'injok kwan'gye kwalli ŭi kyŏrhap (Mothering Experiences of Korean Women in the Industrialization Period: Combining Economic Support, Care Work, and Relation Management for Family)." *P'eminijŭm yŏn'gu (Feminist Studies)* 8, no. 1: 69–123.

Parish, William L., and Robert J. Willis. 1993. "Daughters, Education, and Family Budgets: Taiwan Experiences." *The Journal of Human Resources* 28: 863–898. https://doi.org/10.2307/146296

Salaff, Janet W. 1981. *Working Daughters of Hong Kong: Filial Piety or Power in the Family?* New York: Columbia University Press.

Yi Hyojae, and Kim Chusuk. 1976. "Yŏsŏng kyŏngje hwaltong mit ch'wiŏp e kwanhan yŏn'gu-1960-70nyŏndae ŭi ch'ui (A Study on the Economic Activities and Employment of Women in the 1960s and 1970s in South Korea)." *Ihwanonjip (Ewha Journal)* 27: 267–293.

Yi Jŏngŭn. 2010. "Kukche kyŏrhon kajŏng ŭi oegugin shinbu wa chiyŏk sahoe hwaltong (Foreign Brides of International Families and their Community Activities)." *Chungang minsok'hak (Central Folklore Studies)* 15: 127–171.

Yi Mijŏng. 1998. "Kajok nae ŭi sŏngch'abyŏlchŏk kyoyuk T'uja (Gender-segregated Educational Investment in Family)." *Han'guk sahoehak (Korean Sociology)* 3: 63–97.

Conclusion

Gender, Class, and State–Society Relations

This final chapter revisits its earlier discussions on the domestication of rural women's labor during South Korean industrialization. This study addresses the following research questions: How did the Park Chung Hee regime interact with rural women in the 1960s and 1970s when South Korea faced urban-centered industrialization? What do the interactions between the state and rural women, who were marginalized social actors, tell us about the growth of the middle class and the dis(continuities) of gender relations during the industrialization of the 1960s and 1970s in South Korea?

This chapter starts with a discussion of the continuity of gender hierarchies during the Park Chung Hee regime, under which "traditional" gender norms were newly packaged as "modern" using terms such as "modernization" and "development". Given its systematic yet informal everyday-life interventions and the consequences of these interventions on the formation of social values of the middle class for all women, including working-class women, the politics of the Park Chung Hee regime were distinctly gendered. The second section revisits Maria Mies' housewifization theory for its applicability to the housewifization process of rural women in South Korea. It discusses how the housewife ideology of the middle class came to be embraced by working-class women and how this process was closely connected to the growth of the middle class in South Korea. Moreover, using the concept of "patriarchal bargain" (Kandiyoti 1988), this research analyzes how gender relations were not (re)constructed, despite women's growing negotiating capacity. Next, state–society relations in South Korea during industrialization in the 1960s and 1970s will be reconsidered. Finally, the chapter summarizes the main findings and contributions of the research and suggests avenues for future research.

The Park Chung Hee Regime and Gender: The Institutionalization of Gender Relations and Middle-Classness

Scholarship in cultural studies has attempted to understand patriarchal gender orders in family relations and the workplace in East Asia from a Confucianism view (see Brinton 2001; Brinton et al. 1995). Women in East Asia are expected to be "wise mothers and good wives" who take good care of the well-being of the family in the domestic sphere, physically and emotionally. Married women's complete devotion to children's physical and mental development, including academic

DOI: 10.4324/9781003110538-8

achievement and career success are considered particularly important aspects of motherhood. In the Korean context, there have also been scholarly attempts to analyze gender relations from the Confucianism perspective (Kim 2005; Kim Suyŏng 2001). Even though Confucianism can provide great insights into understanding the relationship between the past and the present in gender relations in East Asia, Moon (2002) maintains that "this explanation fails to investigate why the Confucian tradition persists and how 'tradition' itself is constructed" (ibid., 82). That is, she raises the question of the ahistorical nature of the cultural approach. Thus, she notes the necessity to focus on the engagement of various social actors in the development of the housewife ideology process in specific cultural contexts. Similarly, the analysis of the (re)construction of gender relations should not rely on cultural elements but should be contextualized within a class-based, cultural, and historical background (Moore 1988).

Traditionalization of Modernity

It is necessary to go back to the era of Japanese colonial rule and US military administration to understand how gender ideology was (re)institutionalized for women during the Park Chung Hee regime. How the concept of "family" changed and how the role of women within the family was newly defined during the Japanese colonial era remains controversial. One scholarly view maintains that the introduction of the legal system weakened the "traditional" family patriarchy and helped develop a "modern" family system (Kim Duhŏn 1969). Another view posits that Japan's patriarchal system further strengthened the patriarchal system in Korea (Pak Pyŏngho 1986). Kim Hyegyŏng (2006) focuses on the introduction of modern school systems and laws on women's status within the family as the institutional foundation that changed family structures and the roles of women within the family during the Japanese colonial era. Myriad factors contributed to the creation of the new image of women based on the concepts of "motherhood" and "housewife". The concept of "children" as entities to be protected, cared for, and educated was also introduced alongside the modern concept of "motherhood". With the spread of disciplines such as home economics and early childhood education, the concept of the "housewife", which meant a woman in charge of managing a family, became widespread. Furthermore, the Japanese colonial regime and educated modern intellectuals, upper-class women, and activists who attempted to make use of the reform of the family system for national liberation movements were involved in the dissemination of such gender norms. In the modernization process in Japan, the concept of "good wife, wise mother" was proliferated as one of the disciplines of the Meiji government (1868–1912).

After the liberation in 1945, the first national administrative department in charge of women's welfare was established. The US military government, which began to rule after the liberation, set up a Women's Bureau in the Health and Welfare Department in charge of women-related agendas in 1946. The Bureau was established, "first, to improve the social, economic, political, and cultural aspects of Korean women; second, investigate and collect materials on the status and welfare of Korean women; third, establish basic policies to promote the well-being of Korean women" (Ministry of Health and Social Welfare 1987, 51).

Hwang Chŏngmi (2001, 36–44) considers the background of the establishment of the Women's Bureau and clarifies the fundamental ideas behind the foundation of this administrative department, finding that the establishment of such a women-related administrative agency positioned women as part of the "socially vulnerable". The Women's Bureau was among the departments founded when the Health and Social Welfare Department was expanded from the Division of Sanitation of the Police Bureau under the rule of the Government-General of Korea during the Japanese colonial period. The Health and Social Welfare Department was mainly in charge of managing so-called "socially vulnerable people", such as the poor, children, the unemployed, and prostitutes.

The birth of the Women's Bureau reflected ideas from the US government about welfare and women. The Women's Bureau was mainly engaged in enlightenment activities centered on the improvement of health and hygiene conditions, food, clothing, and shelter. There was the perception of an urgent need to enlighten "ignorant" Korean women with Western values, such as "democracy", "equality", the "creation of a rational living environment", "childcare", "education", and the "nurturing of motherhood". Thus, women were positioned as objects to be "guided" and "monitored" (Hwang Chŏngmi 1999, 178). Similarly, the policy interventions initiated by the US military government did not mean positioning women as "individuals" but as a collective entity; that is, a "good mother, good wife, good daughter" within a "family-centered approach" (Shin Hyŏnok 1999, 42). Among these roles, "good mother" was particularly emphasized, as women were considered responsible for family welfare and childcare. This idea was often demonstrated in a bulletin called *sae sallim* (New Household), published from 1947 to 1949, and such a position appears in the congratulatory address of the chief of the Health and Social Welfare Department: "There are many problems that must be resolved urgently for our people. Among them, it is vital to nurture "good mothers" by enlightening, protecting, and guiding them, as they are responsible for their family life" (Health and Social Welfare Department 1987, 58).

These fundamental ideas were inherited and systematically developed by the Korean government, established in 1948. "Modernization" in all realms of life, including clothing, food, housing, and health and hygiene improvement was promoted in earnest with the establishment of the Life Improvement Division in the Women's Bureau (Hwang Chŏngmi 2001, 46). In this process, "traditional" rituals and customs were deemed "old bad customs". That is, "tradition" was regarded as a concept contrary to the "modernity" of a rational, scientific, and modernized Western world (Shin Hyŏnok 1999).

Even after the inauguration of the Park Chung Hee regime, there was no significant change in the framework of the organizations and the content of women-related administration. Women were positioned as being mainly responsible for the welfare of their family members through their gendered roles as wives and mothers. Family planning projects were used as a means of poverty alleviation rather than improving women's decision-making on their reproductive behaviors.

The Park Chung Hee regime's policy on rural women in the 1960s was greatly influenced by the administration of the US military government and its welfare approach to women. The Park Chung Hee regime's perspective on rural women changed in the 1970s along with the progress of rapid urbanization and industrialization and the sharp decrease in the working population from the latter half of the 1960s to the 1970s. Following such shifts, the Park Chung Hee regime positioned rural women as workers and family managers in the local community through the New Community Movement by building a new image of "modern" rural women.

However, the fact that the Park Chung Hee regime expanded the area of activity of rural women from the home to the community did not necessarily mean women were recognized as leaders in the family or community. As discussed in this book, women were assigned the role of conveyors of information for the "modernization of the kitchen", and the scope of their domestic labor expanded to the local community. The role of a "wise mother and good wife" in charge of the home was expanded to include responsibility for the welfare of the local community, with women becoming responsible for joint cooking, daycare management, environmental improvement projects of the New Community Movement, and the preparation of banquets for the elderly. Furthermore, the role of "wise mother and good wife" was "natural" and "correct" and was a cornerstone of the modernization of the motherland. Hence, the Park regime's gender ideology for women demonstrated duality: while it championed modernity, its "modern" gender roles were based on the continuity of "traditional" ones. As with the definition of "tradition", "modernity" was ill-defined, fluid, mobile, and contradictory (Rofel 1994, 1999). "'Tradition' and 'modernity' are complex categories that are often defined only in opposition to one another" (Ashford 2020, 61). Thus, these two categories were rife with multiplicities, contradictions, and complexities during the Park Chung Hee era (Kim Ŭnshil 1999).

Middle-Classness and the Institutionalization of Becoming a Housewife in Everyday Life for "All" Women

The importance of the continuity of gender politics under the Park Chung Hee regime, dating to the Japanese colonialism and US military occupation periods, in understanding (un)changing gender relations in South Korea cannot be underestimated. However, it is also necessary to examine the (re)construction of gender relations during the 1960s and 1970s, as these periods were central to the institutionalization of housewifization. Among the most distinctive features of the (re)construction process of gender relations during the Park Chung Hee regime is that "being or becoming a modern woman" was regulated by the state as a major part of modern nation-state building politics (Kim Hyŏnmi 2000; Kim Ŭnshil 1999; Yi Suja 2000). From a formal institutional perspective, Moon (2002) maintains that Korean family law from 1960 through 1990 reinforced the breadwinner ideology for males and the housewife ideology for women by legally recognizing every married man as a household authority. Some studies have attempted to unpack gender relations in Korea by highlighting the informal institutionalizing of the housewife ideology during industrialization (Chang Migyŏng 2007; Kim Yŏnchu and Yi Chaekyŏng 2013). Meanwhile, there have been few scholarly attempts to shed light on the experiences of becoming a housewife among lower- and working-class women during industrialization in South Korea, even though most women in this period belonged to these social class categories. In this sense, an analysis of the informal institutional dimension of the state's social management of making rural women housewives – which was firmly embedded into the everyday lives of rural women, as already noted – provides an important insight into understanding how gender roles were legitimatized in everyday life.

In elaborating on womanhood during the Park Chung Hee regime, it is important to remember that middle-class women and, indeed, *all* women were redefined as housewives, regardless of whether they were *de facto* housewives (Kim Hyegyŏng 2009). In this regard, "being/becoming a housewife" was central to discourses on modern womanhood in Korea in the 1960s and 1970s. In short, it is the period when the "normative gender constructs of husband-provider and housewife became firmly established" (Moon 2002, 85). First, gender norms for middle-class women had become *the* norms and indicators for *all* women regarding the value of labor, consumer practices, leisure, savings, and mothering practices. As already discussed, even though rural women were considered indispensable productive labor given the lack of a rural labor force during the period of rapid urbanization, the value of rural women's labor was depreciated and seen as auxiliary and subordinate to men's labor. The gendered division of domestic labor was clearly defined through wide-ranging rural development projects (see Chapter 2). Rural women were the main targets for family planning, and "good" motherhood was defined as a reduction in the number of children (see Chapter 3). Through savings initiatives and state-led organizational activities, rural women were expected to take charge of the home and national economies (see Chapter 4). Hence, to facilitate this goal, they were organized, instructed, and monitored by the state through organizational activities (see Chapter 5). The making of rural women into housewives also holds special significance in shaping the meaning of middle-classness for the general populace. Regarding the persistent involvement of the state in the proliferation of the housewife ideology, there are similarities with imperial Japan regarding the development of the housewife ideology during the Park Chung Hee regime. Lu (2013) notes the "fluidness" of the definition of "good" middle-class women during imperial Japan, with a special focus on Japanese emigrant women in Manchuria and California. For instance, while the labor of emigrant women who migrated to Manchuria as "continent brides" was highly praised for supporting Japan's expansionism, labor by Japanese female migrant workers on the Western coast of the United States was heavily criticized as a national shame because it failed to realize the US' middle-class housewife ideology. Despite the constant fluidness in defining the "ideal" middle-classness of women, the state's claim was consistent in that it aimed to disseminate a middle-class hegemony by instilling a housewife ideology in *all* women.

Similarly, even though discourses on "ideal" housewives during the Park Chung Hee regime were somewhat inconsistent and contradictory in their approaches to urban and rural women, as discussed elsewhere in this book, state intervention in women's everyday lives was consistent, as the idea persistently existed that women should be controlled, monitored, and disciplined as "housewives". Hence, state intervention was expected to contribute to the modernization of the motherland. Institutions are perceived as "desirable, proper, [and] appropriate within some socially constructed system of norms, values, beliefs, and definitions" (Suchman 1995, 574). Likewise, the state as an institutional actor plays a crucial role in constructing beliefs and norms, and the involvement of the state is related to institutionalization and the legitimacy of social discourse.

Revisiting the Housewifization Theory

As Maria Mies (1998) demonstrates, the domestication of women is a common phenomenon that accompanies modernization. Mies' (ibid.) research contributes to the identification of "labor by women" in general and "labor by women in the late-industrializing countries", marginalized in discussions on the political economy of capitalism, as labor in the informal sector is predominant in the late-industrializing countries.

Despite many years since Mies' (1998) work, it still provides great insights today. Regarding women's labor market participation, the theory still reflects the current situation women face. Despite the conspicuous feminization of the labor market, women are overrepresented in the informal sectors and are concentrated in low-paid labor under neoliberal labor market reform. The situation women in South Korea face is no different. For instance, during the COVID-19 pandemic, many female workers have been required to "come back home" given the increasing demand for care and the growing cost of caretaking. Approximately 476,000 female workers had to leave the labor market in South Korea in 2020 given the growing demand for care and the collapse of the women-dominated service sector (Kwon 2021). Similar to foreign workers in the care and emotional labor sectors at the global level, women in late-industrializing countries suffer from exploitative working conditions (Boris and Parreñas 2010; Romero, Preston, and Giles 2014). The housewifization theory provides a meaningful theoretical framework to better understand the "feminization" of labor in the labor market and the household. Tilly and Scott (1989) clarify the unchanging gender relations despite the participation of working-class women during industrialization in France and the United Kingdom. However, the "'housewifization' of women at a global level does not take place everywhere in an identical manner" (Moon 2002, 84).

Women's Domestication and Class: Urban and Rural Housewives

Previous research on the domestication of women's labor shows that the housewife ideology was actively embraced by upper-, middle-, and working-class women as their new identities. It is important to pay attention to the relations of middle- and working-class women within the housewife ideology because middle-class women became an "ideal" of middle-classness for rural working-class women. Focusing on the domestication process of working-class women during industrialization in

Great Britain, Bourke (1994) depicts how working-class married women "increasingly came to define themselves primarily as housewives" (168) and how they often thought that "housewifery was a good – even the *best* – option" (171).[1]

This active acceptance of the housewife ideology by working-class women can be interpreted within the context of the emergence of full-time housewives who were free from the burden of domestic labor. As Duchen (1991) illustrates, working women's labor was usually represented as "underqualified, underpaid, [and] doing jobs without interest, career prospects or responsibility" (ibid., 9); therefore, "working-class women were sometimes relieved to give up paid employment (ibid., 9)." Garon (2010) also argues that many Japanese women were pleased to identify themselves as full-time housewives, as they perceived it as "a status that struck most women as a marked improvement from their previous lives of hard physical labour" (ibid., 330–331). Chang Migyŏng (2007) maintains that middle-class housewives could make a living by performing only housework, unlike lower-class working women who had to do formal labor and housework. While home for middle-class women had a symbolic value as an "economic and emotional universe" (Duchen 1991, 9), home for working-class women "represented the double shift rather [than] the haven from the world of work" (ibid., 8). In this contrast, the home was a societal space symbolizing social status for middle-class women. Liberation from arduous productive labor, although limited, allowed women to enjoy a degree of comfort they had never experienced before. Chang Migyŏng (2007) maintains that relative to lower working-class women, the economic freedom and physical comfort of middle-class women would have made them satisfied with their lives as husband-dependent beings.

As Pae Ŭn'kyŏng states (2008), it was in the late 1970s that the modern gendered division of labor and modern housewives emerged in Korean society. As the Korean economy continued to grow rapidly until the mid-1970s, male workers who were stably employed in high-wage jobs began to emerge as a group that could earn enough income to support an entire family. This confluence of factors enabled the establishment of the modern Korean nuclear family. Meanwhile, as discussed, it is important to consider how "labor" had been newly defined within the housewife ideology and how the middle-class housewife was rigidly established as a strong "imaginary" exemplar for working-class women by the mid-1970s. In her anthropological research on the upward social aspirations of women during industrialization in the 1960s and 1970s in South Korea, Abelmann (2002) depicts the paradoxical mindset of an interviewee who relates that even though she appreciates her labor as a means for her family's upward social mobility, she devalues it as being at odds with the values of the upper- and middle-class and women in general.

Previous research notes the significant contributions of the rural populace toward economic development (see Chang 2010; Kim Suyŏng 2001). Regarding women's contributions in terms of economic growth, Abelmann (2002) maintains in her anthropological research that the desires of women during industrialization functioned as a driving force in the formation of the middle class in South Korea. This book portrays the mechanisms by which rural women, who were the bulk of the female populace at that time, attempted to achieve middle-class status by partly accepting and partly resisting the ideology of housewife suggested by the state; that is, actions that contributed to laying down a solid foundation for the formation of the middle class in South Korea and the construction of a middle-class identity.

The examination of relations between middle- and working-class women in the prevalence of the housewife ideology is important to understand the (re)construction of gender relations in South Korea. Chang Migyŏng (2007) maintains that traditional patriarchy could be carried over to modern patriarchy without any resistance from middle-class women, as they embraced the housewife ideology and were somewhat satisfied with their liberation from physical labor and with their newfound social status as household managers. Their social position was further legitimized through modern terms such as "childcare", "children's education", "motherhood", and "nuclear family" (Chang Migyŏng 2007). As middle-class women were viewed as role models for working-class women, rural women assumedly aimed for the practices and social values of housewives and their family relations. For instance, as discussed in Chapter 3, rural women admired intensive mothering, though it was impossible for them to fully concentrate on their children's education given the time constraints placed on them by their gendered labor. Hays (1996) argues that intensive motherhood is a set of highly gendered practices given the unequally distributed gender roles in children's education. Furthermore, she maintains that the full devotion of a mother to her children is likely to be practiced by middle- and upper-class mothers with more time, energy, and resources. In this context, however, the ideal motherhood of middle-class women was, ultimately, shared by lower-class mothers because of the increasingly popular social norm of the meaning of a "good" mother.

Aspirations toward Becoming a Housewife and the Middle Class: Gender and Class

Yang (2018, 14) notes that the middle class in South Korea should be understood in the context of "social narratives", as "concepts of the middle class in Korea were expressed, discussed, represented, and imagined in public discourses". Thus, it is essential to pay special attention to the fact that social narratives concerning middle-classness were proliferated among a still rural and agricultural populace. This fact is a crucial facet of the historical process of the formation of the middle class in South Korea, even more so than specific socioeconomic indicators of social class (Roberts 1993).

Pahl (1989) argues that the analysis of class should shift its focus "from the categorization of individuals, families, and households by their *attributes* to a categorization according to their *attitudes* and values" (ibid., 713, italics in original). Thus, class is not a fixed and static term that can be defined based on economic factors but a fluid entity that can be constructed and reconstructed by people in everyday life. Within this approach, the understanding of class shifts from class action and consciousness to the notion of "identity". It means that people try to *do* class within a broad spectrum of everyday life practices to identify themselves in specific ways in various dimensions and evaluate and categorize others who do not share similar socioeconomic and cultural practices.

This understanding of class is useful in analyzing women. First, it sheds light on noneconomic factors such as lifestyle, residency, consumer practices, belonging in particular neighborhoods, and mothering practices (see Reay 2005; Savage et al. 2005; Skeggs 2004). It is particularly meaningful, as women's social class is typically discussed via either the socioeconomic status of their husbands or male relatives (Reay 1998). Feminist sociologists have attempted to expand the boundaries of social class from being restrained by objective economic measures and labor market participation in the official sphere. For instance, Reay (ibid., 259) argues that "we need to rethink social class as a dynamic mobile aspect of identity that continues to permeate daily interactions" by highlighting mothers' actions and attitudes in children's education.

Second, this approach to class pays more attention to women's subjectivities in constructing and reconstructing the boundaries of social class. Abelmann's (2002) ethnographic research vividly depicts that women's desires during industrialization were the main driving force in the formation of the South Korean middle class. Similarly, the middle class in the 1960s and 1970s in South Korea was not a reflection of society's real class structure but "an aspirational category" (Yang 2018, 21). Understanding class as an aspirational category means the boundaries of class are constantly being defined, restructured, and tested, despite their tangibility and significance (Fernandes and Heller 2006). In the Korean context, the boundaries of the middle class, though unclearly defined, were negotiable and closely related to the dramatic social changes of the 1960s and 1970s. Kendall (2002, 3) states that, from the 1960s through the 1980s, "despite intense political frustration, [there was] a period of optimism marked by a sense that things would get better because, by all visible markers of material life, things were palpably improving". South Korean society shared the idea that it was a society open to social mobility based on the "we were all poor together" mindset in the 1960s and 1970s (Abelmann 2002, 29). South Koreans perceived a sense of openness in this period given the rapid industrialization and urbanization, the improvement of life in general, the outbreak of the Korean War, the shared memory of devastation, land reform, perceptions of rural society as being egalitarian, and repetitive official rhetoric proclaiming equal opportunities for all (ibid.). Finally, the notion of class as an aspirational category provides great insight into understanding how it was "gendered" and how women did, redid, and undid class on a daily-life basis in the South Korean context during industrialization.

(Re)construction of Gender Relations: Negotiation and Agency

According to eminent feminist activist and scholar, Cho Haejoang (2002), women began to identify themselves as "wives who orchestrated nuclear households rather than as mothers who were embedded in a larger family collective" (ibid., 173) since the 1960s. This period was when "the first transition of postcolonial South Korea from traditional patriarchy to modern patriarchy began" (ibid., 167).

In Cho's research, urban middle-class women are depicted as managers of the incomes of their husbands, who invest fully and earnestly in their children's education. Further, they are shown as people who attempt to achieve upward mobility through informal economic activities, such as speculative investment in real estate, organizing informal rotating credit associations, and saving money while shopping. However, middle-class women are also depicted as greedily urging their husbands to make more money by any means, pushing their children to extremes to achieve academic success, and arranging their children's marriages to achieve upward social mobility.

It is important to raise the question of whether the development process of the housewife ideology in urban areas was also applicable to rural women, as most of the population remained rural and agrarian until the early 1960s. As modernity has various forms (Stivens 1998), so are the experiences of modernities of women in "non-Western" countries (Mohanty 1988; Ong 1988). The experiences of modernity are also diverse within a nation. This book clarifies that rural women strongly aspired to reach a particular form of women's middle-classness, including being stay-at-home housewives who were free from burdensome work, engaged in intensive mothering, were managers of household economies, had nuclear families and modern residences, and had husband–wife-centered families without interference from their mothers-in-law. As discussed, some of the aspirations toward "becoming" middle class were achieved. For instance, contrary to the original intentions of the state, family planning was perceived as a path to children's education and intensive mothering practices of middle-class women (Chapter 3). Given the increasing opportunities to engage in organizational activities, rural women's autonomy within the household economy and decision-making capacity greatly expanded (Chapters 3 through Chapter 5). This situation strengthened the bargaining power of women in their relationships with their husbands and mothers-in-law (Chapter 5). Cho (2002), for instance, argues that rural women began to retort to their mothers-in-law under rapidly changing family structures during industrialization and urbanization, as they considered their mothers-in-law to be undereducated and outdated people who might have negative influences on their children's education. Such stories are often cited in newspaper articles reporting on intergenerational conflicts from the end of the 1970s. At the center of the conflicts were married women and their mothers-in-law, with conflicts varying from family planning surgical procedures (*Kyunghyang Shinmun* August 9, 1977) to different ideas on caring for the elderly (*Kyunghyang Shinmun* June 14, 1979) and the growing decision-making power of daughters-in-law in purchasing household goods (*Kyunghyang Shinmun* July 7, 1977). These growing intergenerational conflicts reflect rural women's endeavors to challenge conventional relations within the family.

It is also necessary to investigate constraining factors in rural women's negotiations within the context of the (re)formation of gender relations. Kandiyoti (1988) coined the term "patriarchal bargain" to describe how women challenge, negotiate, and adapt to the set of rules that shape and constrain gender relations. For example, despite their active response to opportunities for their children's education during the Park Chung Hee regime and their efforts to embrace their own intensive motherhood, rural mothers often played the role of mother to their sons, not their daughters, regarding the allocation of educational opportunities and financial resources among children. This disparity was a consequence of the gender-segregated labor market and rural women's strategic patriarchal bargain, considering the unchanged familial structure and the idea that "sons are a woman's most critical resource, ensuring their life-long loyalty is an enduring preoccupation" (ibid, 279). This patriarchal bargain should be understood in the context of the family based Korean capitalist system, where rural-urban migrants and "left-over" (mainly married rural women) family members were codependent in the building of a family based welfare system (Kim Suyŏng 2001).

However, unlike their urban counterparts, rural women were hesitant to achieve a status as "wives". Even though rural women were somewhat active in building husband–wife-centered families, broadening their autonomy in the household economy and adjusting relations with their mothers-in-law, they did not radically change gender relations within the family, as they were caught between new social transformations and conventional gender roles within the family. For instance, regarding the relationship with their mothers-in-law, they were rather careful, as social norms within the family remained "traditional" despite the transformation of the family structure from the extended to nuclear family (Kim Hyeyŏng 2016). Hence, rural women had to bargain between "the cyclical nature of women's power in the household, their anticipation of inheriting the authority of senior women" (Kandiyoti 1988, 279), and the aspiration toward challenging their conventional gender roles as daughters-in-law.

Rethinking the State–Society Relations in South Korea

In discussions on economic development in South Korea, much emphasis has been put on the role of the state (see Amsden 1989), professional bureaucracy (see Evans 1995; Haggard 2004), and state-capitalist relations (see Castells 1992; Johnson 1987). Among these, the state is consistently at the center of discussion (Amsden 1989; Evans 1989; Haggard and Moon 1983; Wade 1990a, 1990b; White and Wade 1988; Zhao and Hall 1994). However, "ordinary" people's engagement in economic development has been overlooked. In particular, the role of women, who supported the family-based capitalist system in South Korea during industrialization, has been under-researched (Kim Suyŏng 2001). This book addresses this oversight by investigating state–society interactions, with a special focus on rural women. Accordingly, it furnishes a better grasp of a specific picture of economic development, not as a "visible" achievement figured in numbers and graphs, but as an "invisible" accumulation of people's experiences and aspirations, aspirations that shaped the middle class in South Korea.

The literature has also focused on the autonomy of the state in the modernization process in South Korea. However, as Park (2010, 581) notes, "how these developmental states have sought to define societal projects and mobilize people around these goals" has been little discussed. This book examines state–society relations not as "static" and "fixed" but as "negotiable" and "dynamic". This work considers how rural women were instructed by the state to "learn" to be or become middle-class women from managing the kitchen to reducing the number of children. Moreover, the modernization of rural villages was directly connected with the modernization of the nation. This state-led social management process resonates with the modernization process in Japan (see Garon 1997). Hence, the boundary between the private and the public was ambiguous and ill-defined, as is commonly seen in the Asian context (Moon 2002).

Finally, state–society relations were not one-directional, but interactive. Thus, state autonomy in East Asia was "not simply passive compliance from the people but the enthusiastic participation of many private groups in its ambitious programs to manage society" (Garon 1997, xv). From the study analyses, rural women were identified as "rural housewives"; however, their active engagement with state intervention contributed to forming the middle class, constructing middle-class identity in South Korea, and (re)constructing gender relations at the national level.

Findings and Future Research

The work has highlighted the dynamic interactions between the strong developmental state and society during the Korean industrialization in the 1960s and 1970s by shedding light on a marginalized social group from a scholarly point of view: rural women. By analyzing the aspiration toward becoming middle class by rural women and (re)constructing gender relations during industrialization, this research suggests a multilayered approach to analyzing state–society relations. It has demonstrated that the housewife ideology was promoted by the Park Chung Hee regime in the daily lives of rural women as a means of modernizing the motherland. Even though the image of "becoming housewives" was originally intended to assist urban-centered industrialization and reconcile state–society relations in rural areas, rural women attempted to embrace the housewife ideology as a measure for social upward mobility, namely, the aspiration of "becoming middle class". Therefore, the development process of the housewife ideology for lower-, working-class women in South Korea should be understood as an "aspirational category". Nonetheless, rural women's adaptations and negotiations and the challenges they posed to state intervention in their daily lives are significant to understanding the formation of the middle class and the construction of middle-class identity in South Korea. Finally, on a theoretical level, this research has attempted to further systematize Maria Mies' housewifization theory using a historical, sociocultural, and class-based approach.

While the findings of this book contribute insight into the state–society relations, aspirations of the working class toward city-based virtues of the middle class, and the (re)construction of gender relations during the industrialization of the 1960s and 1970s South Korea, the research has several limitations. First, even though this research clarified the process of how gender relations were (re)constructed during this period, it did not discuss the interconnectedness of gender relations in the present. For instance, despite the continual gender inequalities in the labor market, the preference for sons regarding birth has improved in recent years. A more detailed discussion on the continuities and changes in gender relations should be followed. Next, though the research focused on rural women's aspiration as a collective imaginary category, the differences among rural women, such as educational background, regionality, and political preferences, were not reflected in how these differences influenced responses to governmental intervention and the discourses on the middle-class aspiration. Finally, Western countries were partly depicted in this book as a unified, fixed, and static entity comprising a dichotomous relationship with societies in Asia. A more careful analysis of the domestication process of women in the Western context and a detailed comparative perspective is necessary.

Note

1 Similarly, Gordon (1997) notes that the number of wives of working-class families engaged in wage labor was small, as they were pleased to identify themselves as housewives in Japan. He notes that "it is important to recognize how many women were 'ready' to hear the movement's messages by virtue of their place in the social structure" (269). He pinpoints how women's positive reactions to the proliferation of the housewife ideology can be understood given that women appreciated the state intervention and middle-class reformers' encouragement through the New Life Movement in Japan to be an opportunity "to make their work more efficient, more 'modern', more scientific, and by implication, more respected" (270).

Bibliography

Abelmann, Nancy. 2002. "Women, Mobility, and Desire: Narrating Class and Gender in South Korea." In *Under Construction: The Gendering of Modernity, Class, and Consumption in the Republic of Korea*, edited by Laurel Kendall, 25–53. Honolulu: University of Hawai'i Press.

Amsden, Alice. 1989. *Asia's Next Giant: South Korea and Late Industrialization*. New York: Oxford University Press. https://doi.org/10.1016/0305-750X(94)90111-2

Ashford, Holly Rose. 2020. "Modern Motherhood, Masculinity, and Family Planning in Ghana, 1960–75." *Journal of West African History* 6, no. 2: 61–91. https://doi.org/10.14321/jwestafrihist.6.2.0061

Boris, Eileen, and Rhacel Salazar Parreñas (eds.). 2010. *Intimate Labors: Cultures, Technologies, and the Politics of Care*. Stanford: Stanford University Press.

Bourke, Joanna. 1994. "Housewifery in Working-Class England 1960–1914." *Past & Present* 143: 167–197.

Brinton, Mary. 2001. "Married Women's Labour in East Asian Economies." In *Women's Working Lives in East Asia*, edited by Mary Brinton, 1–37. Stanford: Stanford University Press.

Brinton, Mary, Yeon-Ju Lee, and William L. Parish. 1995. "Married Women's Employment in Rapidly Industrialized Societies: Examples from East Asia." *The American Journal of Sociology* 100, no. 5: 1099–1130. https://doi.org/10.1086/230633

Castells, Manuell. 1992. "Four Asian Tigers with a Dragon Head: A Comparative Analysis of the State, Economy, and Society in the Asia Pacific Rim." In *State and Development in the Asian Pacific Rim*, edited by Jeffrey W. Henderson and Richard P. Appelbaum, 33–70. London: Sage Publications.

Chang, Kyung-sup. 2010. *South Korea under Compressed Modernity: Familial Political Economy in Transition*. London and New York: Routledge.

Chang Migyŏng. 2007. "1960–70nyŏndae kajŏngjubu (anae) ŭi hyŏngsŏng gwa chendŏ jŏngch'i": 'yŏwŏn', 'chubu saenghwal' japchi tamnon ŭl chungshim ŭro (The Formation of Housewives and Institutional Politics: Focusing on Magazine Discourse, 'yŏwŏn' and 'chubu saenghwal')." *Sahoe gwahak yŏn'gu (Social Science Research)* 15, no. 1: 142–180.

Cho, Haejoang. 2002. "Living with Conflicting Subjectivities: Mother, motherly Wife, and Sexy Woman in the Transition from Colonial-modern to Postmodern Korea." In *Under Construction: The Gendering of Modernity, Class, and Consumption in the Republic of Korea*, edited by Laurel Kendall, 165–195. Honolulu: University of Hawai'i Press.

Duchen, Claire. 1991. "Occupation Housewife: The Domestic Ideal in 1950s France." *French Cultural Studies* 2: 1–11. https://doi.org/10.1177/095715589100200401

Evans, Peter. 1989. "Predatory, Developmental, and Other Apparatuses: A Comparative Political Economy Perspective on the Third World State." *Sociological Forum* 4, no. 4: 561–587.

Evans, Peter. 1995. *Embedded Autonomy: States and Industrial Transformation*. Princeton: Princeton University Press.

Fernandes, Leela, and Patrick Heller. 2006. "Hegemonic Aspirations: New Middle Class Politics and India's Democracy in Comparative Perspective." *Critical Asian Studies* 38, no. 4: 495–522. https://doi.org/10.1080/14672710601073028

Garon, Sheldon. 1997. *Molding Japanese Minds: The State in Everyday Life*. Princeton: Princeton University Press.

Garon, Sheldon. 2010. "State and Family in Modern Japan: A Historical Perspective." *Economy and Society* 39, no. 3: 317–336. https://doi.org/10.1080/03085147.2010.486214

Gordon, Andrew. 1997. "Managing the Japanese Household: The New Life Movement in Postwar Japan." *Social Politics: International Studies in Gender, State & Society* 4, no. 2: 245–283. https://doi.org/10.1093/sp/4.2.245

Haggard, Stephan. 2004. "Institutions and Growth in East Asia." *Studies in Comparative International Development* 38, no. 4: 53–81. https://doi.org/10.1007/BF02686328

Haggard, Stephan, and Chung-In Moon. 1983. "Liberal, Dependent or Mercantile? The South Korean State in the International System." In *The Antinomies of Interdependence*, edited by John Gerard Ruggle, 131–190. New York: Columbia University Press.

Hays, Sharon. 1996. *The Cultural Contradictions of Motherhood*. New Haven: Yale University Press.

Health and Social Welfare Department. 1987. *Punyŏ haengjŏng 40nyŏnsa*. Seoul: Ministry of Health and Social Welfare.

Hwang Chŏngmi. 1999. "Palchŏn kukka wa mosŏng: 1960–70nyŏndae punyŏ haengjŏng ŭl chungshimŭro (The Developmental State and Motherhood: Policy on Women and Children in the 1960s and 1970s)." In *Mosŏng ŭi tamnon kwa hyŏnshil (Discourses on Motherhood versus Reality)*, edited by Shin Yŏnghŭi, Chŏng Chinsŏng, and Yun Chŏngno, 167–195. Seoul: Nanam ch'ulp'ansa.

Hwang Chŏngmi. 2001. "Kaebal kukka ŭi yŏsŏng chŏngch'aek e kwanhan yŏn'gu: 1960–70 nyŏndae han'guk punyŏ haengjŏng ŭl chungshimŭro (Women and the Developmental State: State Policy on Women in Korea in the 1960s and 1970s)." Doctoral diss., Seoul National University.

Johnson, Chalmers. 1987. "Political Institutions and Economic Performance: The Government-Business Relations in Japan, South Korea, Taiwan." In *The Political Economy of the New Asian Industrialism*, edited by Frederic C. Deyo, 136–164. Ithaca: Cornell University Press.

Kandiyoti, Deniz. 1988. "Bargaining with Patriarchy." *Gender and Society* 2, no. 3: 274–290.

Kendall, Laurel. 2002. "Introduction." In *Under Construction: The Gendering of Modernity, Class, and Consumption in the Republic of Korea*, edited by Laurel Kendall, 1–24. Honolulu: University of Hawai'i Press.

Kim Duhŏn. 1969. *Han'guk kajok chedo ŭi yŏn'gu (A Study on Family Systems in Korea)*. Seoul: Seoul National University Press.

Kim Hyegyŏng. 2006. *Shingminji ha kŭndae kajok ŭi hyŏngsŏng kwa chendŏ (The Formation of Modern Family and Gender under Japanese Colonial Rule)*. Seoul: Ch'angjak kwa pip'yŏng.

Kim Hyegyŏng. 2009. "Pak chŏnghŭi ch'eje ha 'haekkajok tamnon ŭi pyŏnhwa gwajŏng gwa iwŏn gujo yŏn'gu (Discourses on the Nuclear Family and the Double Structure during the Park Chung Hee Era)." *Sahoe wa yŏksa (Society and History)* 82: 169–212.

Kim Hyeyŏng. 2016. "Tongwŏndoen kajok chuŭi ŭi shidae esŏ kajok wihŏm ŭi sahoero (From the Era of Mobilized Familism to Familism with Risk)." *Han'guk sahoe (Korean Society)* 17, no. 2: 3–44.

Kim Hyŏnmi. 2000. "Han'guk ŭi kŭndaesŏng gwa yŏsŏng ŭi nodonggwŏn (Modernity and Women's Working Rights in South Korea)." *Han'guk yŏsŏnghak (Korean Women's Studies)* 16, no. 1: 37–64.

Kim Suyŏng. 2001. "Han'guk ŭi sanŏp'wa gwajŏng gwa kajok, yŏsŏng (Family and Women in Industrialization)." *Chinbo p'yŏngnon (Progressive Critique)* 7: 57–75.

Kim Ŭnshil. 1999. "Han'guk kŭndaehwa p'ŭrojekt'ŭ ŭi munhwa nolli wa kabujangsŏng (The Culture and Patriarchy Embedded in the Korean Modernization Project)." *Tangdae bip'yŏng (Contemporary Criticism)* 88: 79–100.

Kim Yŏnchu, and Yi Chaekyŏng. 2013. "Kŭndae 'kajŏng jubu' doegi kkwajŏng gwa toshi chungsanch'ŭng kajog ŭi hyŏngsŏng (The Process of Becoming a Modern Housewife and the Construction of the Urban Middle-class Family)." *Kajok gwa munhwa (Family and Culture)* 25, no. 2: 29–61.

Kim, Yun-Jung. 2005. "Reconciling Work and Motherhood: The Experiences of Korean Working Mothers." Doctoral diss., University of Bath.

Kwon, Yong. 2021. "The Long Shadow of the Asian Financial Crisis in South Korea: Seoul's Approach to Pandemic Relief is Colored by the Formative Experience of the 1997–1998 Crisis." *The Diplomat*, December 6.

Kyunghyang Shinmun. 1977. "Puŏk sallim ŭi sae igi (New Modern Home Appliances in the Kitchen)." July 7.

Kyunghyang Shinmun. 1977. "Pyŏnhwa sok sŏng munhwa (Social Changes and Sexual Practices in Rural Areas)." August 9.

Kyunghyang Shinmun. 1979. "Kobugan ŭi kaltŭng haesodoelkka (Intergenerational Conflicts between Daughters-in-law and Mothers-in-law)." June 14.

Lu, Sidney Xu. 2013. "Good Women for Empire: Educating Overseas Female Emigrants in Imperial Japan, 1900–45." *Journal of Global History* 8, no. 3: 436–460. https://doi.org/10.1017/S1740022813000363

Mies, Maria. 1998. *Patriarchy and Accumulation on a World Scale: Women in the International Division of Labour*. London: Zed Books.

Ministry of Health and Social Welfare. 1987. *Punyŏ haengjŏng 40nyŏnsa (40 Years of History in Policy on Women)*. Seoul: Ministry of Health and Social Welfare.

Mohanty, Chandra. 1988. "Under Western Eyes: Feminist Scholarship and Colonial Discourses." *Feminist Review* 30: 61–88. https://doi.org/10.1057/fr.1988.42

Moon, Seungsook. 2002. "The Production and Subversion of Hegemonic Masculinity: Reconfiguring Gender Hierarchy in Contemporary South Korea." In *Under Construction: The Gendering of Modernity, Class, and Consumption in the Republic of Korea*, edited by Laurel Kendall, 79–113. Honolulu: University of Hawai'i Press.

Moore, Henrietta L. 1988. *Feminism and Anthropology*. Minneapolis: University of Minnesota Press.

Ong, Aihwa. 1988. "Colonialism and Modernity: Feminist Representations of Women in Non-western Societies." *Inscriptions* 3, no. 4: 79–93.

Pae Ŭnkyŏng. 2008. "Kusul saengaesa rŭl t'onghae pon sanŏp'wa shigi han'guk ŏmŏni ŭi mosŏng kyŏnghŏm kyŏngjejŏk kiyŏ wa tolbom nodong, ch'injok kwan'gye kwalli ŭi kyŏrhap (Mothering Experiences of Korean Women in the Industrialization Period: Combining Economic Support, Care Work, and Relation Management for Family)." *P'eminijŭm yŏn'gu (Feminist Studies)* 8, no. 1: 69–123.

Pahl, Raymond Edward. 1989. "Is the Emperor Naked? Some Questions on the Adequacy of Sociological Theory in Urban and Regional Research." *International Journal of Urban and Regional Research* 13, no. 4: 709–720. https://doi.org/10.1111/j.1468-2427.1989.tb00143.x

Pak Pyŏngho. 1986. "Han'guk kabujanggwŏn pŏpche ŭi sajŏk koch'al (The History of Patriarchism in Korea)." *Han'guk Yŏsŏnghak (Korean Women's Studies)* 2: 50–84.

Park, Sang-Young. 2010. "Crafting and Dismantling the Egalitarian Social Contract: The Changing State-Society Relations in Globalizing Korea." *The Pacific Review* 23, no. 5: 579–601. https://doi.org/10.1080/09512748.2010.522247

Reay, Diane. 1998. "Rethinking Social Class: Social Qualitative Perspectives on Class and Gender." *Sociology* 32, no. 2: 259–275.

Reay, Diane. 2005. "Emotional Capital, Women and Social Class." In *Feminists Evaluate Bourdieu*, edited by Beverley Skeggs and Lisa Adkins, 57–74. London: Blackwell.

Roberts, Helen. 1993. "Women and the Class Debate." In *Debates in Sociology*, edited by David Morgan and Liz Stanley, 52–70. Manchester: Manchester University Press.

Rofel, Lisa. 1994. "Liberation Nostalgia and a Yearning for Modernity." In *Engendering China: Women, Culture, and the State*, edited by Christina K. Gilmartin, Gail Hershatter, Lisa Rofel, and Tyrene White, 226–249. Cambridge: Harvard University Press.

Rofel, Lisa. 1999. *Other Modernities, Gendered Yearnings in China after Socialism*. Berkeley: University of California Press.

Romero, Mary, Valerie Preston, and Wenona Giles. 2014. "Care Work in a Globalizing World." In *When Care Work Goes Global: Locating the Social Relations of Domestic Work*, edited by Mary Romero, Valerie Preston, and Wenona Giles, 1–28. London and New York: Routledge.

Savage, Mike, Gaynor Bagnall, and Brian Longhurst. 2005. *Globalisation and Belonging*. London: Sage Publications.

Shin Hyŏnok. 1999. "Kukka kaebal chŏngch'aek kwa nongch'on chiyŏk ŭi yŏsŏng chojik e kwanhan yŏn'gu (National Development Policy and Women's Organizations in Rural Areas)." Doctoral diss., Seoul: Yonsei University.

Skeggs, Beverley. 2004. *Class, Self, Culture*. London: Routledge.

Stivens, Maila. 1998. "Theorising Gender, Power and Modernity." In *Gender and Power in Affluent Asia*, edited by Krishna Sen and Maila Stivens, 1–34. London: Routledge.

Suchman, Mark C. 1995. "Managing Legitimacy: Strategic and Institutional Approaches." *The Academy of Management Review* 20, no. 3: 571–610. https://doi.org/10.5465/amr.1995.9508080331

Tilly, Louise, and Joan W. Scott. 1989. *Women, Work, and Family*. Abingdon: Routledge.

Wade, Robert. 1990a. *Governing the Market: Economic Theory and the Role of Government in East Asian Industrialization*. Princeton: Princeton University Press.

Wade, Robert. 1990b. "Industrial Policy in East Asia: Does it Lead or Follow the Market?" In *Manufacturing Miracles: Paths of Industrialization in Latin America and East Asia*, edited by G. Gereffi and D. L. Wyman, 231–266. Princeton: Princeton University Press.

White, Gordon, and Robert Wade. 1988. "Developmental State and Markets in East Asia: An Introduction." In *Developmental States in East Asia*, edited by Gordon White, 1–29. London: Palgrave Macmillan.

Yang, Myungji. 2018. *From Miracle to Mirage: The Making and Unmaking of the Korean Middle Class, 1960–2015*. Ithaca and London: Cornell University Press.

Yi Suja. 2000. "Han'guk sahoe ŭi kŭndaesŏng e taehan yŏsŏng chuŭi munhwaronjŏk sŏngch'al (Feminist Cultural Reflections on the Modernity of Korean Society)." *Yŏsŏng yŏn'gu nonch'ong (Journal of Women's Studies)* 1: 169–188.

Zhao, Ding-Xin, and John A. Hall. 1994. "State Power and Patterns of Late Development." *Sociology* 28, no. 1: 211–229. https://doi.org/10.1177/0038038594028001013

Index

Milton Keynes UK
Ingram Content Group UK Ltd.
UKHW051908230624
444477UK00005B/136

9 780367 627195